PRESCRIPTIONS AND POLICIES

PRESCRIPTIONS AND POLICIES

The Social Well-Being of African Americans in the 1990s

Edited by

Dionne J. Jones

Transaction Publishers
New Brunswick (U.S.A.) and London (U.K.)

Library of Congress Catalog Number: 90–46178
ISBN: 0–88738–883–3
Printed in the United States of America

Library of Congress Cataloging-in-Publication Data

Presciptions and policies: the social well-being of African Americans in the
    1990s / edited by Dionne J. Jones.
        p. cm.
    "Originally published as a special issue of The Urban League reviews,
summer 1989; winter 1989–90" — T.p. verso.
    ISBN 0–88738–883–3
    1. Afro-Americans — Social conditions — 1975 — 2. Afro-Americans —
Government policy. I. Jones, Dionne J.
E185.86.P68   1991
323.1'196073 — dc20   90–46178
                                                                  CIP

CONTENTS

PRESCRIPTIONS AND POLICIES: RACIAL VIOLENCE

PRESCRIPTIONS AND POLICIES

Prescriptions and Policies: The Social Well-Being of African Americans in the 1990s

Dionne J. Jones

The 1980s will be remembered as a decade of retrogression in the nation's provisions for ensuring the social well-being of disadvantaged groups. In particular, the needs of African Americans were severely neglected. This circumstance was one of the regrettable hallmarks of the Reagan era and that administration's philosophy of limited government involvement in meeting human needs. Rationalized on the basis of fiscal responsibility and the compensating role of private, voluntary initiatives in alleviating the nation's social problems, the philosophy was expressed in the form of massive reductions in social spending—in employment and training, housing, education, income maintenance, and other vital areas. The spending reductions embodied in the Omnibus Budget Reconciliation Act (OBRA) of 1981 were merely the beginning of a broader pattern of retrenchment.

The retrenchment was also manifest in highly conservative, regressive actions in the area of civil rights. Propounding the view that the society had become "color blind," the Reagan administration waged a sustained assault on affirmative action and evidenced a general relaxation of federal enforcement of existing equal opportunity mandates. This development occurred despite the fact that racial discrimination is still a pervasive problem in our national life. The resurgence of racial antipathy and violence toward African Americans during the 1980s was one of the more poignant indicators that the ideal of color blindness remains a distant goal. One cannot help but wonder how much the previously mentioned government policies and initiatives in the civil rights area might have contributed to the climate of hostility that marked the decade.

The persistence of inequalities in the status and well-being of African Americans and whites makes it imperative that the nation's leadership pursue a much more progressive social agenda in the 1990s. Indeed, one analysis suggests that, on a number of critical measures, racial parity is not likely to occur for an inordinate time into the future, if ever, unless more is done to close the continuing gaps.[1] At stake is the well-being of the nation as a whole as well as that of African Americans.

Through his call for a "kinder and gentler America," President Bush has voiced the kind of sensitivity to social issues that was lost through most of the 1980s. Thus far, however, the new administration has fallen short in providing the resouces required to effectively meet the needs of African Americans and other disadvantaged groups. This divergence between rhetoric and reality must be rectified if the nation is to move into the 21st century strong and unified.

Given that the African American civilian labor force growth by the year 2000 is projected to be 96.2 percent more than the white workforce growth,[2] it is clear that more aggressive actions are required to train and prepare African American workers. African Americans continued to experience disproportionate unemployment during 1989. The official unemployment rate for African Americans (11.3%) was more than double that for whites (4.3%).[3] African American teenagers continue to be jobless at rates exceeding levels of the Great Depression.

Our youth are our future, and every effort must be made for them to develop their human potential, thereby becoming gainfully employed. Herein lies the crux of the problem, as the vicious cycle of poverty revolves. In order for African American youth to be gainfully employed, they must be educated and adequately prepared and trained for the labor market. This is not happening in nearly large enough proportions. Public schools are failing to stimulate and educate too many African American students,[4] as is evidenced by dropout rates that are as high as 50 percent in some urban school districts. In fact, only 64.9 percent of African American youth aged 18 to 19 had completed high school in 1986.[5] Yet, this figure is only a 9.1 percent increase from the 1974 school completion rate for 18- to 19-year-old African Americans.

It follows that if young people (indeed, people of any age) are idle with no legitimate source of income, they will easily fall prey to the lure of extralegal activities. Overwhelming evidence attests to this: for example, there is heightened drug use, abuse, and sales; crime, particularly homicide; prostitution; and so forth.[6] The devastating effects of substance abuse are being witnessed in increasingly alarming proportions in African American communities. Homicide rates are mounting in inner cities, where many innocent bystanders are being caught in the cross fire. Almost as shocking is the fact that the drug traffickers and lookouts are becoming increasingly younger.

What are the prescriptions for alleviating these conditions? There is no one simple answer. A multifaceted approach will have to be taken. More far-reaching problems such as poverty and unemployment must be addressed at the national, state, and local government levels. In addition, a variety of community services will have to be offered in schools, cultural awareness activities will have to be undertaken, and the development of racial pride will have to be nurtured. To save our youth, we must offer them a viable, exciting alternative. Schools can help by revamping the educational curriculum so that it is more meaningful for African American students.

Of course, the problems of African American youth are inextricably intertwined with the adversities faced by African American families and communities in general. Disparities continue to exist between African Americans and whites. What public policies and private initiatives are required to bring about parity in the social well-being of African Americans and whites?

The articles in this special edition of the *Review* offer prescriptions and policies for improving the social well-being of African Americans in key areas. Under the heading "Policy Issues: Prescriptions for Empowerment," the first two articles deal with national policy issues. "Fiscal Strategy, Public Policy, and the Social Agenda," by Lenneal J. Henderson, Jr., illustrates the changing philosophy of fiscal support for the poor. Henderson analyses the emerging framework of fiscal ethics and its implications for African Americans and the poor. He urges that the moral struggle to attain equity and financial choice for African Americans, Hispanics, women, and the poor should escalate. The second article is "Aiding African American Communities in the Post-Reagan Era: How to Get More African Americans in Government" by Hanes Walton, Jr., Daniel Brantley, and Willie E. Johnson. The authors note that the scarcity of African American and minority officials handicaps state efforts to help African American and minority communities that are already deprived of federal aid. They urge governors and legislatures to ensure that more minorities are appointed to government positions and that minority officials have a mandate to help needy communities.

The next group of articles are subsumed under the heading "Prescriptions and Policies: Family Issues." In "Will Welfare Be Reformed? The Possible Effects of the Family Support Act on Children," Lynn C. Burbridge analyzes the provisions of the Family Support Act of 1988 and discusses implications they have for children. She notes that the primary focus of policymakers and others working with children and their families should be on the well-being of children, rather than on debating the need for the self-sufficiency of welfare grant recipients.

The second article on family issues is "African American Family Policy or National Family Policy: Are They Different?" by Jean M. Granger. Granger addresses the need for African Americans to join forces with other groups to push for a family policy for all Americans. Observing that because of racist attitudes, policymakers and others are reluctant to move on issues that are represented as African American issues, Granger urges support for a national family policy. With passage of such legislation, she notes, African Americans will need to work with the committees to ensure that the specific needs of African Americans are addressed.

"Prescriptions and Policies: Health Issues" is the next area, which contains four articles. "The Implications of Demographic Changes in the African American Aged Population for Formal and Informal Care Systems in the 21st Century," by Jacqueline Marie Smith addresses the current underutilization of formal health care facilities by the African American aged. Smith cautions that with changing demographic trends in the African American population, the heavy burden currently placed on the informal care system (family and friends) may cease to be a viable option for the African American aged in the future. She offers recommendations for improvements in the formal health care system so that it can accommodate the anticipated needs of the African American aged.

Health care issues extend beyond the individual to the environment. Of critical concern is the dumping of toxic waste and the resultant hazards that ensue for residents of neighboring communities. In "Toxic Waste and the African American Community,'' Robert D. Bullard and Beverly H. Wright address the wanton disregard for African American life. They report that toxic waste sites are disproportionately located in African American and Hispanic communities, while large commercial hazardous waste landfills and disposal facilities tend to be in rural communities in the southern black belt. Bullard and Wright suggest that African Americans need to collaborate with other concerned groups to lobby against and vociferously denounce such inhumane practices.

Another troubling health issue for African Americans is raised by Ivor L. Livingston and Ronald J. Marshall. In their article ''Cardiac Reactivity and Elevated Blood Pressure Levels among Young African Americans: The Importance of Stress,'' they use a model developed by Livingston to show the interrelationship among hypertension, stress, and race. They show that African American youth have a proclivity to experience greater stress than their white counterparts because of the prevailing conditions that exist in urban neighborhoods. They call for the initiation of preventive strategies to help African American youth develop greater resistance to environmental pressures.

Omowale Amuleru-Marshall's article ''Substance Abuse among America's Urban Youth'' is the fourth article under health issues. Amuleru-Marshall notes that when African American youth feel shut out of the mainstream of society and are confronted with life options of idleness, brought on in large part by high unemployment, these youth find the drug culture an easy alternative. Pointing to some shortcomings of current substance abuse prevention and treatment programs, Amuleru-Marshall offers alternative approaches for helping African American youth in treatment.

Two articles are presented under ''Prescriptions and Policies: Education.'' In ''The Coloring of IQ Testing: A New Name for an Old Phenomenon,'' Donna Y. Ford, J. John Harris III, and Duvon G. Winborne revisit the issue of bias in IQ testing as it relates to African Americans. These authors contend that IQ testing is but one mechanism for maintaining racism, prejudice, and inequality in the United States. In addition, they point to differential explanations for superior intelligence test performance between whites and African Americans and between Asian Americans and whites. Thus, they conclude ''paradigmatic paralysis'' continues to dominate professional thinking.

The second article on educational issues is ''Between a Rock and a Hard Place: Drugs and Schools in African American Communities,'' by William B. Harvey, Paul F. Bitting, and Tracy L. Robinson. The authors decry the educational system as being meaningless and irrelevant for African American students. Thus, with the diminishing perceived utility and value placed on schooling, there is heightened social acceptability of drugs for African American students. Harvey et al. contend that the educational system must be reconstructed to embrace the cultural diversity of all students. Meaningful participation in an educational program, they insist, is a necessary and viable approach for fighting the ''war on drugs.''

The final area covered in this edition of the *Review* is ''Prescriptions and Policies: Racial Violence'' under which two articles are presented. Dionne J. Jones's article, ''The College Campus as a Microcosm of U.S. Society: The Issue of Racially Motivated Violence,'' discusses the rise in racial incidents on predominantly white college campuses. An analysis is made of some of the causal factors of these incidents, and the responses of African American students on these campuses are discussed. Finally, recommendations are made for alleviating this problem.

The article by Ronald Walters, ''White Racial Nationalism in the United States,'' puts the problem of racially motivated violence in historical political perspective. Walters shows how nationalism by whites has been a reaction to pressure by African Americans and others for social change since World War II. Feeling disempowered and determined to maintain the status quo, the conservative movement garnered its forces and finally brought Reagan to power. Walters warns that institutional racism and white nationalism must be reversed in order for America to remain free and democratic.

The analyses presented in this edition agree that there is a need for drastic shifts in public and social policies to ease the burden placed on African Americans. Policymakers can no longer turn a blind eye to racist or dysfunctional policies. They must work aggressively to make social well-being a reality for all Americans.

NOTES

1. Billy J. Tidwell, *Stalling Out: The Relative Progress of African Americans* (Washington, DC: National Urban League, Inc., 1989).

2. Monica L. Jackson, ed., ''African Americans to Be Larger Share of the Workforce in the Year 2000,'' *Quarterly Economic Report on the African American Worker*, National Urban League Research Department Report no. 20 (Washington, DC: National Urban League, Inc., May 1989), 1.

3. U.S. Department of Labor, Bureau of Labor Statistics, Unpubished data, 1990.

4. Dionne J. Jones, ''The Increasing Significance of Race: The Educational Condition of Blacks,'' *Journal of Social and Behavioral Sciences* (forthcoming).

5. U.S. Department of Education, National Center for Education Statistics, Office of Education Research and Improvement, *1989 Education Indicators* (Washington, DC: Government Printing Office, 1989), Table 1:9–1, 160.

6. Janet Dewart, ed., *The State of Black America 1989.* (New York: National Urban League, Inc., 1989).

1

Fiscal Strategy, Public Policy, and the Social Agenda

Lenneal J. Henderson, Jr.

Fiscal policy reflects one key dimension of the struggle over resources in America. This is particularly essential for African Americans, Hispanics, and others highly dependent on public monies for basic necessities. The new fiscal strategy reflects a preoccupation with budget deficits, tax reform capable of generating more revenues, and reduction of social spending, particularly from discretionary sources, as well as a stress on self-financing or user fee-oriented fiscal policy. States and local governments are asked to bear a greater part of the responsibility to help the poor. The implications for African Americans, Hispanics, and others who comprise the list of target populations include a greater involvement in the politics of fiscal decision making, the continued development of internal expertise in the technicalities of tax and budget policy, and the generation of policy proposals for the poor that emphasize self-financing schemes.

As Charles V. Hamilton aptly argues, the struggle of the 1990s will shift dramatically from past struggles for rights to struggles for resources.[1] Indeed, the struggle for resources will be indistinguishable from the struggle for rights. Chief among those resources are fiscal resources: the public financial transactions of government. Whether its focus is on child care, the underclass, the homeless, teenage pregnancy, housing, health care, care for the elderly, transportation, or natural resource policy, no advocacy, social services, or public agency can escape the need to incorporate its agenda in federal, state, or local fiscal strategy.

Mikesell includes all portions of the budget cycle; the tax, charges, and aid processes of revenue generation; administration of the government debt; bonds; procurement policy; public enterprise; and the creation and use of various trust accounts within the meaning and scope of fiscal policy.[2] If politics is the authoritative allocation of values, then fiscal policy is the authoritative distribution and redistribution of value through money.

This article posits five interrelated issues. First, African Americans, Hispanics, Native Americans, women, and others struggling for financial resources to achieve group ends depend disproportionately on public monies to finance those ends. Second, these groups are experiencing a radical shift in the ethical foundation of public policies supporting the financing of their constituency needs. This shift is from direct, significant funding of a variety of social objectives to more circumscribed efficiency objectives and is driven by deficits, tax and expenditure limitations, balance of trade and payment deficits, and adamant political conservatism. Third, given the new ethical framework and its associated fiscal strategies of self-financing, monetary incentives, and privatization, social service agencies, civil rights organizations, churches, state and local governments, and others involved in advocating for the delivery of goods and services to needy populations must update and revise their political and grantsmanship strategies. Fourth, fiscal control policies such as the Balanced Budget and Emergency Deficit Control Act of 1985 (hereinafter referred to as Gramm-Rudman-Hollings [GRH]), its 1987 amendments, the Tax Reform Act of 1986, and the variety of state fiscal responses to tax reform provide the specific, limited context in which social advocacy strategies should begin. Finally, while vigorously seeking to change national, state and local fiscal priorities through such mechanisms as the courts, legislative lobbying, mass media exposure of the executive branch, and electoral politics, advocates of social change should incorporate formal cost-benefit analysis, socioeconomic-impact assessment, and other tools in their arsenal for addressing the new fiscal ethics.

FISCAL STRATEGY AND POLITICAL ECONOMY

To best assess the meaning of these five issues to the agenda of those working with the needy, this article adopts a modified version of the political economy model developed by Warren Ilchman and Norman Uphoff.[3] Ilchman and Uphoff interrelate economic and political decisions through a framework of *resource exchange*.

A resource is anything that has intrinsic value and can, therefore, be exchanged. Money, material goods, and services are but a kind of resource. Other resources, such as human resources, information, technology, infrastructure, status, legitimacy, authority, coercion, and even violence, are more social and political in nature. A social or political resource, such as status or legitimacy, may be exchanged for an economic resource, such as money or commodities. Resources may also be sorted, saved, or given away. Depending upon their value, however, storing or saving resources may cause them to appreciate or depreciate in value. Giving a resource away without some reciprocation or compensation is considered a net loss to the group possessing the resource. Most importantly, *power* in this framework is not necessarily the result of how much of a resource base a group possesses, or even what combination of resources it possesses, but how *strategically* the group utilizes and exchanges those resources that it owns. Strategic use of resources includes cultivation and development of the net value of the group's resources following exchange and, most importantly, the attainment of some ethical or moral value embodied in the goals and objectives of the endowed group.[4]

Each major fiscal decision of a federal, state, or local government entity involves a distribution or a redistributon of both economic and political resources for every actor in the economy and the political system. Concomitantly, each distribution and redistribution of the resources resulting from fiscal decisions culminates in a moral or ethical result capable of making a statement about the values and priorities of the decision-making process and the society.

Consequently, the Congressional Black Caucus, in its *Quality of Life: Fiscal 1990 Alternative Budget*, argues that "a nation's values and concern for social and economic justice are measured by the fiscal priorities established in its national budget."[5] And the League of United Latin American Citizens (LULAC) has repeatedly warned tax experts that failure to incorporate large numbers of unemployed and underemployed Hispanic citizens and aliens represents not only a fiscal failure, but also a moral failure. And the rapidly rising number of women entering the workforce and subject to rising taxes without benefit of adequate child care *and* care for the elderly from those for whom they work makes a loud statement about value priorities and not just fiscal dynamics.[6]

Therefore, the political economy of fiscal strategy is always more than a question of the econometrics of resource distribution and redistribution. It is even more than a question of *morally correct fiscal decisions* made by government. The issue is whether the fiscal decisions of government empower or enable citizens, particularly those with salient needs, to decide on the morality of their own resource-exchange strategies; that is, the attainment of ends that minimize undue dependence on any sector of society and maximize ability to influence the moral course of societal decisions. It is this maxim that drives each of the five issues in this article.

THE FISCAL DEPENDENCY OF THE NEEDY

The first issue raised in this article is that African Americans, other minorities, women, and other disadvantaged groups depend disproportionately on government financing to meet their needs. Paradoxically, African Americans and Hispanics are simultaneously dependent on federal, state, and local governments for most of their financial resources and are subject to regressive tax and revenue policies.[7] Of the more than 300,000 businesses owned and operated by African American and Hispanic entrepreneurs, more than 90 percent of them supply or provide services to government. Fewer than 50 percent of all other enterprises are as dependent on the government dollar.[8] Similarly, African American and Hispanic households are more than twice as dependent on some form of federal, state, or local transfer payment, subsidy, public assistance, or Aid to Families with Dependent Children, as are other households. An African American or Hispanic student in any college or university is almost three times as likely to receive government support as the predominant support for tuition, room, and board as are other students. And African American and Hispanic men and women in the correctional institutions of the nation represent far more than their demographic representation in the population as a whole. Moreover, as Persons, Walton, and other experts on African American elected officials point out, African American elected officials usually serve the state or in jurisdictions containing large numbers of impoverished, poorly housed populations with health care, day care, education, employment, and infrastructural needs that severly strain city, county, or state budgetary resources.[9] Given advancing rates of poverty, homelessness, health care deficiencies, and other social maladies, needy dependency on government will increase.

The civil rights, antipoverty, feminist, and other movements in the 1950s, 1960s, and 1970s thrust an ethic of social responsiveness upon fiscal decision makers unprecedented even during the Great Depression. Through the Manpower Development and Training Act of 1962, the Economic Opportunity Act of 1964, the Cities Demonstration and Metropolitan Development Act of 1966, and others, the alleviation of poverty was placed higher on the public agenda than it had been. The result was a great redistributive impulse: a desire to reallocate the financial resources of the nation through fiscal policy. Walton has pointed out that federal outlays for civil rights regulatory activities increased from $900,000 in 1969 to $3.5 billion in 1976.[10] Also in 1976, the Small Business Act of 1958 was amended to create federal set-aside programs for minority businesses through what has become known as the 8(a) program.

The result of these policy initiatives was to increase dependency on government with the hope of social transformation. Social transformation was to reduce dependency on government by the needy through the creation and management of strong, viable, productive, and more independent institutions and individuals capable of working in any institution. However explicit the doctrine of responsiveness to the poor was, the implicit need for a socially transforming independence among the needy was not and has not been fully accomplished.

THE CHANGING PHILOSOPHY OF FISCAL SUPPORT

The second issue considered is that there has been a radical shift in public policies and fiscal support away from social programs and focusing on deficits, taxation, and so forth. The election of Ronald Reagan to the presidency set the tone for a radical departure from the responsiveness philosophy of the 1960s and 1970s. Before responsiveness could facilitate transition to greater self-determination among the needy, the "Reagan Revolution" moved vigorously to reduce federal spending in many categories of social support while shifting primary responsibility for the poor to states and localities. The key components of Reagan's fiscal strategy were increases in defense spending, cuts in domestic spending, and cuts in taxes.[11] Although Reagan was unable to reduce entitlements, he did reduce discretionary social spending in both real-dollar terms and actual outlays. The Reagan strategy was to be accomplished by four principal administrative mechanisms:

1. People would be appointed to cabinet and subcabinet positions who were loyal to the president and who had no independent standing and could be removed easily if they did not follow directions or "went native."
2. Budget impoundments, reductions, recisions, and deferrals would be implemented to stop or curtail statutorily mandated income maintenance, housing, health, and other programs.

3. There would be a process of reorganization and retrenchment.
4. Rules would be issued curtailing eligibility for entitlement programs; programs would be wholly or partially contracted out, and closer program monitoring would be incorporated into regulations.[12]

However, the combination of tax cuts mandated by the Economic Recovery Tax Act of 1981, increases in social entitlements, and significant increases in defense spending resulted in $400 billion of accumulated deficits between 1981 and 1986. Policy retrenchment, driven by political and economic philosophy, soon gave way to deficit reductions, driven by fiscal necessity.

It is also imperative to emphasize the intergovernmental nature of the change in fiscal philosophy. Even before Reagan's election as president, many states and localities were imposing tax and expenditure limitations on government through initiatives, constitutional amendments, legislative mandates or even recall elections.[13] The famous Proposition 13 in the State of California best symbolized this backlash against taxation, and, indirectly, government spending. Property taxes were rolled back 57 percent and property tax assessments were rolled back from 1978 to 1975–1976 levels. California's cities, counties, and special districts experienced immediate and sharp revenue shortfalls. Discretionary spending, including many social initiatives, were reduced or forever eliminated.[14]

The ethical thrust resulting from most of these retrenchment initiatives was that government's fiscal burdens had become too heavy, that the beleaguered American taxpayer should not be expected to bear the cost of social change, and that citizens should become more vigilant about fiscal decision making. Implicit in this thrust is a rejection of the social transformation ideology apparent in the 1960s. Neither an ethic of governmental responsiveness to the expensive needs of the impoverished nor a tolerance for the time and cost required for responsiveness to result in social transformation is evident in this ethic.

However, it is important to emphasize that government itself did not go away in this ground swell of dissatisfaction. Federal defense spending continued to escalate, states bailed out troubled localities, and states and localities invented or extended user fees, public enterprises, and consolidated financing to extend their operations in lieu of property taxes.

THE EMERGING FRAMEWORK OF FISCAL ETHICS

The new ethical framework and its associated fiscal strategies of self-financing, monetary incentives, and privatization are the third issue of concern. Given pervasive concerns about the nature and extent of government spending at the federal level, within the 50 states, 3,043 counties, 17,000 municipalities, 16,500 villages, hamlets, and townships, 15,500 independent school districts, and 31,000 special districts,[15] a new fiscal ethic emerges with profound implications for racial and ethnic groups and the needy. This ethic is built on four salient foundations. First, deficit reduction, particularly at the federal level, must be taken seriously, not just to balance the budget, but to facilitate the restoration of America's position as an international economic and trading force. Second, government functions that are purely tax-supported must be reduced, and replaced with those that are as self-financing as possible. The greater the degree of self-financing, the less fiscal burden on government. Third, monetary incentives to achieve administrative efficiencies must be provided. The objective is to reduce these burdens on government bureaucracy that do not accomplish social ends effectively. Fourth, responding to the needs of the poor should be accomplished through the states and localities, as well as through a network of nonprofit, church, and other benevolent organizations. All four principles minimize or subtract government from the fiscal equation. If government is present at all, it is as a seed-funding source or as the other part of a matching arrangement.

America has reached a level of obsession with its declining position in the world economy. A continuous and negative balance of trade and balance of payments; increasing foreign, particularly European and Japanese, investment in American states and cities; and persistent problems of petroleum, uranium, and other raw material dependencies jam daily newspaper headlines. The federal deficit and federal debt are frequently cited as major contributions to, if not sources of, American economic decline.[16] Declining federal, state, and local tax and revenue yields have been associated with industrial and commercial decline.

To reduce tax burdens and to free up money for investment in U.S. enterprise, many have argued that new ways of financing government are needed. Some have suggested greater use of user fees, so that those using government services pay at the time they are provided such services.[17] Others suggest that public enterprises or government corporations be established or extended to thrust government more effectively into the marketplace as a producer of goods or services. Presumably, revenues from these enterprises would offset their costs of operation.

In addition to the two aforementioned proposals, experiments using monetary incentives to achieve government efficiencies have been utilized. These incentives, or "shared savings" approaches, reward government agencies attaining higher levels of efficiency either by giving direct cash awards or by putting a share of the savings realized from the efficiency into the budget of the agency. For example, to alleviate overcrowding in pretrial detention facilities, New York City established a program offering substantial budgetary increments to those district attorneys' offices in the city that reduced the number of long-term detainee cases.[18] Frequently, effectiveness is sacrificed for efficiency in many of these experiments. The aim is often not quality of service, but reduced quantity of burden.

Thus, social service agencies, civil rights organizations, churches, state and local governments, and others involved in advocating for the delivery of goods and services to needy populations must update and revise their political and grantsmanship strategies.

THE RAVAGES OF FISCAL CONTROL POLICIES

The fourth issue raised is that the austere, conservative fiscal policies provide the context for social advocacy strategies to begin. The emerging fiscal ethic reflects an obsession with the politics and economics of fiscal control. The deficit has insinuated itself into almost every debate and controversy over federal public policy. Every public policy proposal, regardless of its inherent value or ethical imperative, is subjected to the severe deficit-addition test: To what extent will it exacerbate or alleviate the federal budget deficit?

Both Gramm-Rudman-Hollings and its 1987 amendments and the Tax Reform Act of 1986 reflect impulsive fiscal-control tendencies. GRH resulted from congressional frustration with its inability to substantially reduce the federal deficit. The deficit had grown from $60 billion in 1980 to $220.5 billion at the end of 1985, increasing from 2.3 to 5.3 percent of the gross national product (GNP) of the United States. Deeply concerned about the economic and political implications of continued deficits, about the failure of the Economic Recovery Tax Act of 1981 and other measures designed to stimulate economic growth, and about the impact of these aggregate failures on upcoming 1986 and eventual 1988 elections, Congress assigned a high priority to deficit reduction in 1985.

Despite considerable efforts to reduce the budget, Congress and both President Reagan and President Bush have fallen far short of projected deficit-reduction targets. President Reagan's proposed fiscal year 1987 budget included a 5.9 percent real growth in defense, no tax increases, and massive domestic spending reductions, including termination of the federal school lunch program, Job Corps program, Work Incentive Program (WIN), Urban Development Action Grants (UDAG), revenue sharing program, and mass transit assistance program. Congress, in its Omnibus Reconciliation package of 1987, found these cuts both economically and politically unacceptable. Both the economic and political resources of many political constituencies—Republican and Democratic, regional, racial, gender, labor, and business—were jeopardized. Congress knew that these constituencies would use remaining economic and political resources against incumbents if the president's program was adopted.[19]

GRH sets a series of deficit ceilings designed to eliminate the budget deficit by fiscal year 1991 and provides a framework for across-the-board reductions (sequesters) in controllable domestic programs if the president and Congress cannot agree to a budget within the prescribed ceiling. GRH classifies federal programs into four categories: (1) Exempt, (2) Category I (indexed), (3) Health Services, and (4) Category II (controllable).

Programs in the first category, that is, exempt programs, may not be mandatorily reduced. These include Social Security, interest on the federal debt, the earned income tax credit, prior-year obligations, and judicially ordered claims against the federal government, as well as antipoverty programs such as Aid to Families with Dependent Children (AFDC), food stamps, child nutrition programs, Special Supplemental Food Program for Women, Infants, and Children (WIC), community health centers, and Medicaid.

Category I designates a series of indexed programs and calls for up to half of all required savings to come from reductions in cost-of-living adjusted increases for these programs. Cuts in the base of these programs are prohibited. In essence, Category I froze programs at fiscal year 1985 levels. Of these programs, civil and military retirement and Special Milk programs, for example, would experience a direct reduction, and real-dollar reductions due to inflation resulting from direct reductions.

In the Health Services category, GRH provides for reductions of up to 1 percent in fiscal year 1986 and 2 percent per annum thereafter in five health services programs, including Medicare. Given rapid increases in health care costs and failures in many health services areas to contain such costs, and given the emergency nature of health care inadequacies in poor and nonwhite communities, the real impact of these reductions will exceed the 7 percent level through 1991.

Category II, the controllable category, subjects all other defense and domestic programs to across-the-board reductions if deficit targets specifically identified in the statute are not met. The absolute size of these reductions are determined by the relationship of proposed budgets to budget targets established in the law. This process, known as *sequestration*, automatically executes across-the-board spending reductions in Category II programs.

Under sequestering, the difference between the estimate and the target is automatically reduced with one-half of the excess being canceled from defense accounts and the other half from civilian accounts, with numerous exceptions.[20] Thelwell estimates that in the fiscal year 1990 budget, 70 percent of the outlays are exempt from sequestering.[21]

In the original GRH, the sequestration-triggering decisions were left to the Congressional Budget Office (CBO), the Office of Management and Budget (OMB), and the General Accounting Office (GAO). CBO and OMB were to jointly estimate the size of the deficit for the upcoming fiscal year and to determine whether the deficit exceeded the specified limit by more than $10 billion. If so, CBO and OMB were required to calculate the two uniform percentages—one for defense and one for domestic programs—by which affected programs would have to be reduced in order to close the gap. This so-called snapshot of the federal budget situation was to take place on 15 August of every year. It would then be sent to the GAO for verification and transmitted to the president and Congress by 25 August.

In preamended form, GRH set severe deficit-reduction targets and all but eliminated the congressional budgetary role (see Table 1). However, the Supreme Court, in the case of *Bowsher v. Synar* in July 1986, invalidated the automatic sequestration provision that required the comptroller general, the head of the GAO, to perform an executive function assigned by the Constitution to the Congress.[22] The act, however, contained an alternative that provided for presidential sequestration on enactment of a joint resolution—a procedure that, while not automatic, was constitutional.[23]

TABLE 1
Deficit Targets under Gramm-Rudman-Hollings
Fiscal Years 1986-1991

Fiscal Year	Deficit Level
1986	$171.9 Billion
1987	144 Billion
1988	108 Billion
1989	72 Billion
1990	36 Billion
1991	0

Source: Balanced Budget and Emergency Deficit Control Act of 1985 (P.L. 99-177)

The import of the Supreme Court's *Synar* decision for social advocacy is threefold. First, it restores congressional responsibility for deficit reduction. Congress remains the primary legal and political arena for difficult budgetary decisions, including both discretionary and nondiscretionary spending. Second, by reinforcing the constitutional role of Congress to make budgets, expertise about budgets and their socioeconomic impacts shift from the GAO to the CBO. Social advocates must not only follow the congressional debate in key Senate and House committees, but they also must track the analyses and proposals of the CBO, particularly those most likely to influence congressional thinking. Analyses become as critical for those supporting continued or increased levels of support for the needy as the ethical debate. And, third, because the mechanical role of the GAO was eliminated by the courts, direct conflicts between the Congress and the presidency over deficit priorities become sharper. Who prevails in such a conflict depends upon the strategies each party adopts and the constellations of interests each party is inclined to work with. However, neither Congress nor the presidency has taken a deficit policy stance that will take the federal budget deeply into social intervention or that sustains all discretionary social programming at current funding levels plus inflation.

Fiscal Control Strategies II: The Tax Reform Act of 1986

If the GRH was the major legislative initiative on deficit reduction, the Tax Reform Act of 1986 was the leading legislative action on revenue. The policy objectives of the act included fairness, revenue growth, simplification of tax regulations and forms, elimination of multiple tax shelters for those itemizing, increased taxes on capital gains from real estate sales, removal of more than six million poor households from the tax pools, a separate standard deduction for households headed by a single parent, low-income housing depreciation, retroactive repeal of the investment tax credit, and continued deductibility of state and local income taxes.

The Tax Reform Act of 1986 illustrates the interconnection of budget and tax policies. Tax provisions were designed both to simplify tax compliance and, most importantly, to generate greater and more predictable revenues to address the budget deficit. And, as Lynn Burbridge rightly argues:

> At the same time the tax law was encouraging more investment in low-income housing, the federal government was cutting its financial commitment to low-income housing in half. So whatever gain was made on one side was taken away on the other. Further, most tax economists agree that providing tax incentives for low-income housing is less efficient than directly subsidizing it.[24]

Furthermore, reduction of charitable expense deductions combined with real-dollar declines in a variety of income transfer programs tend to exacerbate poverty among those with income, employment, and occupational problems. As Darity and Myers indicate:

> Blacks unequivocally rely in disproportionate numbers on such programs for income. One-quarter of all blacks are enrolled in the Medicaid program, one-quarter receive food stamps, 20% receive support from the AFDC program, and one in seven blacks live in federally-subsidized housing. One-quarter of black households with school children 5 to 18 years old receive free or reduced-price school lunches.[25]

Income losses in any household translate into revenue losses for federal, state, and local governments. Revenue losses constrain policy responsiveness to the poor as reflected in public budgets, even when the will to be responsive is present.

Moreover, the psychological and administrative barrier created between taxpayer and government was severely exacerbated by the confusion over both tax provisions and tax forms following the enactment of the Tax Reform Act. Several versions of the 1040 Individual Tax Form were issued before the confusion abated. Phased-in elimination of the consumer interest provisions seemed complicated, and the backlog of cases at the Internal Revenue Service (IRS) involving the new tax law belied its policy objective of simplifying the law. The result was a frustration of revenue generation and a smaller-than-anticipated contribution of the new tax provisions to deficit reduction.

Finally, it is also essential to understand the intergovernmental consequences of both federal budget and tax policy. "Tax conformity," the extent to which state income tax law reflected federal policy alternatives, became an immediate issue following enactment of the Tax Reform Act. States most intent on reflecting federal tax reform realized a revenue windfall at the expense of state taxpayers, particularly the poor. Those adopting a more gradualist approach displayed a sensitivity to the voter intolerance of higher state taxes than was exhibited in most of the tax revolts of the 1970s and 1980s.

On the expenditure side, the elimination of state and local revenue sharing funds and the reduction in most categories of block grant funding distributed from federal to state and local governments was both economically and politically expensive to nonwhites and advocates of the poor.[26] Need increased in cities, counties, school districts, and states where African Americans, Hispanics, and women hold more than 90 percent of the elective offices.

Consequently, both GRH and tax reform are having significant effects on the distribution and redistribution of economic and political resources among African Americans, Hispanics, and the other needy, and between the needy and other Americans. Indeed, there is a quantitative impact on the resource level of those who need, as well as a qualitative impact on both their standards of living and on the ethical orientation of American society as a whole. They imply an agenda for public officials, social service deliverers, advocates of the poor, and others with a strong fiscal component.

TOWARDS AN ETHICAL FISCAL STRATEGY

The fifth issue addressed here is that advocates for social change should incorporate formal cost-benefit analysis and socioeconomic-impact assessment among other strategies as they address the new fiscal ethics. It is essential to maintain both the values implied in the struggle of nonwhite and poor Americans seeking fiscal alternatives and the related criteria for good fiscal policies. At a minimum, good fiscal policies include the principles of *productivity, equity,* and *elasticity.* A productive fiscal policy generates sufficient revenues to meet governmental needs on the tax side and makes investment in human needs, economic development, and defense on the spending side. If tax policies fail to generate adequate revenue, more public monies must be spent on borrowing, with a subsequent effect on interest rates and economic growth.

An equitable fiscal policy is fair to both taxpayers and to specific public constituencies benefiting from public expenditures. In tax policy, economists refer to two kinds of equity—*horizontal* and *vertical*. Horizontal equity means that taxpayers who have the same amounts of income should be taxed at the same rate. Vertical equity implies that wealthier people should pay more taxes than poorer people. A related principle is that tax should be *progressive*: taxes increase as income increases. *Proportional* principles of taxation increase taxes in exact and direct proportion to increases in income. *Regressive* taxes are those that impose greater burdens on taxpayers least able to pay or that increase as income decreases.[27]

Although traditionally applied to taxes, notions of progressivity, proportionality, and regressivity also have a budgetary counterpart. Fiscal policies that tend to benefit the least needy and deprive the most needy are budgetarily regressive. Generally, GRH is regressive in its impacts on African Americans and Hispanics, because it utilizes budget bases that were already retrenched before 1985 as baselines for GRH-mandated cuts, and because needs continue to rise as funding levels decline.

Finally, an elastic fiscal system is one that is flexible enough to address its revenue and spending needs regardless of macroeconomic changes in economic conditions. Taxes and spending make a contribution to the stabilization of the economy, as well as to the stability of socioeconomic components of society.

As the Congressional Black Caucus *Quality of Life: Fiscal 1990 Alternative Budget* and work by organizations such as the Center for Budget Priorities point out, when GRH and the Tax Reform Act are considered together, they are fiscally regressive for African American and Hispanic households, individuals, and institutions. Strict enforcement of the Tax Reform Act objectives is generally progressive for low-income families and households. However, anticipated reductions in GRH Categories I and II, minuscule growth in exempted programs, and increased demands for both exempt and retrenched programs erode most of the benefits of tax reform for lowest-income households.

Moreover, in considering the ethics of good fiscal policy, it is also essential to consider the reciprocal relationship between households and institutions. Institutions such as charitable organizations, businesses, advocacy organizations, municipal, county, and state governments, trade unions, and others provide essential services to their members and constituencies. Conversely, these institutions justify their existence and draw money and other resources from households. If fiscal policies adversely affect households, institutions are profoundly affected. Similarly, if fiscal policies damage institutions, households suffer.

Consequently, the ethical budget holds as its principal mission both responsiveness to the needy in the United States and economic and political empowerment. It is aimed at a redistribution of resources that only temporarily charges more affluent members for subsidies so that the less affluent members eventually become more affluent. Human capital is as essential as physical capital. And, long-term investments in human captial development are perceived as realizing multiple returns to society that will more than pay for the investments.

CONCLUSIONS AND POLICY IMPLICATIONS

What policy advocacy implications do the new fiscal ethics hold? What strategies of human services delivery and advocacy for the poor seem appropriate? How can the double bind of dependency on public finance by both the poor and the middle class be reduced?[28]

First, the moral struggle to attain equity and financial choice for African Americans, Hispanics, women, and the poor should escalate. Majority Americans have as great a stake, if not greater, in the outcome of the moral struggle as do those who are needy. The ultimate financial and moral beneficiaries of this struggle are the majority businesses, educational institutions, and public agencies, because the poor buy from them.

Second, local, state, and federal fiscal monitoring should continue and increase. Components of such monitoring include the following:

1. Regular assessment of spending and taxing policies, proposals, and plans for the current and potential impacts they have on the needy
2. Analysis of procurement and contracting practices to determine whether, and to what extent, small, minority- and female-owned business utilization plans are in place;

3. Where privatization occurs, or is proposed, transitional plans including mandates to private owners to continue inclusion of the needy

Third, expanded use of formal policy and impact assessments should be used to advance the needs of the poor in legislative hearings, public rule-making and regulatory processes, and judicial proceedings.[29]

All of these points underscore the need for social policy advocates to carefully acquire, utilize, and work with *experts*. Policy expertise comes from many disciplines, and it is the major weapon of interested parties whose ethical preferences prevail in policy. The new fiscal ethics are, therefore, best met by a new and more effective use of expertise.[30]

NOTES

1. Charles V. Hamilton, "The Welfare of Black Americans," *Political Science Quarterly* 101, (2) (1986): 253.

2. John L. Mikesell, *Fiscal Administration: Analysis and Applications for the Public Sector*, 2nd ed. (Chicago: The Dorsey Press, 1986), *x*.

3. Warren F. Ilchman and Norman T. Uphoff, *The Political Economy of Change* (Berkeley and Los Angeles: The University of California Press, 1969).

4. On the issue of ethics and public finance, see B. J. Reed and John W. Swain, *Public Finance Administration* (Englewood Cliffs, NJ: Prentice-Hall, Inc., 1990), 195–96.

5. The Congressional Black Caucus, *The Quality of Life: Fiscal 1990 Alternative Budget* (Washington, DC:, Congressional Black Caucus, 1989), *i*.

6. Margaret C. Simms, ed., *Black Economic Progress: An Agenda for the 1990s* (Washington, DC: The Joint Center for Political Studies, 1988).

7. For example, see Congressional Tax Force on Federal Excise Taxes, *Analyzing the Possible Impact of Federal Excise Taxes on the Poor, Including Blacks and Other Minorities* (Washington, DC: Voter Education and Registration Action, Inc., July 1987).

8. Small Business Administration, *State of Small Business, 1989* (Washington, DC: Government Printing Office, 1989).

9. Georgia A. Persons, "Blacks in State and Local Government: Progress and Constraints," *The State of Black America, 1987*, (New York: National Urban League, Inc., 1988), 167–92; Georgia A. Persons, "Reflections on Mayoral Leadership: The Impact of Changing Issues and Changing Times," *Phylon* 41 (3) (Sept. 1985): 205–18; Hanes Walton, *Black Politics: A Theoretical and Structural Analysis* (Philadelphia: J. B. Lippincott, Inc., 1972).

10. Hanes Walton, *When the Marching Stopped: The Politics of Civil Rights Regulatory Agencies* (Albany: State University of New York Press, 1988), 59.

11. Mark S. Kamlet, David C. Mowery, and Tsai-Tsu Su, "Upsetting National Priorities: The Reagan Administration's Budgetary Strategy," *The American Political Science Review* 82 (4) (December 1988): 1,293–1,307.

12. Adapted from Irene S. Rubin, *Shrinking the Federal Government: The Effect of Cutbacks on Five Federal Agencies* (New York and London: Longman, Inc., 1985), 27.

13. Paul David Schumaker, Russell W. Getter, and Terry Nichols Clark, *Policy Responsiveness and Fiscal Strain in 51 American Communities* (Washington, DC: The American Political Science Association, 1983).

14. Lenneal J. Henderson, *Proposition 13: Managing the Income Security Impacts* (Washington, DC: National Institute of Public Management, 1979).

15. Bureau of the Census, *Census of Governments, 1987* (Washington, DC: Government Printing Office, 1988).

16. Linda Williams, "Gramm-Rudman and the Politics of Defict Reduction," *The Urban League Review* 10 (2) (Winter 1986–87): 72–83.

17. Carol E. Cohen, "State Fiscal Capacity and Effort: An Update," *Intergovernmental Perspective* 15 (2) (Spring 1989): 15–23.

18. Thomas W. Church and Milton Heumann, "The Underexamined Assumptions of the Invisible Hand: Monetary Incentives as Policy Instruments," *Journal of Policy Analysis and Management* 8 (4) (Fall 1989): 641.

19. Lenneal J. Henderson, "Blacks, Budgets, and Taxes: Assessing the Impact of Budget Deficit Reduction and Tax Reform on Blacks," in *The State of Black America 1987*, ed. Janet Dewart, (New York: The National Urban League, Inc., 1987), 75–95.

20. Henderson, "Blacks, Budgets, and Taxes," 79.

21. Raphael Thelwell, "Gramm-Rudman-Hollings Four Years Later: A Fable (Unpublished paper, Washington, DC, Sept. 1989), 3.

22. *Bowsher v. Synar*, 54 USLW 5064.

23. Thelwell, *Gramm-Rudman-Hollings*, 4.

24. Lynn Burbridge, "Tax Reform: A Minimalist Approach for Assisting the Low-Income," *The Urban League Review* 10 (2) (Winter 1986–87): 101–12.

25. William Darity, Jr., and Samuel Myers, Jr., "Distress v. Dependency: Changing Income Support Programs," *The Urban League Review* 10 (2) (Winter 1986–87): 24–33.

26. Vincent Marando, "Revenue-Sharing and American Cities" (Paper delivered at the annual meeting of the American Political Science Association, Aug. 1989).

27. Henderson, "Blacks, Budgets, and Taxes," 84.

28. Darity and Myers, "Distress v. Dependency," 26.

29. See, for example, Robert V. Bartlett, "Policy and Impact Assessment: An Introduction," *Policy Studies Review* (Sept. 1988): 73–74.

30. On the role and value of policy expertise, See Stuart S. Nagel, *Policy Studies: Integration and Evaluation* (Westport, CT: Greenwood Press, Inc., 1988).

2

Aiding African American Communities in the Post-Reagan Era: How to Get More African Americans in Government

Hanes Walton, Jr., Daniel Brantley, and Willie E. Johnson

The scarcity of African American and minority officials handicaps state efforts to help African American and minority communities already deprived of federal aid. Governors and legislatures could, however, cooperate to see that more minorities are appointed to government positions and that minority officials have a mandate to help needy communities.

Critical for the amelioration of African American communities after the Reagan era is a rethinking and restructuring of political resources as well as linkages. Reagan's chief legacy will be the deficit, John Chubb and Paul Peterson predict in *The New Directions in American Politics*.[1] They see this reality dominating the post-Reagan national agenda and budget. The deficit's size and influence compels attention from federal officials.

What then are the options and alternatives available to minority communities? We propose a partial solution that governors can employ to better enable minority appointees to help solve the problems of minority communities in the post-Reagan era.

Unfortunately, minorities are seldom appointed to state boards, comissions, and authorities, as Table 1 attests.

PLANNING INSTEAD OF POLITICAL SYMBOLISM

The data in Table 1 reveal that very few African Americans hold appointed positions. One possibility for the scarcity of minority officials, including African Americans, is that there has been no concerted effort to recruit more minorities or to have minority officials handle the problems of minority communities. A second possibility is that minority communities apparently are a low priority for state officials.

TABLE 1
The African American Presence on State Boards,
Commissions and Agencies in Georgia: 1986

State Boards	Number of Appointive Positions	Number of African Americans	Percentage of African Americans
Pardons and Parole Board	5	1	20
Board of Corrections	15	3	20
Board of Natural Resources	15	3	20
Human Resources Board	15	4	27
Transportation Board [a]	10	1	10
Education Board	10	1	10
Board of Regents	15	3	20
Community Affairs Board	15	3	20
Workers Compensa- tion Board	3	0	0
Public Safety Board	10	1	10
County Registrars	477	4	0.8
County Heads of Election Board	13	1	7.7

Source: Adapted from data collected by Georgia Rep. Tyrone Brooks.
[a]State Board of Transportation elected from congressional district by delegation members.

Governors have the power to turn around this situation by appointing more minorities to their administrations and, thus, indicating that minority communities will receive the priority they merit. Governors have yet to do so, however. Instead, the politics of symbolism has resulted in appointment of African Americans, Hispanics, and Asians to highly visible positions in state government. Subsequently, such officials typically have lacked the authority to be effective leaders and resolve problems in minority communities.

Key state officials such as governors, lieutenant governors, and legislative leaders make numerous political appointments to statewide boards, commissions, authorities, and agencies. Many appointments are apparently used to payoff political deals and garner political support. However, slightly, African American and other minority communities have benefited from the practice of partisan and patronage politics. But, in the post-Reagan era, the politics of symbolism has to give way to the realization that we must use our resources more effectively, including minority appointees. As a constructive alternative to politics as usual, we propose an administrative strategy to use minority appointees more effeciently to plan, set priorities, and implement programs to ameliorate conditions in minority communities.

Leadership in drafting and implementing such a plan should come from the governor's staff, a governor-elect's transition team, or a legislative minority caucus. The plan should be an aid in determining the priority of appointing minorities to boards, commissions, authorities, and agencies.

Indeed, a bold initiative is needed because of the relatively worsening economic and social conditions in minority communities. For instance, corporations shun counties with African American populations of 35 percent or more when locating manufacturing and industrial facilities, according to Margaret Edds in *Free at Last*.[2] Edds's findings were confirmed by Dr. Lawrence Hanks in *Black Political Empowerment in Three Georgia Counties*[3] and Professor K. C. Morrison in *Black Political Mobilization*.[4] They also demonstrated that it is exceedingly difficult, if not impossible, for these counties to attract any jobs, industry, or other means of development. Hence, these findings by a journalist and African American and white scholars alike clearly suggest the strong need for African Americans to be appointed to state rural development boards.

Likewise, other studies strongly document the need for African American political appointees to urban redevelopment and inner-city boards. The growing numbers of homeless further indicate how many needs are going unmet. These findings and their social indications are not being addressed by any plan or priorities to relieve the plight of urban and rural minority communities. Therefore, we believe an administrative system that would aid these communities would be of great value and worth states considering. The core of this plan is coordination.

Our proposal calls for the governor's office to work together with state minority legislative caucuses. First, they should hold sessions to develop linkages and plan strategies on how to effectively handle problems and crises facing minority communities. This goes beyond the common practice of appointing minority officials who may lack a sense of service to their respective communities and a willngness to work together. Coordination and cooperation—between the political appointees, the legislative minority caucus, and the governor's staffers—are vital to successful efforts to solve pressing problems in minority communities.

We propose that politicians should follow a deliberate policy of appointing minorities to governmental bodies to allow them to resolve pressing problems in their communities. This mechanism, once in place, should attract and increase the effectiveness of federal aid to states for minority concerns.

The crucial component of the plan is the governor's involvement by appointing members to statewide governmental bodies. Previous efforts at coordination have been on an ad hoc basis among key minority lawmakers, prominent members of minority communities, and state house staffers. But these temporary coalitions have lacked strong support from the chief executive and, consequently, have quickly vanished. Georgia State Representative Robert Holmes, a professor at Atlanta University, in a seminal paper on the relationship between the governor's office and the African American legislative caucuses, examined five different administrative-legislative relationships.[5] Holmes concluded that these relations left much to be desired because cooperation was sporadic.

To build more permanent and more consistent minority relationships, many governors have appointed minorities as their special assistants and/or advisors. These individuals are sometimes able to maintain a sustaining relationship. In many instances, only the governor's office has the prestige and the formal power to introduce and implement such a plan. For this reason, we stress the importance of the governor's office in the appointment of minority officials and the coordination, in conjunction with the legislative branch, of an administrative plan designed to solve the problems of minority communities.

A COORDINATING MECHANISM

The appointment-coordination mechanism which we proposed is a device to assist minority and African American communities in an era of a huge national deficit. It is not offered as a panacea (nothing can replace adequate funding levels), but as a modest proposal. A careful rethinking of how states can better coordinate and manage resources — through planning and distributing limited resources and skillfully deploying manpower — doubtlessly will go a long way to solve problems faced by minority and other communities.

Moreover, such an approach is an additional way to make the government more responsive to the people, especially to minority communities. And, most important, highly visible role models in political offices will help minorities, many of whom only were able to vote as a result of the 1965 Voting Rights Act, to better understand that the political process can be made to work for them.

Finally, it establishes a mechanism for the governor to maximize the state resources which typically go to minority communities. All this can be accomplished with procedures to recruit and increase the effectiveness of minority officials in serving minority constituencies.

NOTES

1. John Chubb and Paul Peterson, eds., *The New Directions in American Politics* (Washington, DC: Brookings Institution, 1985).
2. Margaret Edds, *Free at Last: What Really Happened When Civil Rights Came to Southern Politics* (Maryland: Adler and Adler, 1987).
3. Lawrence Hanks, *Black Political Empowerment in Three Georgia Counties* (Knoxville: University of Tennessee Press, 1987).

4. K. C. Morrison, *Black Political Mobilization: Leadership, Power, and Mass Behavior* (Albany: State University of New York Press, 1987).

5. Robert Holmes, ''The Georgia Legislative Black Caucus and the Office of Governor,'' in *Black Politics and Black Political Behavior*, ed. Hanes Walton, Jr. (California: Borgo Press, forthcoming).

3

Will Welfare Be Reformed?
The Possible Effects of the Family
Support Act on Children

Lynn C. Burbridge

The welfare reform debate focuses more on whether or not welfare grant recipients want to be self-sufficient than on antipoverty and child welfare concerns. This article contends that the focus of welfare reform should be the well-being of children. Thus, welfare reform must be evaluated in terms of how it addresses the needs of children. Welfare for children in the United States varies from state to state. There are no minimum benefit standards for children, and proposals to provide minimum national benefits for poor families with children have been rejected by Congress. The Family Support Act of 1988 consists of seven titles. Each title is examined and implications for children are discussed.

Many have said that there is a new consensus about welfare reform, that both liberals and conservatives now agree on the ultimate goal of welfare reform: self-sufficiency. Underlying this consensus, however, have been differing ideas as to the meaning of self-sufficiency and how it should be attained. Nobody would deny that it is better to be independent than dependent, all things remaining equal. But the poorer one is, the less meaningful self-sufficiency becomes both economically and psychologically. This is particularly true for families where the primary concern is, or should be, the well-being of children in the family unit. No matter how independent-minded one is, children need to be fed, clothed, and housed. A key question is how to balance the value placed on self-sufficiency with concerns for mitigating the consequences of poverty. Further, even if a family head is not independent-minded, children still need to be fed, clothed, and housed. Another fundamental question, therefore, is the extent to which there is a social obligation to children whether or not their parents conform to behavioral norms.

These antipoverty and child welfare concerns have played a relatively small role in the welfare reform debate of recent years. If there has been a consensus, it has been to avoid these issues and to focus on whether or not welfare grant recipients want to be self-sufficient. Liberals by and large assert that recipients want to work but need assistance in removing barriers that prevent them from doing so. Conservatives are more likely to argue that recipients have become too used to welfare and need a push to get off the welfare rolls. Little has been said about whether self-sufficiency in poverty is acceptable; very little has been said about children.

This article will not enter the debate about the causes of poverty, the increase in the number of female-headed households, the reasons for long-term welfare receipt, or whether welfare recipients want to work; not because these are unimportant issues, but because they have constituted the bulk of the discussion concerning welfare reform. Rather, this article takes as its premise that there is a fundamental social obligation to children and that welfare reform should be evaluated in terms of how it addresses the needs of children. Self-sufficiency, while still important, is examined in terms of the benefits it can bring to children. The consensus for welfare reform is discussed in terms of a consensus to fulfill child welfare goals.

The next section provides a brief discussion of child welfare as a goal for social policy and the well-being of children in the United States. A detailed examination of the Family Support Act and its possible impact on child welfare follows. The last section discusses implications for public policy.

WELFARE FOR CHILDREN

Prior to the Family Support Act

Aid to Families with Dependent Children (AFDC) began as a program just for children. Originally Aid to Dependent Children (ADC), it was established by the 1935 Social Security Act, enabling states to provide cash assistance to poor children without fathers. Under the current AFDC program, children's caretakers are also included in the grant. Until the passage of the Family Support Act of 1988, however, the provision of benefits to two-parent families was a state option; 25 states and the District of Columbia exercised this option—called Aid to Families with Dependent Children of Unemployed Parents (AFDC-UP) and only for two-parent families in which the principal earner was unemployed—and 25 states maintained AFDC as a program for single parents. In these states, poor children in two-parent families could not receive benefits. The new law requires all states to have an Unemployed Parents program at least six months out of the year. For AFDC or AFDC-UP eligibility for federal assistance ends on a child's 18th birthday.

There are also income-related eligibility requirements; AFDC is very much a categorical program. Each state sets its own standard of need, benefit levels, and income and resource limits. The standard of need and benefit levels can be and are below the poverty level. The federal government provides matching funds to the states for the AFDC program based on state per capita income. The federal match ranges from 20 percent to 80 percent and averages about 50 percent. Poorer states generally have low benefit levels and high federal matches.

In determining eligibility and benefits, the federal government requires states to follow certain guidelines regarding the treatment of earnings and work-related expenses. States must also provide Medicaid for AFDC recipients, also through a federal-state cost-sharing formula. Most recipients are eligible for food stamps as well. In addition, many states also provide public assistance to poor, single individuals without children. These programs do not receive federal funds, however, and are initiated by the state or the county.

Since 1967, states have been required by the federal government to operate an employment and training program for recipients—the Work Incentive Program (WIN). Through the years, WIN has changed from a voluntary program to a mandatory one and has periodically changed its emphasis on long-term versus short-term training. Since 1981, WIN has experienced a 75 percent cut in funding, making anything but short-term job search assistance extremely difficult for states to provide without supplementary funding from state revenues. The Reagan Administration also tried to mandate "workfare," under which recipients would be required to work off their grant in public services employment. Because of opposition to workfare, a national mandatory program was never passed by the Congress. The Community Work Experience Program (CWEP) was made an option to the states, however, if they wanted a workfare component in addition to WIN. States were also given more freedom in the design and administration of work programs than they had had prior to the 1980s.

Since the states are given a great deal of discretion in determining their AFDC benefits and the kinds of services offered to recipients, it is not surprising that there is considerable variation across states in the benefits and services received by AFDC grantees. According to a recent study by the Center on Budget and Policy Priorities, AFDC benefits range from 15.6 percent of the poverty line in Alabama to 83.3 percent of the poverty line in California.[1] The kinds of employment, training, and support services vary greatly as well. For example, some states offer access to expensive education and training programs with extended daycare and Medicaid, while others offer little except job search or workfare.[2] These differences are justified on the grounds that the states are better able to judge the level of need in their region, and that welfare programs should reflect the cultural norms within the state. These state-by-state differences, however, are responsible for significant horizontal inequity in how the poor are treated in this country. What this has come to mean for children is that their well-being not only depends on their luck in being born to the right parents (that is, those with nonpoverty incomes), but also in being born to parents in the right state.

There are no national minimum-benefit standards for children. This omission is particularly striking when U.S. social policy for children is compared to that found in the rest of tl > Western world. It is also very different from U.S. policy for the aged. These are discussed in the next section.

Comparisons

In comparing U.S. social policy to that in other Western countries, Sheila Kamerman and Alfred Kahn note that "unlike the situation in several other countries, children's economic well-being has never been high on the agenda of either political party in the

United States, nor has any one party been known as a special champion of children.''[3]
Their research indicates that the United States is one of the only industrial countries that
does not provide a universal, public, child benefit or family allowance. While it does
have a family tax allowance, it can only be used by those above pretax threshold. Nor
does the United States have a means-tested cash program for *all* poor children. Not all
poor children are covered by AFDC, because need standards are generally below the
poverty level and because there are restrictions on aiding poor children in two-parent
families where the primary earner is employed.

Most other industrial countries provide a universal cash benefit or refundable tax
credit based on the number of children in the family. Many European countries are also
providing a guaranteed minimum child support payment to one-parent families so that
custodial parents will not be vulnerable to irregular payments from the absent parent.
The government, in turn, assumes responsibility for collecting child support. These
provisions ensure a minimum living standard for all children in these countries and
child support for female-headed households.

A study of Organization for Economic Cooperation and Development (OECD) countries by Michael O'Higgins indicates that the per capita value of family benefits are
lowest in the United States.[4] The United States also has the lowest tax benefits for
children as a percentage of gross earnings. Interestingly, when total social program
expenditures are taken as a percentage of gross domestic product, the United States has
the third-lowest ranking, above Japan and Australia. The reason for this higher ranking
in total expenditures is that the United States spends more for the elderly than do Japan
and Australia (as well as Great Britain). So, in spite of its low family and child benefits,
the U.S. treatment of the elderly prevents it from ranking last in terms of total social
expenditures.

The treatment of the elderly also presents an interesting contrast when one evaluates
the U.S. commitment to children. Every proposal to provide a minimum national
benefit for poor families with children has been rejected by Congress. Yet, the Supplemental Security Income Act of 1973 ''established what was a uniform basic minimum pension'' for the elderly (that is, SSI).[5] There is also a universal health program
for the elderly, Medicare, while 13 million children are without any insurance coverage
at all.[6] Medicaid is provided to families on AFDC, but it is a state option to provide
Medicaid coverage to all poor children. Thus, children of the working poor are often
uninsured or underinsured. Virtually all other industrial countries provide some form of
national, universal health coverage.

Various reasons have been cited for the greater generosity of children's programs in
other countries. Kamerman and Kahn note that the pro-nationalism of the Right combined with the concerns for social equity on the Left created a consensus for children's
program in these countries. This was strengthened by concerns for social solidarity
following the devastation of World War II. The United States, in contrast, has never
had a strong pro-nationalism movement and suffered considerably less that did its

European counterparts in the war. Also mentioned has been a greater commitment to the free market in the United States, a resistance to government interference, and assertion of states' rights in setting social policy goals.

While all of these explanations have merit, relatively little attention has been paid to the role of race. Kamerman and Kahn note that at the time European countries were struggling to provide greater social equity for all children, the United States was involved in a civil rights revolution to redress centuries of racism and discrimination against African Americans. Social solidarity has been a difficult concept to sell in the racially and ethnically divided United States. Even with the elimination of the most egregious Jim Crow laws, poverty is still generally considered a minoirty problem, and solutions for it are often considered minority solutions. As long as the poor are considered "the others," there is indifference, if not outright hostility, to policies directed toward ameliorating or ending poverty. The social homogeneity of other industrial countries has enabled them to adopt generous and universal children's programs, which have been difficult to realize in the United States. Regardless of the reason, however, the lack of a clear commitment to the well-being of children has made them very vulnerable to changes in economic and political winds. This is discussed as the next section.

The Well-Being of Children

About one in five children in the United States is poor. This represents a one-third increase in the child poverty rate since the 1970s. Various reasons have been given for this: a poor economy including back-to-back recessions in 1980 and 1981–1982, declines in the real value of AFDC benefits as a result of inflation, and reductions in government spending for social programs during the Reagan presidency. Sheldon Danzinger decomposed the contribution of different factors explaining increases in family poverty. He found that among families with an unmarried head, 75 percent of the increase can be attributed to welfare program changes, whereas among married-couple families, 70 percent result from changes in market income.[7] Thus, both political and economic factors were at work, the impact varying by family type.

Among African American children—particularly those in female-headed households—poverty rates are extremely high. Sixty percent of African American and Hispanic children living with their mothers are poor, compared to 40 percent of white non-Hispanic children living with their mother. Further, Danzinger noted that a welfare reform policy targeted on one-sixth of the poor—notably long-term AFDC recipients—would affect one-third of all poor children and one-half to two-thirds of poor African American children.

Poverty rates are not the only index of child welfare. Haveman et al. examined four measures of well-being of children: family income, family net financial assets, family tangible assets (financial assets and real assets) and parental time available to the child.[8] They found that between 1962 and 1983, income, assets, and parental time per child increased overall. These increases in well-being would not have occurred—by and large—were it not for decreases in family size, however. Of greater concern was the authors' finding that inequality in wealth was very high across as well as within groups. In addition, within-group inequality in per-child parental time had increased.

Further, studies using the Panel Study of Income Dynamics (PSID) indicate that poor or near-poor families experience considerable instability in income, with frequent moves above and below the poverty line.[9] Little work has been done on income instability and its impact on children, however. Research indicates that it has a significant effect on family breakups, indicating that variations in income can be just as important as levels of income.[10]

Time and space do not permit an examination of noneconomic indices of well-being such as education, housing, health status, and so on. But they are no less important when assessing the status of children in the United States.

THE FAMILY SUPPORT ACT OF 1988

There are seven titles to the Family Support Act of 1988. Title I deals with child support. Title II deals with the JOBS program, Title III deals with transitional assistance, Title IV deals with related AFDC amendments, Title V authorizes family support demonstrations, Title VI contains other miscellaneous provisions, and Title VII addresses the funding provisions. Each title is discussed below with special attention to the possible impact on children.

Title I—Child Support and Establishment of Paternity

The federal Child Support Enforcement (CSE) Program was enacted in 1975 and included as a new part D to Title IV of the Social Security Act. Subsequent amendments to the law in 1981, 1984, and 1985 strengthened the enforcement activities specified in the original legislation. The law provides federal matching funds to the states for obtaining and enforcing of child support obligations, establishing paternity, and locating absent parents. The states must make efforts to secure support for children on AFDC, and the assignment of rights to child support is a conditon for eligibility to the program. The states must also make available their services to non-AFDC families upon application by a custodial parent.

Prior to the Family Support Act, the primary enforcement tools included the garnishing of federal and state income tax returns for delinquent child support payments and mandatory wage withholding, which could be required if support payments were one month delinquent. The 1985 amendments also required all states to establish expedited processes for obtaining and enforcing child support.

The federal matching rate for the administrative costs of the program was 68 percent in 1988 and is to be reduced to 66 percent in fiscal year (FY) 1990. In addition, each state receives incentive payments: 6 percent of the state's AFDC collections and 6 percent of its non-AFDC collections. An even larger incentive payment can be received—

up to 10 percent of collections—if collections exceed total administrative costs. Incentives paid for non-AFDC collections were capped at 105 percent of the incentive for AFDC collections in 1988, and increased to 110 percent in 1989 and 115 percent in 1990. Thus, the incentives are geared to ensure that considerable efforts are made to obtain child support for AFDC cases.

In spite of these efforts, data for 1983 indicate that a little more than half of families with an absent father had a child support order. Only half of these received all the child support that was due them. Thus, only 25 percent of children in families with an absent parent received full child support payments. Further, about a third of the families with an absent father were below the poverty level; only about a third of these had a child support agreement; and of those with orders, 62 percent actually received payments. In addition, only 18 percent of never-married women were awarded child support payments, compared to 76 percent of divorced women; and only 34 percent of African American mothers were awarded child support payments, compared to 67 percent of white mothers and 41 percent of Hispanic mothers.

The Family Support Act strengthens child support enforcement tools. For example, judges and other officials would be required to use state guidelines for child support, and the state must provide for immediate wage withholdings for all cases—not just AFDC cases of those involving delinquent payments. There are several exceptions, however, so the extent to which states will actually change their practices is unclear. Within five years of enactment, states will have to adjust awards for AFDC cases every three years and non-AFDC cases at the request of a parent. In addition, states would have to meet federal performance standards for the establishment of paternity. The provision affecting the most families, however, is the requirement that both parents' social security numbers must be acquired by the state when issuing birth certificates (thus making it easier to track absent parents.)[11] The Congressional Budget Office (CBO) estimates that these provisions will result in a net savings of $170 million federal dollars.

Implications for Children. Perhaps the most interesting aspect of this title is that it is included in a welfare reform bill and contains provisions affecting AFDC and non-AFDC cases alike. There is at least an implicit recognition that welfare reform should be closely tied to *child* support, which, in turn, is a universal concern, not just a concern that only arises out of concern for the costs of welfare. Nevertheless, the emphasis is on AFDC cases and retrieving some of the revenue expended on welfare families.

While cost savings are not a trivial issue at a time of high budget deficits, it is not clear that AFDC families will benefit substantially from child support enforcement. Robert Lerman cites data from the National Longitudinal Survey indicating that 21-to-29-year-old absent fathers have a median income of $10,700; $8,400 for the typical African American absent father.[12] Fathers of AFDC children probably have even lower median earnings. Thus, the contribution they may make to their families is small. Further, a simulation analysis conducted by Phillip K. Robins indicates that "AFDC dependency is quite insensitive to changes in child support policies."[13] This is not to suggest that absent fathers of AFDC families cannot or should not contribute to the support of their families, only that—from the point of view of child welfare—the impact of these contributions on AFDC children is likely to be small.

It can be argued, of course, that even if families cannot get off welfare, the ability of government to recoup some of the costs of the program will make greater expansion of the program more politically feasible. It has also been argued that stricter enforcement of child support will inhibit family breakups; that is, fathers will be less likely to desert their families if they are held accountable for child support.[14] Thus, the fewer desertions there are, the fewer families will end up on AFDC. Further, non-AFDC families on the margins of poverty many benefit significantly from stricter enforcement, particularly when the absent father has an adequate salary. For these families, child support represents a real gain in income, unlike for AFDC recipients who only gain if the support is enough money to bring total family income above the AFDC grant level. (Currently, AFDC recipients can disregard from income $50 of their child support, so they are only $50 richer unless child support payments are high enough to bring them off the roles.)

Title II—Job Opportunities and Basic Skills Training Program (JOBS)

Currently the most-talked-about component of the Family Support Act, JOBS would supersede the WIN program that was discussed earlier. According to the new law, every state must operate a JOBS program providing at least two of the following four activities: job search, CWEP (work experience), grant diversion, or on-the-job training (OJT). Thus workfare (CWEP) remains an option to the state.

Like WIN, JOBS is a mandatory program, but JOBS is mandatory for women with children over three, instead of for women with children over six, as was WIN. Thus, a larger group of women will be classified as mandatories. States must guarantee child care for women with children between three and six, however. States can also require recipients under the age of 20 to participate in education if they have not obtained a general equivalency diploma (GED) or high school diploma. Thus, child care must be provided for these parents as well.

Federal matching would change from the 90 percent under WIN. The first $126 million (the WIN allocation for 1987) will have a 90–10 match; any additional funds would be matched at the lower Medicaid matching rate with a minimum federal match of 60 percent for nonadministrative costs. The cap on funding was $600 million in FY 1989, going up to $1.3 billion in FY 1995. While this is a considerable sum, it only represents a cap; the federal government does not have to spend these funds for training. There are also explicit incentives to serve hard-to-serve groups, namely, dropouts, those with little work experience, families in which the youngest child is within two years of being ineligible for assistance, and long-term recipients. Volunteers for the program must be considered first within these target groups.

JOBS also has participation performance standards, although they will not be difficult for most states to attain.

Implications for Children. As noted earlier, the emphasis in the welfare reform debate has been on the adults in the system rather than the children. The purpose of JOBS — as with WIN that preceded it — is to encourage or force AFDC parents to become more self-sufficient. The arguments against this approach are that (1) people cannot be forced to be self-sufficient; and (2) clients and their families are often worse off when they work than when they are on AFDC.

In regards to the first point, the states will have considerable discretion in how they intend to enforce the work requirements. Under WIN, state practices regarding enforcement ranged from swift sanctioning of noncooperative clients to the operation of an essentially voluntary program. This is unlikely to change under JOBS, because of the discretion given to the states.

One of the reasons most often given for clients' resistance to participation is low wages in the labor market. This, combined with the cost of daycare and the loss of Medicaid, often makes clients worse off when employed than when they are on welfare. The Family Support Act will provide extended daycare and Medicaid benefits, which shall be discussed in the next section on Title III. Of concern here is whether the training provided under JOBS will make recipients competitive in the labor market and provide more income for their families.

The experience from other employment and training programs has not been encouraging.[15] By and large, women — including AFDC recipients — have been trained for low-wage, sex-stereotyped jobs. The greatest impact of these programs has been on women with little labor-market experiences, for whom even low-paying clerical jobs represent an improvement in labor-market experience. Even with gains in employment and reductions in grant levels, however, most programs have had no effect on overall welfare dependency. In other words, women have increased their employment but do not earn enough to get off welfare.

From a child welfare point of view, however, the ability of women to bring in any additional funds to support their families is a good thing. Further, if working and receiving welfare makes them better off than just working or just being on welfare, then this may be the preferred alternative. Welfare families have often been better off under this option, because recipients do not lose benefits dollar-for-dollar for increased earnings and may receive daycare or have daycare costs subtracted from income in the benefit calculation, and because they keep their Medicaid while on welfare.[16]

While this has changed somewhat with the new law, it is still the case that children will be better off if the mother is both working and receiving benefits. Not only is there more income, but there is also more stability in income. For if the mother loses her job, increased benefits automatically kick in. Little attention has been devoted to the greater stability and security achieved under this scenario, but its advantages cannot have escaped the attention of most welfare recipients.

In addition, women will still be able to upgrade or maintain their work skills, so that when their children grow up they will not be unprepared for the labor market. More care and attention must be given to the quality of training, however, since ultimately it would be desirable to impart the skills necessary to move AFDC women out of the low-wage labor market. It is unlikely, however, that there will be sufficient funds to make this possible for large numbers of women.

Title III—Transitional Assistance for Families after Loss of AFDC Eligibility

Perhaps the most significant element of the new law is the provision of transitional child care and Medicaid benefits for women who find employment and terminate their benefits. The federal government, however, took the lead from the states, many of which had begun using state funds for transitional support services.

The law says that the state should provide transitional child care if it determines that it is necessary for employment. It can be provided for up to one year after the client leaves AFDC as a result of employment. Since it is the state that determines what is "necessary," there will most likely be considerable variation in the use of transitional child care. States can also pay for child care provided by relatives, an important concern since many AFDC recipients rely on relatives for child care. This is particularly true for women with very young children, more of whom would be required to participate as a result of the lowering of the mandatory age of youngest child from six to three. The federal matching rate would be the Medicaid rate.

Medicaid can be extended for one year for those losing their benefits as a result of employment, as well. The first six months would be provided free. In the second six months, states have the option of establishing copayments.

Implications for Children. These provisions provide additional incentives for women to work, but the benefits are short-lived. If within a year women are able to find jobs with medical benefits and increase their earnings sufficiently to meet daycare costs comfortably, there will be an overall improvement in family well-being. If not, recidivism to welfare at the end of the year may be the consequence.

Nevertheless, these provisions are an important step forward. They acknowledge that child care and health benefits are an important concern of families, female-headed families especially. At least for one year, they remove the disincentives to work, or to work only part-time, so that the client can keep daycare and Medicaid benefits associated with AFDC receipt. Quality child care and health coverage for the working poor are important components of a welfare policy that supports self-sufficiency and child welfare.

Title IV—Related AFDC Amendments

This title contains several provisions that will affect children. First it mandates that all states have an AFDC-UP program at least six months out of the year. Second, it permits states to require minor parents to live with their parent, or a suitable guardian, in order to obtain benefits. Third, it authorizes a study of proposals for minimum AFDC benefits. Fourth, this title also raises the disregard for child care from $160 to $175 per month ($200 per month for infants). The disregard for work-related expenses was increased from $75 to $90. The law also stated that the Earned Income Tax Credit (EITC) should be disregarded.

Implications for Children. The first provision, mandating AFDC-UP in all states, is a victory of sorts for those pushing for national AFDC standards. Prior to this, only 26 states provided benefits to two-parent families. Now all states must do this at least six months out of the year, provided the principal earner is unemployed. On the down side, many poor families will still be without benefits. Working poor families will still receive nothing, need standards will still be below the poverty level, and even AFDC-UP families may only be covered for part of the year. Nevertheless, according to CBO estimates, this will make poor children in 450,000 families eligible for welfare.[17] It represents a step towards treating all poor children equally.

The second provision allowing states to require minor parents to stay at home in order to receive benefits affects children with children. While research has found little relationship between welfare receipt and female-headedness, there have been indications that the availability of welfare encourages the formation of new households.[18] This provision is evidently designed to discourage this. It may also, however, make it difficult for minor parents and their children to escape an abusive family situation. This is an issue that requires further study.

The third provision, for a study of proposals for minimum benefits, keeps alive an important issue: how to bring greater equity in the way children are treated across states. An attempt to include in this law incentives to states to raise their benefits failed as a result of continued congressional resistance. Unfortunately, some of the most important child welfare issues are included either as studies or as special demonstration projects.

Finally, the increases in disregard amounts for child care and work-related expenses, as well as the EITC disregard, will make it easier for parents to pursue quality daycare. In addition, this provision provides further work incentives. What is missing, is any change in the earnings disregard. Prior to the AFDC changes in 1981, the first $30 and one-third of income could be disregarded in the calculation of the AFDC benefit. This essentially represents a tax rate on earnings of 67 percent. Under the Reagan-sponsored changes in 1981, the one-third disregard was only permitted for 4 months and the $30 deduction only lasts for 12 months. After that point, AFDC recipients can only disregard daycare and work-related expenses; the tax rate is essentially 100 percent on whatever is above these deductions. Prior to 1981, there was considerable evidence to support the contention that labor supply is affected by the tax rates on earning in the AFDC calculation: the lower the tax rate, the greater the incentive.[19] Nevertheless, studies of the 1981 changes indicated that those who were cut from welfare as a result of changes in the earnings disregard did not return to the roles.[20] As a result, Congress has felt less pressure to change the earnings disregard. It should be pointed out, however, that while these families did not return to the roles, they were considerably poorer when they lost their benefits.

Title V—Demonstration Projects

As indicated earlier, some of the most important child welfare concerns are included as studies or demonstrations. Under Title V, demonstration projects would be authorized on education and training programs for children, early-childhood development programs, and projects to provide counseling and services to high-risk teenagers, among others.

Title VI—Miscellaneous Provisions

Since these deal primarily with reporting requirements and quality control, they will not be discussed in this article.

Title VII—Funding Provisions

Since this title addresses various tax-related charges to generate funds, they will not be discussed in this article.

CONCLUSION

This article has deliberately avoided an examination of the costs of the child welfare policy implied by the above discussion. Obviously, the large federal deficit will make implementing a more equitable system of benefits very difficult, even without any political opposition. The purpose of the article is, however, to indicate the kinds of concerns that the new welfare reform act—or any relevant policy—should consider when the frame of reference is the well-being of children and greater equity in the opportunities for children. How to implement such a policy—both politically and economically—is the subject of another article.

NOTES

1. Center on Budget and Policy Priorities, *Holes in the Safety Nets: Poverty Programs and Policies in the States* (Washington, DC: Center on Budget and Policy Priorities, 1988).

2. See, for example, Demetra Nightingale and Lynn C. Burbridge, *State Work-Welfare Programs in 1986: Implications for Policy* (Washington, DC: The Urban Institute, 1987).

3. Sheila B. Kamerman and Alfred J. Kahn, "Social Policy and Children in the United States and Europe," in *The Vulnerable*, ed. John Palmer, Timothy Smeeding, and Barbara Torrey (Washington, DC: The Urban Institute Press, 1988), 351–80.

4. Michael O'Higgins, "Beyond Income and Poverty: Trends in Social Welfare among Children and the Elderly since the 1960s" in *The Vulnerable*, ed. John Palmer, Timothy Smeeding, and Barbara Torrey (Washington, DC: The Urban Institute Press, 1988).

5. Gosta Esping-Anderson, Lee Rainwater, and Martin Rein, "Institutional and Political Factors Affecting the Well-Being of the Elderly," in *The Vulnerable*, ed. John Palmer, Timothy Smeeding, and Barbara Torrey (Washington, DC: The Urban Institute Press, 1988), 333–41.

6. Katherine Swartz, "The Uninsured and Workers without Employer-Group Health Insurance," The Urban Institute Working Paper no. 3789-02, Aug. 1988.

7. Sheldon Danzinger, "Antipoverty Policy and Welfare Reform," (Paper presented at the Conference for Welfare Reform Alternatives, Williamsburg, VA, Feb. 1988).

8. Robert Haverman et al., "Disparities in Well-Being among U.S. Children over Two Decades: 1962–1983," in *The Vulnerable*, ed. John Palmer, Timothy Smeeding, and Barbara Torrey. (Washington, DC: The Urban Institute Press, 1988).

9. For example, see Frank Levy, "How Big Is the American Underclass," The Urban Institute Working Paper no. 0090-1, Sept. 1977.

10. Heather L. Ross and Isabel Sawhill, *Time of Transition* (Washington, DC: The Urban Institute Press, 1975).

11. Not discussed here are various other miscellaneous provisions dealing with administration, reporting requirements, special demonstration programs, and so on not relevant to this article.

12. Robert Lerman, "Child Support Policies as a Nonwelfare Approach to Helping the Poor" (Paper presented at the Conference for Welfare Reform Alternatives, Williamsburg, VA, Feb. 1988).

13. Phillip K. Robins, "Child Support, Welfare Dependency, and Poverty," *American Economic Review* Sept. 1986: 785.

14. Sanford Schram and Michael Wiseman, "Should Families Be Protected from AFDC-UP?" Institute for Research on Poverty, Policy Paper no. 860–88, 1988.

15. For example, see Lynn C. Burbridge, "Black Women in Employment and Training Programs," *Review of Black Political Economy* Fall-Winter 1985–86.

16. The tax rate on earnings (the amount the grant is reduced for every dollar of earnings) changes after four months.

17. Congressional Budget Office, *Reducing Poverty Among Children*, May 1985.

18. David T. Ellwood and Mary Jo Bane, "Impact of AFDC on Family Structure and Living Arrangements" (Report prepared for the U.S. Department of Health and Human Services under grant no. 92A-82, 1984).

19. For example, see SRI International, *Final Report of the Seattle-Denver Income Maintenance Experiment*, vol. 1, *Design and Results* (Menlo Park, CA: SRI International, May 1983).

20. Douglas Wolf and Robert Moffitt, "The Effect of the 1981 Omnibus Reconciliation Act on Welfare Recipients and Work Incentives in AFDC," *Social Services Review* June 1987.

4

African American Family Policy or National Family Policy: Are They Different?

Jean M. Granger

African American families have unique needs due to institutionalized oppression and racism. These needs are not met in the United States, which remains one of the few industralized countries without a national family policy. Although African American families would be helped by policies specifically targeted to the African American community, African Americans acting alone do not have the resources to address this national issue. The author argues that African Americans should join other groups to develop a national family policy that will assist all families.

The African American family appears to be in trouble, but it remains a strong institution providing nurturance and maintenance for family members. Several centuries of perpetuation of negative myths concerning African Americans and their families have served to provide the rest of American society with a rationale for oppression of and discrimination against African Americans. Oppression and lack of opportunity have contributed to African American poverty and family breakdown. African American and white professionals and publications frequently refer to statistics concerning the increasing rate of African American adolescent pregnancies, suicide and homicide, unemployment, family problems, and children being raised in poverty. Clearly it is important for us to continue to seek solutions for these problems.

Justifiably, there is also tremendous concern for the number of African American children who have lost, or who are at risk of losing, their families because of poverty and other societal ills impacting upon families. This situation has been exacerbated by racism, or at the least, by a lack of recognition, understanding, and acceptance of cultural differences and a variety of types of family structures, both in society generally and, more specifically, by agency workers in child welfare, family services, and public assistance. We must continue to confront these issues and concentrate on maintaining and reuniting children with their families, wherever possible.

But we are faced with unfortunate complications. Extensive evidence exists concerning these problems, with documentation of societal contributions to the causation and perpetuation of the problems.[1] Solutions have been suggested and many have been tested and found to work.[2] Careful analysis of publications about these issues demonstrates that most of the researchers, authors, and other persons involved are African American. Special conferences are arranged, and primary attendance is by African Americans. Federal and other funding is made available sporadically for projects, but invariably, such funding is insufficient and/or does not continue long enough. Similar issues exist with other ethnic-minority groups. However, other members of society use statistics in their publications in a way that increases negative attitudes toward African Americans. The result is national, state, and local recommendations and actions that are basically punitive and hostile to African Americans, other ethnic minorities, and poor persons.

Rarely is it indicated that, in spite of all of the societal obstacles, the largest percentage of African American families—whether low, middle, or upper income, whether single-parent, nuclear, or extended in structure—continue to function and furnish productive members of this society[3] Moreover, when suggestions are made for an African American family policy, too often the idea that certain services should be made available to all African Americans (as needed) due to societal conditions is ignored in favor of focusing on assisting African American families who have already developed problems.

Is it possible that singling out African American family problems and suggesting an African American family policy are counterproductive? By emphasizing our concerns over the problems noted above, are we adding our voices to forces in the larger society that use the available information to suggest that African American families are increasingly "pathological," and that provision of services is a "waste" of funds? Is the information we are furnishing achieving the purpose of making the rest of society empathetic toward the African American experience? Or are we providing more ammunition to those controlling societal forces that shape policies and practices that are destructive to African Americans (and other ethnic minorities and families)? Do we need to develop a larger perspective in working for societal change, by reminding others that many of these problems are shared by all American groups, while at the same time not losing our concern for African American families and those matters of particular importance to us?

This article addresses these issues and suggests some other avenues of approach. With the end of the Reagan era, renewed interests in family policy could produce support for ways to resolve some of the dilemmas faced by African American families.

FAMILY POLICY ISSUES

In our concern about African American families, we have tended to lose sight of a major point: the growing problems and concerns listed in the preceding section do not apply only to African American families. Disproportionately more African American families, considering our overall population numbers, are involved because of poverty, oppression, and discrimination. However, these problems are part of a national malaise affecting American families. It is more appropriate to say that the American family is still strong, but in trouble. Programs for African American families will be affected by societal attitudes toward American families, in general, as well as by the attitudes toward African Americans, in particular.

Highly industrialized, complex societies increasingly have acknowledged that all governmental (and private) policies impact on families, frequently in negative ways. Therefore, decisions have been made that nationally mandated family policies and programs are necessary to fortify and sustain families as well as to prevent problems that can lead to family breakdown.[4]

The United States remains one of the few industrialized countries that does not have a national family policy.[5] Many recommendations were made between the late 1960s and early 1980s for an American national family policy that would contain specific goals for strengthening families and for implementing policies and programs to achieve these goals. A national family policy could consist of multiple goals, policies, and programs in all major areas affecting the daily lives of families (for example, child care, personal social services, guaranteed family income, housing, health, education, reformation of social security, employment). Or a national family policy could address one of these areas as a major family priority and focus on policies and programs to achieve the stated goals of that priority.[6]

One of the major reasons that the United States has not implemented a national family policy, in spite of recommendations in this regard, is our country's historical bias against governmental involvement in the personal welfare of citizens. This bias has resulted in a lack of cohesive national policies and programs for families and residual, poorly planned, and inadequately funded services at the local, state, and federal levels.[7]

Another reason for the lack of national family policy is the fragmented, residual nature of social policy in this country, which exists because of three major considerations that take precedence in any social policy decisions and actions. These are the desires of powerful interest groups that represent their members' attitudes and beliefs; economic factors; and the prevention of major alteration of the societal structure.[8] Thus, despite demographic data, research outcomes, and social realities that indicate great family need, social and political forces, serving the prespectives of special-interest groups, conspire against an effective family policy.

The situation is further complicated by attitudes about family structures, the needs of American families, and the role of government with regard to families that often divide along the liberal-conservative continuum. Conservatives' proposals are focused on returning families to the "traditional nuclear family" and reducing the role of government in families.[9] Liberals' proposals accept the plurality of family forms and recommend federally mandated, cohesive family policy and preventive programs that anticipate family needs.[10]

Biases, attitudes, and special interests are also impacted by the actual outcomes of empirical data, and affect the interpretations of those outcomes, concerning programs with the potential for becoming part of a national family policy. Because of the abundance of studies and information in these areas, only three examples will be given.

Provision of child care is affected by beliefs that maternal employment outside the home is "bad for children"[11] or partially responsible for the breakdown of family live.[12] Consequently, with the increase of (white) maternal employment, much research attention has focused on its effects and/or the effects of child care by paid providers outside the home on the social and emotional development of children. But analysis of this research[13] finds conflicting outcomes: maternal employment has positive and negative effects upon children; and child care contributes to positive and negative social growth and develoment in children.

In the guaranteed-minimum-income experiments, negative results were reported that contributed to the decisions not to reform the public welfare system to a national policy of guaranteed incomes for families. It was reported that guaranteed incomes led to decreased work on the part of family members and increased rates of marital breakups. What was not publicized was that when work decreased it was among young wives and adolescents, who concentrated on increasing their parenting and coping skills and pursuing additional education to increase employment skills. Breakups of marriages were lower where income supports were higher, serving to support the many studies reporting relationships between family stability and income or employment stability.[14]

The study indicating that Headstart and other preschool programs for children from disadvantaged backgrounds had no lasting results was much publicized and used as one of the reasons to cut back such programs.[15] However, other studies, some of which were longitudinal in nature, found that compared to control groups, Headstart children scored higher on achievement tests and had higher rates of high school and college completion and employment.[16]

Clearly, any national family policy proposals are likely to be affected by controversies such as those surrounding the three areas of child care, education, and a guaranteed family income. It is important to note that the latter two examples—that is, studies concerning guaranteed income and preschool programs—contained numbers of ethnic-minority participants. Moreover, previous federally mandated child care plans that did not come to fruition were perceived as furnishing assistance to large numbers of ethnic-minority children.[17] The current child care policies under discussion are, in large part, the results of pressures from a number of white interest groups. It is possible that the more positive societal responses are related to perceptions that whites, as well as other racial groups, will benefit.

Given the complexity of the issues involved in any area of potential family policy, policymakers, family policy and child welfare experts, and members of the public have strong attitudes about governmental family policy. Since these attitudes will significantly shape the nature of family policy in the years to come, it is important to know what evidence exists concerning attitudes toward governmental provision of family programs.

ATTITUDES TOWARD FAMILY POLICY

In spite of the importance of attitudes, little empirical evidence exists concerning the attitudes among comparative societal groups toward an explicit governmental family policy. Two studies concerning attitudes toward family policy have been identified.

Zimmerman, Matessich, and Leik surveyed Minnesota state legislators about their attitudes toward family policy.[18] These legislators were generally favorable toward the idea of family policy, but viewed such policy as helping families with problems (for example, child abuse). Of 12 goals for family policy, they ranked assisting families with young children as 12th in appropriateness, and helping all families as 11th. They felt that government should confine itself to helping families, financially and otherwise, only when absolutely necessary. Legislators' age, education, income, family experience, marital status, and political party affiliation significantly influenced their attitudes toward family policy. For example, Republicans were less likely than Democrats to perceive helping all families as an appropriate goal of family policy, and were more likely to restrict government help only to families with problems.

Granger compared attitudes among national family policy experts, California career professionals in family services, and members of the general public (other citizens) toward three suggested components of a national family policy.[19] These components were supportive services for families: a guaranteed minimum income, personal social services, and child care. Respondents were asked if they supported universal provision of these services for all families, as needed. Although favorableness toward these measures generally was exhibited in the expected rank order of experts, career professionals, and other citizens, all three groups were found to be favorable toward the universal provision of personal social services and, even more so, of child care (for working parents and parents having difficulty coping) as preventive and interventive measures for family problems. They were also favorable toward tax credits and tax changes as methods for guaranteeing that families would have an income no less than the governmental poverty level.

Responses were affected by the possibility of tax increases to implement the programs and the respondents' degree of liberalism-conservatism and educational levels. When income taxes were required to implement these programs, experts remained favorable, career professionals became uncertain, and members of the general public became slightly unfavorable toward these programs. Liberals and persons with higher educational levels were more favorable toward the measures than were conservatives and persons with lower educational levels, regardless of whether implementation required increases in personal income taxes. These outcomes are similar to those found in the survey by Zimmerman, Mattesich, and Leik[20] and other surveys concerning social welfare expenditures discussed below.

In the Granger study, even though support for social services decreased when income tax increases were required to fund programs, the fact that members of the public became only slightly unfavorable was encouraging. The majority (86%) of the respondents were white and had older children. (Demographic data for white and ethnic-minority respondents were very similar.) Thirty-six percent of the other citizens and 56 percent of the career professionals lived in a very fiscally and politically conservative county, and 100 percent of the career professionals worked in such a county. Moreover, both of the counties primarily involved have large and growing ethnic-minority populations.

There is significantly more empirical evidence available, including the results of national public opinion surveys, on attitudes toward present social welfare expenditures. These attitudes could also be expected to impact upon the development of a national family policy. They have impacted upon services for members of ethnic minorities and poor persons for many years.

Studies of the public's attitudes toward social and public welfare expenditures indicate ambivalence and inconsistency in these attitudes. American citizens support, in varying degrees, social welfare programs, but tend to be more favorable toward programs such as Social Security and health care programs for the elderly and disabled than they are toward programs viewed as serving "less deserving" groups (for example, single parents or ethnic minorities). Many respondents were found to believe, erroneously, that most poor persons and public assistance recipients were members of ethnic-minority groups.[21]

Americans also have been found, generally, to be positive toward social welfare programs, but reluctant to fund them if they require additional personal income taxes. Persons with higher educational levels have been more likely than have others to have positive attitudes about funding social welfare services.[22]

Liberalism or conservatism has also affected attitudes toward the provision of social welfare programs.[23] Liberal respondents (usually Democrats) have been more likely to be favorable toward social welfare expenditures; conservative respondents (usually Republicans) have been more likely to be unfavorable toward such expenditures.

IMPLICATIONS FOR AFRICAN AMERICAN FAMILIES AND NATIONAL FAMILY POLICY

Generalizations cannot be made for the Zimmerman, Mattessich, and Leik study or the Granger study concerning attitudes toward family policy because of sampling issues (for example, response rate and demographic similarities among groups). More empirical data are needed since an understanding of which groups and types of individuals might support family policy proposals could help develop the strategy needed to advocate for family policy. However, these outcomes, combined with the results of other studies and the continuing interest in family policy and family needs, do suggest some avenues of pursuit for African Americans.

Historically, it has been the case that when African Americans make socioeconomic, political, or any other types of gains, there follows a period where the larger society returns to repressive measures and attempts to neutralize gains. Therefore, it is no longer useful to believe that American society will heed the needs of African American families and deal with our issues and problems. Nor do we (or any other single group) have the resources to resolve private problems that are caused by unresolved national, public issues. Consequently, we must focus on issues as they relate to all American families. In spite of ambivalent attitudes toward governmental assistance to families, tremendous pressures have increasingly been brought to bear upon the larger society, by white Americans, to furnish supportive and fortifying services for families.

The outcomes of studies of attitudes suggest two opposite but related attitudes. First, if Americans believe that policy and programs will benefit only certain types of families (for example, ethnic-minority families), they will be less willing, or unwilling, to fund or pursue such programs. Second, if they are convinced that policies and programs furnish benefits for all families, as needed, American citizens will be more likely to support such programs.

One crucial factor will be funding and its impact upon personal finances, for example, a raise in personal income taxes. But there is already extensive evidence, gathered by African American and other researchers and family policy and service experts, that it is more cost effective, financially and emotionally, to sustain families and avoid problems than it is to remove children and/or provide rehabilitation services for families after serious problems have developed.[24] However, the American public has limited awareness of the facts.

It would seem, then, that, as African Americans, our public focus should be directed toward the needs and problems of all American families, not just African American families. A national family policy would be primarily preventive (rather than residual), and holistic (focusing on the entire family constellation). Family policy, properly implemented, would take into account differences in culture and family structures. In an inherently racist society, emphasizing the needs of ethnic minorities makes it more likely that such issues will be ignored or will result in punitive measures and cutbacks in services, such as those carried out during the Reagan years. A national family policy that addresses one or several of the areas of recommendation (for example, child care, personal social services, guaranteed family income, housing, health, education, reformation of social security, and employment) for all families, as needed, will automatically benefit African American families. Our concentration could then be directed toward the types of policies needing development and the manner in which these policies are implemented so that the impact upon African American families is appropriate and positive.

Perhaps we also must form coalitions with other ethnic-minority groups and white women. For example, the most recent national focus and funding for research and discussion has been upon working families, child care, and the impact of both upon families and children. Although these issues have been important to African Americans for decades, it is only since the majority of white mothers have entered the workforce and the numbers of white single parents has grown that these concerns have become a matter for public pressure. For the first time, white researchers are acknowledging that, not only is systematic research lacking in these areas, but African American families have coped, usually successfully, with work and child care for years, and should be studied for their coping skills.[25] These issues might be a good starting point for coalitions and family policy proposals, particularly those concerning child care and full employment. The child care proposals presently under discussion in the 101st Congress represent only a beginning attempt to address child care needs.

Concerted efforts need to be made to reach groups that research demonstrated would provide support (for example, family policy experts, citizens with older families, and persons who are more liberal and have higher educational levels) for family policy efforts. On the other hand, campaigns to educate all citizens concerning all families' needs could also contribute to support from other groups.

It is possible that organizing efforts directed to the American public could produce support for cohesive, national family policies.[26] Concern about families and family needs are growing in the United States and it might, therefore, be timely to advocate for universally available family programs. Further, it is also likely that the dissemination of information and the organizing of activities concerning a national family policy (its purposes, what it would accomplish, what it would cost, and how it could be actualized) would find support among the public generally.

Ultimately, the implementation of a comprehensive national family policy would address many of the needs and problems of African American families. More specifically, a national family policy would permit African American social workers, researchers, and other interested persons to focus their efforts and funding on problems in the African American community that remained insufficiently resolved by the national family policy

NOTES

1. Andrew Billingsley, *Black Families in White America* (Englewood Cliffs, NJ: Prentice Hall, 1968); Joseph L. White, *The Psychology of Blacks: An Afro-American Perspective* (Englewood Cliffs, NJ: Prentice Hall, 1984); Patricia E. Bauknight and Reginald S. Avery, "Reganomics and Black Children: Social Policy Considerations," *Black Caucus* 15 (1984–85): 3–6; June Hopps, "Oppression Based on Color," *Social Work* 27 (January 1982): 3–6; Lawrence E. Gary and Bogart R. Leashore "High-Risk Status of Black Men," *Social Work* 27 (January 1982): 54–58; Harriet P. McAdoo, "Demographic Trends of People of Color," *Social Work* 27 (January 1982): 15–23; James A. Moss, "Unemployment among Black Youths," *Social Work* 27 (January 1982): 47–53; Harriet P. McAdoo, ed., *Black Families* (Beverly Hills: Sage Publications, 1981).

2. Sadye M. L. Logan, Edith M. Freeman, and Ruth G. McRoy, *Social Work Practice with Black Families: A Culturally Specific Perspective* (New York: Longman, 1980); Doman Lum, *Social Work Practice and People of Color: A Process-Stage Approach* (Monterey, CA: Brooks/Cole Publishing Co., 1986); Barbara Solomon, *Black Empowerment: Social Work in Oppressed Communities* (New York: Columbia University Press, 1976); Lawrence E. Gary, Lula A. Beatty, Greta L., Berry, and Mary D. Price, *Stable Black Families* (Washington, DC: Institute for Urban Affairs and Research, 1983).

3. See note 2.

4. For extensive discussions of these topics, see, for example, John Dempsey, *The Family and Public Policy: The Issue of the 80s* (Baltimore: Paul Brooks, 1980); Alfred Kahn and Sheila Kamerman, *Child Support: From Debt Collection to Social Policy* (Beverley Hills: Sage Publications, 1988); Sheila Kamerman and Alfred Kahn, *Family Policy: Government and Families in Fourteen Countries* (New York: Columbia University Press, 1978); National Commission on Families and Public Policies, *Families and Public Policies: Final Report of the Commission* (Washington, DC: National conference on Social Welfare, 1978); Edward F. Zigler, Sharon L. Kagan, and Edgar Klugman, eds., *Children, Families, and Government: Perspectives on American Social Policy* (Cambridge: Cambridge University Press, 1983); Kenneth Kenniston and the Carnegie Council on Children. *All Our Children: The American Family Under Pressure* (New York: Harcourt Brace Jovanovich, 1977); White House Conference on Families, *The Report: Listening to America's Families.* (Washington, DC: White House Conference on Families, 1980).

5. See note 4.

6. See note 4.

7. See note 4.

8. Carol H. Weiss, "Policy Research in the Context of Diffuse Decision Making," in *Policy Studies Review Annual*, vol. 6, ed. Ray C. Rist (Beverly Hills: Sage Publications, 1982).

9. Dempsey, *The Family and Public Policy*; John Scanzoni, *Shaping Tomorrow's Family: Theory and Policy for the 21st Century* (Beverly Hills: Sage Publications, 1983).

10. See note 9.

11. H. Lauer, "Jobs in the 1980s: A Sourcebook for Policy Makers," in *The World At Work*, ed. D. Yankelovich, H. Zetterberg, B. Strumpel, and M. Shanks (New York: Octagon Books, 1985).

12. General Mills Family Report, *Families at Work: Strengthens and Strains* (Minneapolis: General Mills, Inc., 1981).

13. Sheila Kamerman and Cheryl Hayes, eds., *Families That Work: Children in a Changing World* (Washington, DC: National Academy Press, 1982); Lois Hoffman, "Maternal Employment and the Young Child," in *Parent-Child Interaction and Parent-Child Relations in Child Development: The Minnesota Symposium on Child Psychology*, vol. 17, ed. Mark Perlmutter (Hillsdale, NJ: Lawrence Erlbaum, 1985).

14. Philip K. Robins, ed. *A Guranteed Annual Income: Evidence from a Social Experiment* (New York: Academic Press, 1980).

15. Shirley L. Zimmerman, "Public Policies and Family Outcomes: Empirical Evidence or Ideology," *Social Casework* 64 (March 1983): 138–46.

16. Ibid.

17. Cheryl Hayes, ed. *Making Policies for Children: A Study of the Federal Process* (Washington, DC: National Academy Press, 1982).

18. Shirley L. Zimmerman, Paul Mattessich, and Robert Leik "Legislator's Attitudes toward Family Policy," *Journal of Marriage and the Family* 41 (August 1979): 507–17.

19. Jean M. Granger, "Attitudes toward Supportive Services for Families," *The Journal of Applied Social Sciences* 12 (Spring-Summer 1988): 222–49.

20. Zimmerman, Mattessich, and Leik, "Legislator's Attitudes."

21. Fay L. Cook, *Who Should Be Helped? Public Support for Social Services* (Beverly Hills: Sage Publications, 1979); Richard M. Coughlin, *Ideology, Public Opinion, and Welfare Policy: Attitudes toward Taxes and Spending in Industrialized Societies* (Berkeley: University of California, 1980); David J. Kallen and Dorothy Miller, "Public Attitudes toward Public Welfare," *Social Work* 16 (July 1971): 83–90; Evelyn H. Ogren, "Public Opinions about Public Welfare," *Social Work* 18 (January 1973): 101–7; Lucinda L. Roff and David L. Klemack, "Attitudes toward Public Welfare and Welfare Workers," *Social Work Research and Abstracts* 19 (Fall 1983): 29–30.

22. Phillip AuClaire, "Public Attitudes toward Social Welfare Expenditrues," *Social Work* 29 (March-April 1984): 139–45; Coughlin, *Ideology, Public Opinion, and Welfare Policy*; National Opinion Research Center, *General Social Surveys, 1972–1986* (Ann Arbor: University of Michigan, 1986).

23. Paul Abramson, *Political Attitudes in America: Formation and Change* (San Francisco: W. H. Freeman, 1983).

24. Alfred Kadushin and Judith A. Martin, *Child Welfare Services*, 4th ed. (New York: Macmillan Publishing Co., 1988).

25. Cheryl Hayes and Sheila Kamerman, eds., *Children of Working Parents: Experience and Outcomes* (Washington DC: National Academy Press, 1983); Kamerman and Hayes, *Families That Work*.

26. Ellen Hoffman, "Social Policy and Advocacy," in *Children, Families, and Government*, ed. Zigler, Kagan, and Klugman; S. Kagan, E. Klugman, and E. Zigler, "Shaping Child and Family Policies: Criteria and Strategies for a New Decade" in *Children, Families, and Government*, ed. Zigler, Kagan, and Klugman.

5
The Implications of Demographic Changes in the African American Aged Population for Formal and Informal Care Systems in the Twenty-First Century

Jacqueline Marie Smith

Even though aged African Americans have poorer health than white Americans, they make relatively less use of the services provided by the formal health care system (physicians, nursing homes, and extended-care facilities). Studies suggest that the underutilization of nursing homes may be related to a greater use of informal care provided by relatives and friends in the home. The pattern of underutilization of formal care seems likely to change because changes in the size, growth rate, household composition, and marital status of the aged African American population may strain the informal care system. If greater attention is paid to the delivery of services to the very old and frail with highly vulnerable family situations, and selected aspects of homemaker services are reorganized, the formal health care system will be able to respond effectively to the consequences of demographic and social changes for the informal care systems of the African American aged.

Most Americans greatly covet youth, but view old age as highly undesirable. In fact, one out of every three persons believes that the worst years of a person's life are after the 60th birthday.[1] Since most Americans associate old age with bad health, financial problems, loneliness, dependency, and being a burden,[2] the public attitude toward old age is not surprising. While the majority of aged persons do not personally experience these problems, some of the aged do.[3] Twelve percent of persons 65 and over sampled by Harris experienced loneliness as a very serious problem.[4] One out of every five reported that poor health was a very serious problem.[5] Thus, only a relatively small portion of the aged, rather than a majority, fit the stereotype held by the public. For the general population, then, experiencing old age will probably result in casting down some of the burdens from earlier stages of the life course and embarking on new paths to happiness and contentment.

For considerable numbers of aged African Americans, however, becoming old is not a time when they cast down the earlier burdens of life, rest comfortably in the sun, take the time to reflect on their lifetime achievements, and embark on new roads to happiness and contentment. Instead, it is a time when they are forced to shoulder an increasingly heavier burden of poverty. Because at younger ages African Americans experience discrimination and greater unemployment and underemployment[6] than many other groups, they are particularly likely to experience old age as a period of hardship.

Poverty is particularly burdensome to the African American aged. Census data show that the median income for families in which the household is African American and at least 65 years old was $12,456, but the median income for their white counterparts was $20,517.[7] Approximately 38 percent of elderly African American families lived below the poverty level at the time of the 1980 Census.[8]

It seems reasonable to assume that the differential exposure to poverty by racial and ethnic subgroups in the aged population probably contributes to racial and ethnic differences in the utilization of public income-maintenance programs by older African Americans and whites. African Americans are almost three times as likely as whites to rely mainly or solely on Social Security benefits in old age.[9] Whites in old age are more likely than African Americans to rely on income from assets.[10] Thus, because of greater risk of poverty, disproportionate numbers of African Americans rely on public income-maintenance programs.

African Americans are also more likely than some groups to experience poor health in old age. More specifically, African Americans who are 45 years old and over are 1.6 times as likely as their white counterparts to assess their health as fair or poor.[11] In addition, in 1988 they experienced more disabled days in bed per person per year (323 versus 276)[12] than whites. A National Urban League survey[13] of African Americans in the United States showed that the healthy elderly African American household was an exception; instead, nearly all elderly households had some chronically ill member.

But the utilization of health care services by older African Americans is much lower than expected given the number with poor health. Older African Americans, who have relatively poorer health than older whites, made only 5.2 physicians visits per year as compared to 5.4 visits per year by aged whites.[14] Aged African Americans also make less use of nursing home and extended-care facilities than whites. Only 33 of every 1,000 African Americans, compared to 48 of every 1,000 whites, resided in nursing homes.[15]

What kinds of health and social programs and services will be needed in the year 2000? How likely is it that the existing patterns of utilization of care systems (formal, both public and private, and informal home care) will continue in the twenty first century for aged persons, particularly aged African Americans, who have poor health? Will there be a need in the twenty first century for care systems to respond to group differences (by race) in exposure to the hardships of old age by modifying existing services and creating, in some instances, highly innovative programs? This article will attempt to answer these questions by (1) discussing the factors contributing to existing patterns of utilization of health care systems (formal, both public and private, and informal home care) for the aged who have poor health; (2) identifying trends in the demographic characteristics of the aged African American population that may affect its future demand for and level of utilization of existing services; and (3) suggesting ways to modify the existing systems to meet the special needs of the African American aged.

FACTORS CONTRIBUTING TO CURRENT PATTERNS OF UTILIZATION OF SERVICES

Why do older African Americans underutilize health care services, relative to other nonminority groups—particularly nursing home and physician services? Findings from empirical studies suggest that the underutilization of nursing homes by aged African Americans may be related to a greater use of informal care provided at home by members of their households. In a study of home health care, among the noninstitutionalized population at least 75 years old, proportionately more aged African Americans received care at home than whites.[16] Aged African Americans also had fewer short hospital stays, as compared to aged whites.[17]

The underutilization of nursing homes may also be a result of differences in income or ethnic value preferences. Berkanovic and Reeder found a complex interaction between ethnicity and income on health care use.[18] These authors suggest that ethnicity and income create different life experiences, which lead to differences in value preferences, including preferences for health care. Billingsley found that some African Americans did not use public services because they receive sufficient support through kinship networks.[19] Kart and Beckham also found that, for African Americans, the level of use of formal care is not associated with ''need.''[20]

DEMOGRAPHIC TRENDS AND CHANGES AFFECTING FUTURE PATTERNS OF UTILIZATION OF SERVICES

This pattern of underutilization of physician and nursing home services, however, seems likely to change. An examination of recent demographic trends suggests changes in the structure (size, growth rate, and composition) of the African American aged population. These changes in structure seem likely to increase the demand and need for services by the African American aged.

Changes in Size

The first change in the structure of this population is the magnitude of the increase in the numbers of African American aged. From 1960 to 1987 the number of African American persons 65 and over increased by 1.4 million.[21] Much of future increases will probably occur in states with the greatest concentration of African Americans (for example, New York, California, Texas, Illinois, and Georgia). For example, in 1970 in New York State, the census counted 112,720 African Americans who were at least 65.[22] In 1980, this figure stood at 166,000. Based on current fertility and mortality rates, New York's aged African American population is projected to increase to 298,000 by the year 2000.[23] For the United States as a whole by the year 2000, the aged African American population is projected to increase to 3,132,000 a 33 percent increase from the 1980 figure.[24]

The increase in numbers of aged African Americans is accompanied by a change in the rate of the ''aging'' of the African American population. In recent decades, the

TABLE 1
Decennial Percent Increase of the Population in the
Older Ages, by Race and Sex: 1970 to 2010

Age, Race, and Sex	1970– 1980	1980– 1990	1990– 2000	2000– 2010
65 Years and Older				
White American	26.7	22.7	8.9	10.5
Male	22.4	22.1	8.2	11.9
Female	29.8	23.2	9.3	9.5
African American	35.1	22.5	15.4	19.5
Male	26.7	14.2	8.6	18.0
Female	41.5	28.1	28.1	20.3
75 Years and Older				
White American	30.4	34.6	25.6	7.8
Male	19.6	33.0	25.8	7.4
Female	37.2	35.5	25.5	7.9
African American	47.7	46.0	25.6	17.5
Male	34.0	33.5	17.2	11.3
Female	57.3	53.5	30.1	20.5
85 Years and Older				
White American	58.8	44.6	47.3	32.3
Male	39.1	32.3	47.0	33.0
Female	69.1	49.9	47.4	32.0
African American	57.3	58.6	60.3	31.1
Male	38.5	42.6	42.8	23.6
Female	68.8	66.7	67.8	33.8

Source: Bureau of the Census, "Population Estimates and Projections," *Current Population Reports*, Ser. P-25, nos. 917, 952, and 1018 (Washington, DC: Government Printing Office, July 1982, May 1984, January 1989), Tables 2, 6, and 4.

African American population, relative to whites, has aged more rapidly. For example, from 1970 to 1980 the percentage increase, as shown in Table 1, in the white female population 65 and over was 29.8. In contrast, the percentage increase for African American females 65 and over was 41.5 percent.

Thus, even though there are proportionately more older whites in the white population than there are older African Americans in the African American population, aged African Americans were added to the pool of the aged African American population at a greater rate than the rate for whites in this 10-year period.

The more rapid aging of the African American population is due to differences in the age distribution of African Americans and whites. Because of relatively higher African American fertility rates, a larger proportion of African Americans, as compared to whites, tend to be young. If the fertility rates of African Americans fall closer to the rates of whites, the age distribution of African Americans will shift as young African Americans reap the benefits of improvements in life expectancy. Thus, even though there will be greater numbers of aged whites than aged African Americans, as time passes, the greater "youthfulness" of the African American population could result in greater changes in the proportion of African Americans entering old age.

Fraction of the Very Old: A Compositional Shift

The growth of the African American aged population has been particularly rapid for persons of advanced age—75 years and older. Table 1 shows that between 1970 and 1980 there was a 34 percent increase in the number of African American males 75 and over. The increase of persons 85 and over was even greater. There was a 68.8 percent increase for African American females, and a 38.5 percent increase for African American males in the same 10-year period. The large rate of increase is probably a result of increased life expectancy.

Studies also suggest that the age groups with the greatest increases (75 and over, and 85 and over) demonstrate the least capacity for independent living because of physical impairment. Physical performance is usually limited with advanced age. In fact, only 29.7 percent of persons 65 to 74 years old indicated that they had minimal limitations in a study by Nagi.[25] However, a little more than 56 percent of persons 75 and over had comparable limitations. Nagi also demonstrated that the capacity for independent living decreases at advanced ages. Seventy-seven percent of persons age 65 to 74 were not limited in independent living, but, in contrast, only 60 percent of persons 75 and over were not limited in independent living.[26]

Impairment at advanced ages is an important factor in the institutionalization of the aged. A General Accounting Office (GAO) study of well-being status and impairment levels of older persons demonstrated that the institutionalized aged were more likely to be impaired than the noninstitutionalized. Among persons not institutionalized, 23 percent were categorized as "generally to extremely impaired." In contrast, among aged persons who were institutionalized, 91 percent were categorized as "generally to extremely impaired."[27]

Of the noninstitutionalized aged surveyed by the GAO, why were the 23 percent who were impaired not institutionalized? One possible explanation is that living arrangements may intervene in the association of impairment and institutionalization. The aged who live in households with other persons, particularly relatives, are probably less likely to be institutionalized because household or family members assist them. The GAO study of persons 65 and older who were not in institutions such as nursing homes found that the home-help services, such as personal care, homemaking, meal preparation, continuous supervision, and transportation, were provided by family and friends.[28]

Household and Marital Status Compositional Shifts

Chatters, Taylor, and Jackson report that marital status and the presence of children are important arbiters of support relationships among aged African Americans. Indeed, there is a hierarchy of preferred support providers. Because of the "proximity and shared history of mutual obligations and commitment of spouses," aged couples tend to rely on each other for support in old age.[29] Children also have a significant effect on the choice of support helpers among aged African Americans. The presence of children in old age inhibits the selection of siblings and friends as caregivers and helpers in old age.[30] Demographic changes in household composition and marital status suggest that an increasing proportion of African American aged will be in living arrangements that do not foster care at home by family and friends. Increases in the proportion of aged persons never married and the declining fertility of African American women may affect the use of social and health care services because of the effects of these factors on living arrangements and informal support networks. More specifically, changes in these factors may increase the number of aged who live alone.

Currently, persons who live alone are at a greater risk of institutionalization as they become increasingly frail at advanced ages.[31] In the United States, there has been a general increase in the proportion of persons who live alone.[32] This trend is also evident in the population of persons who are 65 and older. Between 1970 and 1981, the proportion of persons who lived alone and who were 65 years and over increased by 48 percent.[33] Recent census data also show that, for the population of persons who live alone, a greater proportion of African Americans of advanced age (that is, age 75 and over) live alone than do whites. More specifically, about 42 percent of African Americans who live alone are of advanced age. In contrast, only 21 percent of whites who live alone are 75 years old and over.[34]

About 65 percent of African American men who are at least 75 years old are widowed. Another 17 percent of these men of advanced age are separated. A much greater proportion (84%) of African American women who are 75 years old are widows who live alone (see Table 2).[35] Persons who live in households with others, particularly in family households, have the advantage of being able to pool income and other resources within the household. The pooling of resources probably enhances the well-being of all household members—aged and nonaged. Thus, aged African Americans who live alone may have fewer resources available for their use.

The above discussion suggests that for African American persons 75 years old and over, the likelihood of living alone is greatest for widowed women and widowed or

TABLE 2
Marital Status by Gender and Age of African Americans,
for Persons Who Live Alone (1988)

Marital Status	African American Males		
	65-74 Years	75+ Years	Total
Separated	25%	17%	55,000
Widowed	43%	65%	132,000
Divorced	25%	10%	48,000
Never married	7%	8%	18,000
Total N	148,000	105,000	253,000

Marital Status	African American Females		
	65-74 Years	75+ Years	Total
Separated	11%	6%	47,000
Widowed	72%	84%	421,000
Divorced	13%	2%	45,000
Never married	5%	8%	35,000
Total N	313,000	235,000	548,000

Note: Percentages were computed using data from the Bureau of the Census, "Marital Status and Living Arrangements: March 1988," *Current Population Reports*, ser. P-20, no. 433 (Washington, DC: Government Printing Office, 1989), Table 6.

separated men. Unfortunately for aged African Americans of the future, the declining fertility rate may result in fewer children to care for aged African American parents. Census data show that in 1970, 17.6 percent of African American families had only one child. By 1987, 25.1 percent of African American families had only one child. The percentage of African American families with no children also increased, from 38.9 percent in 1970 to 41 percent in 1987.[36]

Finally, the increase in the number of African American persons who never married may affect the living arrangements of aged African American women more than aged African American men, and thus indirectly affect the demand for the support of formal institutional care. Between 1981 and 1988, the number of African American aged who were 75 years old and older and who were never married increased from 31,000 to 50,000.[37] In 1981, about 77 percent of persons age 75 years old and older who never married were women. By 1988, approximately 80 percent of African Americans 75 years old and older who never married were women.[38]

African American women who never marry may be less likey than married women to have children. As pointed out earlier, adult children rank high in the hierarchy of informal providers. Thus, never-married African American women, if they are childless, may be more vulnerable to institutionalization when impairment in social functioning occurs at advanced ages.

African American men who never marry may be less likely than African American women who never marry to have children. Or, even if aged African American men who never marry do have children, they may interact with these children on a less frequent basis than African American women who never marry but have children. Females may interact on a more frequent basis because child care roles tend to be assigned on the basis of gender. Empirical studies clearly support the notion that there are gender differences in the receipt of informal social support. Taylor, Chatters, and Mays report that African American men are less likely to receive help from children than African American women.[39]

The preceding discussion also suggests that aged African American men who never marry are unlikely to live in households with extended kin relationships. Bell, Kasschau, and Zellman found that elderly African Americans were significantly more likely than comparable whites to be lodgers.[40] (These researchers incorrectly labeled this pattern of living arrangements as "irregular groups." In fact, these arrangements may represent in some cases, particularly for aged African American men who never marry, a form of a nonconsanguineal "extended family," in which various kinds of resources are pooled by "kin" in a manner similar to the pooling of resources by kin in households where members are related by blood.) If aged African American males are not members of extended households but lodgers, they may not be offered support as their physical impairment increases. Overall, then, recent trends in living arrangements, marital status, and fertility seem likely to increase the numbers of frail aged at risk to institutionalization.

RESPONSES OF THE INFORMAL SYSTEM

Because impaired African American aged make greater use of home care, what is likely to be the response of the informal system of caregivers to increased numbers of impaired aged? The initial response will probably be to "make do." Several authors have pointed out that it is a myth that older people are isolated from their children.[41] Shanas found that, among the aged who did not live with their children, 84 percent saw them at least once a week and lived less than an hour away from at least one child.[42] Taylor, Chatters, and Mays report that aged African Americans demonstrate significant levels of interaction with family, relatively close residential proximity to immediate family, extensive familial affective bonds, and a high degree of satisfaction derived from family life.[43]

For the most part, both the African American and white aged expect their adult children who are also aging to provide protection, care, and economic support.[44] Generally, the children of the aged parents rise to meet these expectations. Anderson found that most widowed African American aged are likely to call on their children when in need of help.[45] Among aged African Americans who feel that they need help, almost 40 percent report that they receive help from their family members.[46] For several reasons, however, increases in the numbers of persons of advanced age may strain the informal care system and overwhelm the caregivers, because the number of caregivers may prove to be insufficient. Particularly for aged African American men who live alone, who are without kin, and who live as lodgers, the pool of informal caregivers may shrink. When only a few people lived to reach advanced ages, the current pattern of utilization of formal and informal care may have been adequate. If greater numbers of persons live to be older than 75, there may not be enough ''helpers'' to carry out the same functions.

A second reason that the pool of available caregivers may shrink is because of increases in the labor-force participation of nonaged African Americans. Recently, some authors observed that the incomes of African Americans are rising. Bianchi and Farley have noted that the greatest improvements are in husband/wife families.[47] In husband/wife families, the improvement in income may be due to the presence of two income earners. Care for an impaired aged adult could result in one of the members of the labor force reducing his or her labor-force participation, or in the institutionalization of the impaired aged family member if there were no available formal in-home support services. Yet, findings from empirical studies demonstrate that the aged African Americans most frequently mention immediate family (spouses, daughters, sons) as the categories of individuals who would assist an elderly person if she or he were sick or disabled.[48]

Unfortunately, even when there appears to be an adequate pool of caregivers, psychological crises that are the consequences of impairment may contribute to considerable strain on the system of informal care. Schmidt points out that, in caring for impaired aged parents, aging children experience the synergistic effects of fatigue and competing role demands.[49] Furthermore, when aging children have a history of resolving difficulties (sibling rivalry, drive for independence from parental control, parental imperfection) by distancing and avoidance, impairment of an aged parent may lead to high levels of stress, depression, and immobilization.[50]

Several empirical studies suggest that these psychological crises can be sustained indefinitely by families only if certain conditions exist. No significant difference was found between families providing care in the community and families who institutionalize the aged person in need of care in their reported willingness to provide help every now and then. Most families reluctantly institutionalize the impaired aged. Symer found that the major difference between these two types of families was the family's self-reported ability to care for the impaired aged as long as needed.[51]

Lowenthal reports that families caring for the mentally impaired had experienced prolonged ''troublesome'' behavior (that is, the aged person demonstrated abnormal fears, hallucinations, or confusion) prior to institutionalization. However, troublesome behavior was merely a predisposing factor. Generally, disruptive and self-destructive behaviors, as well as environmental factors, precipitated institutionalization. Only after unsuccessfully trying several difficult alternatives did families resort to institutionalization.[52] The findings of Zarit, Reeves, and Bach-Peterson suggest that it is not the problems associated with impairment, but the social support networks of the caregivers that reduce the burdens of caregivers in the informal system. Further, the more visits that were paid to the impaired by relatives not living in the household, the less burden was felt by caregivers residing in the same households as the impaired.[53]

RESPONSES OF THE FORMAL CARE SYSTEM

If the final response of the informal care system to increased numbers of impaired African American aged is likely to be more frequent institutionalization, what will probably be the response of the formally organized care system? In the past, the initial response of the service delivery system to massive or sudden social change has been a slowness in the recognition of "social problems" and piecemeal solutions to comprehensive problems. If the increases in the next 15 to 20 years in the population at risk to impairment are characterized as rapid, then the response of the formal care system will be slow and piecemeal. For example, Piven and Cloward's discussion of welfare in the 1960s illustrates this point. These authors point out that when African Americans migrated to urban areas in the 1950s and 1960s, many were unemployed and without income.[54] However, many were ineligible for public assistance because of long-standing residency requirements. In 1967, 17 years after the African American exodus, the residency requirements were overturned by the Supreme Court. Wilkensky and Lebeaux's discussion of employment security for workers during the early stages of industrialization in the United States offers still another example of a piecemeal response.[55]

It seems likely that the characteristics of the formal care system itself will make for a piecemeal response, because there is not a comprehensive system constituting a "continuum of care." Brody points out that the varied health needs of the functionally impaired elderly have been ignored because major public resources have focused on acute medical care, rather than on the needs of those with chronic diseases.[56]

If agencies that serve families rise to the upcoming challenge, some of the strain on the informal care system can be alleviated. Currently, family service organizations are either proprietary or private nonprofit agencies. But there is a strong negative association between the private associations and the provision of services to minorities.[57] Thus, family service agencies are unlikely to meet the needs of African American families unless they broaden their target populations. However, if African American church groups organize their activities in conjunction with such agencies or sponsor such agencies, gaps in service population would be reduced.

MEETING THE CHALLENGES OF THE TWENTY-FIRST CENTURY

Even if family service agencies widen the scope of their focus to include minority aged and their families, these agencies still will have to redefine and expand their target programs. Target programs will have to be focused on those who are in most need—very old, frail individuals with highly vulnerable family situations, lodgers, all adult children in the labor force, and so forth. Target programs, then, will have to focus on supporting the individual in diverse family contexts.

Counseling and support groups, for example, should focus on assisting and counseling intergenerational families coping with some of the physical and psychological changes in members of advanced years so that the burdens of being a caregiver, as well as of receiving care, can be reduced. Families need coping skills for relationships with persons who become senile. Thus, counseling and supportive services should be directed towards attenuating role strain and role conflict because of life-cycle transitions.

Counseling and support groups should also be provided to the elderly so that the transition to this new stage of the life cycle is not experienced as an individual trauma. Persons who age and leave the labor force may need counseling on strategies to reorient themselves to life without paid work. Aged persons who experience the disorienting effects of senility or failing physical functioning need factual information about these processes and help in acquiring coping skills.

Family service agencies should also seek to supervise homemaker services. In many instances, in some areas of the country, homemaker services are supervised by medical care personnel and public welfare agencies. The supervision of those services by family service agencies might serve to enhance the informal support networks available to the elderly who are most vulnerable to institutionalization (separated or divorced men, widowed women, lodgers, the frail, etc.).

Finally, agencies should seek to organize homemaker services for aged persons in such a way that homemakers have (1) a more valued status than they currently do, and (2) an incentive to provide quality services. The relationship between the homecare worker and the impaired aged person has unique sources of strain. Friedman and Kaye point out that in the publicly funded homecare system, the employer-employee relationship is atypical because the client does not pay the worker directly. [58] On the other hand, if the aged person accepts the homecare worker, he or she accepts some critical level of control by a stranger because of the dependency of the impaired on the worker's services.

Currently, women who sell their homemaker services are trapped in a secondary sector of the dual labor market. Women who work as homemakers are viewed as having no skills. They seldom earn enough money to support their own families. It seems reasonable to assume that some of the stresses of this economic system directly affect the worker, and in turn, indirectly affect the aged recipient of their services.

Family service agencies should organize homemaker services with extended career ladders. As homemakers learn about nutrition, communication skills—useful for dealing with their clients—and health care, their salaries should increase. For example, if the functionally limited aged person demonstrated confused or disruptive behavior, workers with general knowledge of the causes of such behavior and trained in certain interpersonal skills are less likely to respond with anger or to quit because of frustration. Homemakers could also work with teenagers and adults in the home on nutritional habits that decrease the severity of some chronic diseases associated with aging. In summary, to meet the challenge of the 21st century, formally organized services will have to creatively reach out and support the old and new forms of family in the African American aged population.

NOTES

1. Louis B. Harris et al., *Myth and Reality of Aging*. (Washington, DC: National Council on Aging, 1975).
2. Ibid.
3. Ibid.
4. Ibid.
5. Ibid.
6. See William G. Bowen and Aldrich T. Finegan, *The Economics of Labor Force Participation* (Princeton, NJ: Princeton University Press, 1969); Howard Wachtel and Charles Betsey, "Unemployment at Low Wage," *Review of Economics and Statistics* (May 1972: 121–29; Glen Cain, "Unemployment and Labor Force Participation of Secondary Workers," *Industrial and Labor Relations* 20 (Jan. 1967): 375–97.
7. Bureau of the Census, "Money Income of Households, Families, and Persons in the United States: 1986," *Current Population Reports*, ser. P-60, no. 159, (Washington, DC: Government Printing Office, 1988), Table 4.
8. Bureau of the Census, "Population Profile of the United States: 1981," *Current Population Source Reports*, ser. P-20, no. 374 (Washington, DC: Government Printing Office, 1982), Table 10-1.
9. Sally R. Sherman, "Notes and Briefs," *Social Security Bulletin* 42 (1) (Jan. 1979): 40.
10. Susan Grad and Karen Foster, "Income of the Population Aged 65 and Older, 1976," *Social Security Bulletin* 42, (7) (July 1979): 25.
11. National Center for Health Statistics, "Current Estimates from the National Health Interview Survey, United States, 1984," *Vital and Health Statistics*, ser. 10. no. 156 (Washington, DC: Government Printing Office, July 1986), Table 70.
12. National Center for Health Statistics, "Disability Days: United States, 1988," *Vital and Health Statistics*, ser. 10, no. 143 (Washington, DC: Government Printing Office, 1988), Table 28.
13. National Urban League, *Preliminary Report on the Status of the Elderly*, (New York: National Urban League, 1981).
14. National Center for Health Statistics, "Current Estimates from the National Health Interview Survey, United States, 1988," *Vital and Health Statistics*, ser. 10, no. 173 (Washington, DC: Government Printing Office, 1988), Table 71.
15. National Center for Health Statistics, "National Nursing Home Survey, 1985," *Summary for the U.S. Vital and Health Statistics*, ser. 13, no. 97 (Washington, DC: Government Printing Office, 1989), Table 7.
16. National Center for Health Statistics, "Home Care for Persons 55 Years and Over, United States, July 1966–June 1968," *Vital and Health Statistics*, ser. 10, no. 73 (Washington, DC: Government Printing Office, July 1972).
17. National Center for Health Statistics, "Current Estimates, 1984," Table 73.
18. E. Berkanovic and L. G. Reeder, "Ethnic, Economic and Social Psychological Factors in the Source of Medical Care," *Social Problems* 20 (Fall 1973): 246–59.
19. Andrew Billingsley, "Family Functioning in the Low Income Black Community," *Social Casework* 50 (1959): 563–72.
20. C. S. Kart and B. Beckham, "Black-White Differentials in the Institutionalization of the Elderly," *Social Forces* 54 (June 1976): 901–10.
21. Bureau of the Census, *Statistical Abstract of the United States, 1989*. (Washington, DC: Government Printing Office, Oct. 1988).
22. Bureau of the Census, *Current Population Reports*, ser. P-25, no. 1017 (Washington, DC: Government Printing Office, 1988).
23. Ibid.
24. Ibid.
25. Federal Council on Aging, Data of Saad Nagi adapted by staff of Federal Council on Aging and presented in *Public Policy and the Frail Elderly, A Staff Report* (U.S. Department of Health, Education, and Welfare, 1978), 27.
26. Ibid.
27. Ibid.
28. Federal Council on Aging, *Public Policy and the Frail Elderly*, 77. The GAO sample of Cleveland and Durham was checked against a similar national study undertaken by the Duke Center for the Study of the Aging and Human Development. The major difference was that GAO sample had at least three times more African Americans.
29. Linda M. Chatters, Robert Joseph Taylor, and James S. Jackson, "Aged Blacks' Choices for an Informal Helper Network," *Journal of Gerontology* 41 (Jan. 1986): 94–100.

30. Ibid.

31. National Center for Health Statistics, "Characteristics of Nursing Home Residents, Health Status and Care Received," *Vital and Health Statistics*, ser. 13, no. 51, DHHS pub. no. (PHS) 81–1712, 1978.

32. Bureau of the Census, "Households, Families, Marital Status and Living Arrangements: March 1985 (Advance Report)," *Current Population Reports*, ser. P-20, no. 371 (Washington, DC: Government Printing Office, 1985), Table 6.

33. Bureau of the Census, "Marital Status and Living Arrangements: March 1981," *Current Population Reports*, ser. P-20, no. 372 (Washington, DC: Government Printing Office, 1982), 5.

34. Bureau of the Census, "Marital Status and Living Arrangements: March 1988," *Current Population Reports*, ser. 20, no. 433 (Washington, DC: Government Printing Office, 1989), Table 6. Computed percentages are based on persons aged 20 and over.

35. Ibid.

36. Bureau of the Census, *Statistical Abstract of the United States, 1989* (Washington, DC: Government Printing Office, 1989), Table 69.

37. Bureau of the Census, "Marital Status: March 1981"; Bureau of the Census, "Marital Status: March 1988."

38. See note 37.

39. Robert Joseph Taylor, Linda M. Chatters, and Vickie Mays, "Parents, Children, Siblings, In-Laws, and Non-Kin as Sources of Emergency Assistance to Black Americans," *Family Relations* 37 (July 1988): 298–304.

40. Duran Bell, Patricia Kasschau, and Gail Zellman, *Delivering Services to Elderly Members of Minority Groups: A Critical Review of the Literature* (Santa Monica, CA: Rand Corporation, 1976).

41. Elizabeth Shanas, "Social Myths as Hypothesis: The Case of Family Relations of Old People," *Gerontologist*, 19 (1) (1979): 3–9; see also Shanas et al., *Old People in Three Industrial Societies* (New York: Atherton Press, 1968); Elaine M. Brody, "The Informal Support System of the Functionally Dependent Elderly," *Proceedings of the Conference on the Changing Needs of Nursing Home Care of the American College of Physicians*, 12–13 June 1980.

42. Shanas, "Social Myths."

43. Taylor, Chatters, and Mays, "Parents, Children, Siblings."

44. Wayne C. Seelkbach, "Filial Responsibility among Aged Parents: A Racial Comparison," *Journal of Minority Aging* 5, (1980): 53–57.

45. Peggye Anderson, "Support Services and Aged Blacks," *Journal of Minority Aging* 3 (1980): 53–57.

46. Robert Taylor, "The Extended Family as a Source of Support to Elderly Blacks," *Gerontologist* 25 (Oct. 1985): 488–95.

47. Suzanne Bianchi and Reynolds Farley, "Racial Differences in Family Living Arrangements and Economic Well-Being: An Analysis of Recent Trends," *Journal of Marriage and the Family* (Aug. 1979): 537–49.

48. Chatters, Taylor, and Jackson, "Aged Blacks' Choices," 98.

49. Mary Gwynne Schmidt, "Failing Parents, Aging Children," *Journal of Gerontological Social Work* 2 (3) (Spring 1980): 259–68; see also G. L. Lieberman, "Children of the Elderly as Natural Helpers," *Psychology* 6 (1978): 489–517.

50. Schmidt, "Failing Parents," 260–267; see also Linda Crossman, Cecila London, and Clemmie Barry, "Older Women for Disabled Spouses: A Model for Supportive Services," *Gerontologist* 21 (1981).

51. Michael A. Symer, "The Differential Usage of Services by the Impaired Elderly," *Journal of Gerontology*, 35 (2) (1980): 249–55; Brody, "The Informal Support System," 157–58.

52. Marjorie Fiske Lowenthal, *Lives in Distress* (New York: Basic Books, 1967), 42–56.

53. Steven H. Zarit, Karen E. Reeves and Julia Bach-Peterson, "Relatives of the Impaired Elderly: Correlates of Feelings of Burden," *Gerontologist* 20 (1980): 649–55.

54. Francis Fox Piven and Richard Cloward, *Regulating the Poor*, (New York: Vintage Books, 1972).

55. Harold Wilkensky and Charles Lebeaux, *Industrial Society Social Welfare*, (New York: Free Press, 1958).

56. Stanley Brody, "The Formal Long Term Support System for the Dependent Elderly," in *Proceedings of the Conference on the Changing Needs of Nursing Home Care*, of the American College of Physicians, 12–13 June 1980.

57. Douglas Holmes et al., "Use of Community Based Services in Long Term Care by Older Persons," *Gerontologist*, 19 (1979): 389–97.

58. Susan Rosenfeld Friedman and Lenard W. Kaye, "Homecare for the Frail Elderly: Implications for an Interactional Relationship," *Journal of Gerontological Social Work* 2 (Winter 1979): 109–25.

6

Toxic Waste and the African American Community

Robert D. Bullard and Beverly H. Wright

The disposal of hazardous waste is one of the most serious problems in the United States. Toxic waste facilities are often located in communities that have high percentages of poor, elderly, young, and minority residents. Specifically, an inordinate concentration of uncontrolled toxic waste sites are found in African American and Hispanic urban communities, while large commercial hazardous waste landfills and disposal facilities are more likely to be found in rural communities in the southern black belt. One-third of the 27 hazardous waste landfills operating in the 48 contiguous states were located in 5 southern states. The total capacity of these 9 landfills represented 59.6 percent of the nation's total hazardous waste landfill capacity. Further, the 4 landfills responsible for 63 percent of the South's total hazardous waste capacity were located in minority zip-code areas. These inequities are even more glaring, if one considers that African Americans comprise a mere 20 percent of the South's total population.

The hazardous waste problem continues to be one of the most "serious problems facing the industrial world."[1] The United States generates over 250 million tons of hazardous waste each year. That is more than one ton of waste per person, or enough hazardous waste to fill the New Orleans Superdome 1,500 times over.[2] This problem has not been fully resolved even with recent environmental legislation.[3] For example, tons of unregulated hazardous household waste end up at municipal landfills designed for household garbage. Moreover, many of the uncontrolled or abandoned toxic waste dumps pose potential risks to nearby residents.[4] African American communities are especially at risk, since they are burdened with a disproportionately large share of these noxious facilities.

TOXIC WASTE DUMPING GROUNDS

Toxic waste facilities are not randomly scattered across the American landscape. They are often located in communities that have high percentages of poor, elderly, young, and minority residents.[5] An inordinate concentration of uncontrolled toxic waste sites can be found in African American and Hispanic urban communities.[6] On the other hand, large commercial hazardous waste landfills and disposal facilities are more likely to be found in rural communities in the southern black belt.[7]

Toxic waste disposal has generated demonstrations in many communities across the country.[8] The first national protest by African Americans on the hazardous waste issue came in 1982 after the mostly African American Warren County, North Carolina, was selected as the burial site for more than 32,000 cubic yards of soil contaminated with the highly toxic PCBs (polychlorinated biphenyls). The soil was illegally dumped along the roadways in 14 North Carolina counties in 1978. African American civil rights activists, political leaders, and area residents marched and protested against the construction of the PCB landfill in the small town of Afton. Why was Warren County selected as the landfill site? The decision made more political sense than environmental sense.[9]

Although the demonstrations were unsuccessful in halting the landfill construction, the protests marked the first time African Americans mobilized a national, broad-based group to protest environmental inequities. The 1982 demonstrations prompted Congressman Walter E. Fauntroy, who had been active in the protest demonstrations, to initiate the 1983 General Accounting Office (GAO) study of hazardous landfill siting in the region.[10] The GAO study observed a strong relationship between the siting of off-site hazardous waste landfills and the race and socioeconomic status of surrounding communities. The 1983 government study identified four off-site hazardous waste landfills in the eight states that comprised the Environmental Protection Agency's (EPA's) Region IV (that is, Alabama, Florida, Georgia, Kentucky, Mississippi, North Carolina, South Carolina, and Tennessee). The data in Table 1 detail the sociodemographic characteristics of the communities where the four hazardous waste landfill sites are located.

The four hazardous waste landfill sites included Chemical Waste Management (Sumter Country, Alabama), SCA Services (Sumter County, South Carolina), Industrial Chemical Company (Chester County, South Carolina), and Warren County PCB Landfill (Warren County, North Carolina). African Americans comprised the majority in three of the four communities where the off-site hazardous waste landfills are located. The GAO study also revealed that more than one-fourth of the population in all four communities had incomes below the poverty level, and most of this population was African American.[11]

When the entire southern United States is the area under study, even more glaring siting disparities emerge. For example, there were 27 hazardous waste landfills operating in the 48 contiguous states, with a total capacity of 127,897 acre-feet in 1987.[12] One-third of these hazardous waste landfills were located in 5 southern states (that is, Alabama, Louisiana, Oklahoma, South Carolina, and Texas). The total capacity of these 9 landfills represented 59.6 percent (76,226 acre-feet) of the nation's total hazardous waste landfill capacity (see Table 2). The 4 landfills in minority zip code areas represented 63 percent of the South's total hazardous waste capacity. Moreover, the landfills located in Emelle (Alabama), Alsen (Louisiana), and Pinewood (South Carolina)

Toxic Waste and the African American Community 69

TABLE 1
**1980 Census Population, Income, and Poverty Data for Census Areas
Where EPA Region IV Hazardous Waste Landfills Are Located (1983)**

Landfill (State)	Population		Mean Family Income		Population Below Poverty Level		
	Number	Percent African American	All Races	African Americans	Number	Percent	Percent African American
Chemical Waste Management (Alabama)	626	90	$11,198	$10,752	265	42	100
SCA Services (South Carolina)	849	38	16,371	6,781	260	31	100
Industrial Chemical Co. (South Carolina)	728	52	18,996	12,941	188	26	92
Warren County PCB Landfill (North Carolina)	804	66	10,367	9,285	256	32	90

Source: General Accounting Office, *Siting of Hazardous Waste Landfills and Their Correlation with Racial and Economic Status of Surrounding Communities* (Washington, DC: Government Printing Office, 1983), 4.

Note: Areas represent subdivisions of political jurisdictions designated by the census for data gathering.

accounted for 58.6 percent of the region's hazardous waste landfill capacity, although African Americans make up only about 20 percent of the South's total population.

It is not coincidental that in 1983 the National Association for the Advancement of Colored People (NAACP), after the national protest demonstration in Warren County, North Carolina, passed its first resolution on the hazardous waste issue. The issues raised by subsequent protest actions were instrumental in getting the New York-based Commission for Racial Justice to sponsor its 1987 national study of toxic wastes and

TABLE 2
Operating Hazardous Waste Landfills in the Southern United States and Ethnicity of Communities (1987)

Facility Name	City/State	Rank Nationally[a]	Current Capacity in Acre-Feet[b]	Percent of Population in Zip Code Area		
				Minority	African American	Hispanic
Chemical Waste Management	Emelle, AL	1	30,000	79.5	78.9	0.0
CESCO International Inc.	Livingston, LA	3	22,400	23.8	21.6	1.8
Rollins Enviornmental Services, Inc.	Scotlandville/ Alsen, LA	4	14,440	94.7	93.0	1.5
Chemical Waste Management Inc.	Carlyss, LA	6	5,656	6.8	4.6	1.7
Texas Ecologist, Inc.	Robstown, TX	9	3,150	78.2	1.6	76.6
GSX Services of South Carolina	Pinewood, SC	18	289	71.6	70.5	1.1
U S Pollution Control Inc.	Waynoka, OK	21	118	37.3	23.2	12.3
Gulf Coast Waste Disposal Autority	Galveston, TX	22	110	4.3	0.0	3.8
Rollins Environmental Services, Inc.	Deer Park, TX	23	103	7.3	0.3	6.2

Source: Commission for Racial Justice, *Hazardous Wastes and Race in the United States: A National Report on the Racial and Socio-Economic Characteristics of Communities with Hazardous Waste Sites* (New York: Commission for Racial Justice, 1987), Table B-10.
[a] The ranking is based on the 27 operating hazardous waste landfills found in the 48 contiguous United States in 1987.
[b] Acre-feet is the volume of water needed to fill one acre to a depth of one foot. The total capacity of the 27 hazardous waste landfills was 127,989 acre-feet in 1987.

race.[13] Environmental equity has now become a part of the agendas of mainstream civil rights organizations. Even poor Third World countries have initiated actions in the United Nations to stem the toxic waste dumping within their borders.[14] These poor nations have become toxic waste havens for industries from the United States and other Western industrial powers.

WINNERS AND LOSERS

Poor and minority communities had the most to gain in the passage of environmental regulations such as the Clean Air Act, since they lived closest to the worst sources of the pollution.[15] These communities, however, continue to be burdened with a dispro-portionately large share of industrial pollution problems, even after the passage of all the governmental regulations. Uneven enforcement of environmental regulations is a contributor to this problem. On the other hand, many low-income African American community residents are engaged in a constant battle with problems they face head-on every day: spiraling crime rates, drug trafficking, deteriorating infrastructures, high unemployment, widespread poverty, and a host of other social ills that threaten their survival. Institutional barriers (housing and employment discrimination; redlining by banks, mortgage companies, and insurance firms; public policies that favor the affluent over the poor; and disparate enforcement of land-use and environmental regulations) relegate a large segment of the African American community to less-than-desirable physical surroundings, reduce housing and residential options, limit mobility, and increase risks from exposure to potentially health-threatening toxins.[16]

Public opposition has been more vocal in middle- and upper-income groups on the issue of siting noxious facilities. The NIMBY (not in my backyard) syndrome has been the usual reaction in these communities. As affluent communities became more active in opposing a certain facility, the siting effort shifted toward more powerless communities.[17] Opposition groups often called for the facilities to be sited ''some-where else.'' The Somewhere, U.S.A., was often in poor, powerless, and minority communities. It is this unequal sharing of benefits and burdens that has engendered feelings that poor and minority communities have received unfair treatment.

EXPLOITATION OF THE LAND AND PEOPLE

Facility siting in the southern United States is largely reflective of the long pattern of treating its African American citizens differently from the larger white community. There is, of course, a ''direct historical connection between the exploitation of the land and the exploitation of people, especially black people.''[18] David R. Goldfield, a southern historian, contends that ''as race relations continue to improve, so will South-ern ecology.''[19] Southern ecology has been shaped by economic boosterism, a blind pro-business climate, and lax enforcement of environmental regulations. Southerners have gone to great lengths to stimulate economic regeneration. Many of their indus-trialization strategies were carried out with reckless disregard for environmental cost.

Rapid and unrestrained production has ruined or threatened the region's unique habitat. A classic example of this ecological destruction is the life-giving Mississippi River, which has been turned into a "deadly mixture of sewage, industrial waste, and insecticide below fire-belching Baton Rouge."[20] The entire Gulf Coast region, especially Mississippi, Alabama, Louisiana, and Texas, has been ravaged by "lax regulations and unbridled production."[21]

Polluting industries have exploited the pro-growth and pro-jobs sentiment exhibited among the poor, working-class, and minority communities.[22] Industries such as paper mills, waste disposal and treatment facilities, and chemical plants, searching for operation space, found the South to be a logical choice for their expansion in the 1970s. This was especially the case for economically depressed communities. These communities and their leaders were seen as having a "Third World" view of development: Any development is better than no development at all. They were also suspicious of environmentalists, a sentiment that aligned many African American and working-class communities with the pro-growth advocates.

The sight and smell of paper mills, toxic waste incinerators, chemical plants, and other industrial operations were promoted as trade-offs for having jobs near "poverty pockets." For example, a paper mill spewing its stench in one of Alabama's poverty-ridden black belt counties led Governor George Wallace to declare: "Yeah, that's the smell of prosperity. Sho' does smell sweet, don't it?"[23] Residents and community leaders in West Virginia's and Louisiana's "chemical corridors" are reported to hold similar views.[24]

The 1980s have seen a shift in the reaction of African American communities on the jobs-environment issue. This shift has revolved around the issue of social equity.[25] These communities have begun to challenge the legitimacy of environmental blackmail and the notion of trade-offs. They are now asking: Are the costs borne by African Americans imposed to spare the larger community? Can environmetal inequities (resulting from industrial siting decisions) be compensated? What are "acceptable" risks? Concern about equity is at the heart of this reaction to industrial siting decisions and locational disputes. In the case of industrial facility siting, there is an "inherent imbalance between localized costs and dispersed benefits."[26]

Compensation, economic incentives, and other monetary inducements have been proposed as equalizers to redress the imbalance.[27] The NIMBY syndrome, however, has trickled down to nearly all communities, even low-income African American communities. Few residents want garbage dumps and landfills in their backyards. The price of siting noxious facilities has skyrocketed in recent years as a result of more stringent federal regulations and the growing militancy among poor, working-class, and minority communities. Many of these communities are no longer considered a pushover for polluting industries. Today, they are unwilling to accept new polluting industries into their midst. Some are busy trying to get existing industries shut down or cleaned up.[28] Compensation appears to hold little promise in mitigating siting conflict and environmental disputes where social justice and environmental equity issues are involved.

PROGNOSIS

Environmental disputes are likely to increase in the future as tighter federal regulations take effect (1984 amendment to the Resource Conservation and Recovery Act). All states will soon be required to have the treatment and disposal capacity to handle the hazardous wastes generated within their borders. Currently, some states ship their wastes out of state. A large share of this waste ends up in the southern United States. The new mandate has the potential for equalizing this imbalance. States are currently hammering out site selection criteria. It is not yet known what type of siting pattern will emerge from the new federal mandate. States, however, will need to respond to the equity issue if they expect to have successful siting strategies. African American communities will need to become more involved in developing facility-siting criteria, plans, and long-range waste management strategies. Some planners see the undeveloped and cheap land in the South as a region ripe for the export of municipal and hazardous wastes.

The disparate siting of noxious facilities is sufficient to take some of the luster off the image of the "new" South. For many African American communities that have been systematically and routinely selected to host hazardous waste facilities and other polluting industries, the new South is more imagery than reality. Progress has been made in broadening the base of the environmental movement and mobilizing a wider segment of the population. Still, too many African American communities lack the organization and resources (financial and personnel) to mount and sustain long-term challenges to industrial polluters, government planners, waste disposal giants, and "midnight dumpers" who target their areas for the production and disposal of toxic materials.

The African American experience in the South is a useful point of reference to explore the emergent environmental equity movement. This movement is characterized by a growing militancy among middle-class and working-class community residents alike. Institutional barriers in the housing market have placed middle-income and low-income residents in close proximity and often in the same residential areas. Residents of these communities are now unwilling to accept second class status when it comes to environmental quality. Government and private industry have been served notice that environmental discrimination will be challenged just as other institutional barriers were met with organized resistance.

There are some encouraging signs that the leadership structure and community network now exist in a growing number of African American communities that are willing to challenge the long-standing facility-siting pattern. In most instances, these challenges are led, organized, and funded by indigenous community institutions. The African American community has received little assistance from outside "elites," including mainstream environmentalists, in their struggle for environmental justice.

Community activists and social justice advocates have begun to marshal their resources in opposition to various kinds of environmental threats. They have borrowed tactics directly out of the pages of the earlier civil rights movement, including protest demonstrations, picketing, lobbying, grass-roots organizing, and litigation. In addition to increased activism, African American communities are now attempting to incorporate environmental safeguards into their agendas for economic development. Although many of these communities are economically vulnerable (they have few business and employment centers that are indigenous to the African American community), a growing segment within the community has begun to demand a strategy that balances development and environmental protection. The promise of jobs and a broadened tax base can no longer be the sole criteria for accepting industry into the community. Moreover, many of these jobs are low paying and are often hazardous to the workers and nearby residents.

The mounting toxic waste problem has now moved from community-industry conflict to one of interstate and international conflict. The controversy has taken on a new twist involving politicians, big business, state agencies, and environmentalists. Again, the issue revolves around equity: namely, one state exporting its toxic waste across its borders to another state. For example, the Texas-Alabama and North Carolina-South Carolina interstate disputes are classic examples of states not wanting to become the dumping grounds for another state's toxic waste.

African American leaders, politicians, and community residents need to pay close attention to these disputes and to the arguments put forth. More important, they need to understand that waste facility siting equity within a given state is just as important as between states. The equity question involving the African American communities within states has not been resolved. Environmental discrimination is still a fact of life for many residents in these communities. Similarly, African American communities do not wish to become the dumping grounds for other communities' waste.

NOTES

1. Samuel S. Epstein, Lester O. Brown, and Carl Pope, *Hazardous Waste in America* (San Francisco: Sierra Club Books, 1983), 33–39.

2. Office of Technology Assessment, *Technologies and Management Strategies for Hazardous Waste Control* (Washington, DC: Government Printing Office, 1983), 3; Environmental Protection Agency, "Birth of a Program," *EPA Journal* 13 (1983): 14–15.

3. Epstein, Brown, and Pope, *Hazardous Waste in America*, 6–11.

4. Michael H. Brown, *Laying Waste: The Poisoning of America by Toxic Chemicals* (New York: Pantheon Books, 1980), 267.

5. R.F. Anderson and Michael R. Greenberg, "Hazardous Waste Facility Siting: A Role of Planners," *Journal of the American Planning Association* 48 (Spring 1982): 204–18.

6. Commission for Racial Justice, *Toxic Waste and Race in the United States: A National Report on the Racial and Socioeconomic Characteristics of Communities with Hazardous Waste Sites* (New York: United Church of Christ, 1987), 23.

7. General Accounting Office, *Siting of Hazardous Waste Landfills and Their Correlation with Racial and Economic Status of Surrounding Communities* (Washington, DC: General Accounting Office, 1983), 2.

8. Sue Pollack and Joann Grozuczak, *Reagan, Toxics, and Minorities* (Washington, DC: Urban Environment Conference, Inc., 1984), 20.

9. Ken Geiser and Gerry Waneck, "PCB and Warren County," *Science for the People* 15 (July/Aug. 1983): 13–17.

10. General Accounting Office, *Siting of Hazardous Waste Landfills*, 1.

11. Ibid., 3.

12. Commission for Racial Justice, *Toxic Wastes and Race*, xi.

13. Ibid., 66.

14. Jim Vallette, *The International Trade in Wastes: A Greenpeace Inventory* (Washington, DC: Greenpeace, 1989), 8–10.

15. Sam Love, "Ecology and Social Justice: Is There a Conflict?" *Environmental Action* 4 (1972): 3–6; Frederick H. Buttel and William L. Flinn, "Social Class and Mass Environmental Beliefs," *Environment and Behavior* 10 (Sept. 1978), 433–50; Julian McCaull, "Discriminatory Air Pollution: If the Poor Don't Breathe," *Environment* 19 (Mar. 1976): 26–32; Robert D. Bullard, "Endangered Environs: The Price of Unplanned Growth in Boomtown Houston," *California Sociologist* 7 (Summer 1984): 84–102.

16. Robert D. Bullard and Beverly H. Wright, "Blacks and the Environment," *Humboldt Journal of Social Relations* 14 (Summer 1987): 165–84.

17. Michael R. Edelstein, *Contaminated Communities: The Social and Psychological Impacts of Residential Toxic Exposure* (Boulder, CO: Westview Press, 1987).

18. David R. Goldfield, *Promised Land: The South Since 1945* (Arlington Heights, IL: Harlan Davidson, 1987), 211–12.

19. Ibid.

20. Michael Brown, *The Toxic Cloud: The Poisoning of America's Air* (New York: Harper and Row, 1987), 161.

21. Goldfield, *Promised Land*, 197.

22. Max Neiman and Ronald O. Loveridge, "Environmentalism and Local Growth Control: A Probe into the Class Bias Thesis," *Environment and Behavior* 13 (1981): 759–72.

23. Quoted in Goldfield, *Promised Land*, 197.

24. Ben A. Franklin, "In the Shadow of the Valley," *Sierra* 71 (May/June 1986): 40–41; Jane Slaughter, "Valley of the Shadow of Death," *The Progressive* 49 (March 1985): 50; Brown, *The Toxic Cloud*, 152–61.

25. John Seley and Julian Wolpert, "Equity and Location," in *Equity in Radioactive Waste Management*, ed. Roger E. Kasperson (Cambridge, MA: Oelgeschlager, Gunn, and Hain, 1983), 69–93.

26. David Morell, "Siting and the Politics of Equity," *Hazardous Waste* 1 (1980): 555–79.

27. Kent E. Portney, "The Potential of the Theory of Compensation for Mitigating Public Opposition to Hazardous Waste Siting: Some Evidence from Five Massachusetts Communities," *Policy Studies Journal* 14 (1985): 81–89.

28. Robert D. Bullard and Beverly H. Wright, "Environmentalism and the Politics of Equity," *Mid-America Review of Sociology* 12 (Winter 1987): 21–37.

7

Cardiac Reactivity and Elevated Blood Pressure Levels among Young African Americans: The Importance of Stress

Ivor Lensworth Livingston and Ronald J. Marshall

Compared with white Americans, African Americans are afflicted twice as much by high blood pressure (HBP) or hypertension and its devastating health-related outcomes. Interracial differences in HBP begin to show their insidious presence very early in the life cycle, especially around the adolescent period. There is no known etiology for (essential) hypertension. Thus, the major focus of this is to show that stress (operationalized from a sociopsychological perspective, leading over time, to cardiac reactivity in the body) is a salient contributing factor to the etiology and, possibly, exacerbation of elevated arterial blood pressure (BP) in the African American adolescent. A sociopsychophysiological model of the stress process is used as a framework in which to (1) understand how young African Americans are predisposed to view their life experiences as stressful, (2) see how their bodily systems react to stress, and (3) see how it is possible, over time, for certain effects, such as hypertension, to manifest themselves if stress is not abated. Preventive strategies are discussed and policy-oriented recommendations are made that could reduce the severity of the morbidity and mortality related to hypertension, especially in the at-risk African American adolescent population.

This article explores the racial differences in elevated arterial (that is, systolic and diastolic) blood pressure (BP) between African American youth, especially adolescents, and their white counterparts. Although the etiology of high blood pressure (HPB) or hypertension is multifaceted,[1] it is argued that African American adolescents' perception of day-to-day stress and, subsequently, their cardiac reactivity in response to such stress, are important contributors to the onset and possible exacerbation of elevated arterial BP. A conceptual model of the sociopsychophysiological stress process is used to provide the framework for the discussion of how stress, and subsequent cardiac reactivity, can lead, over time, to elevated arterial BP.

DISTRIBUTION AND CHARACTERISTICS OF ELEVATED BLOOD PRESSURE

In the United States, it has been estimated that HPB affects 23 to 60 million people, depending on the criteria used to define it.[2] Whatever the criteria (for example, a reading of 140/90 mmHg), the consensus of empirical research is that BP increases with advancing age. It has been said that there is a progressive rise of approximately 1.5 mmHg systolic and 1 mmHg diastolic pressure per year of age. The incidence of

HBP is twice as high among African Americans as among white Americans. African Americans also experience a disproportionately higher affliction of irreversible organ damage, which is a direct outgrowth of chronic elevated BP.[3]

Given its public health importance, great efforts have been made to determine the etiology or origins of hypertension. Despite these efforts, however, approximately 90 percent of all hypertensives are diagnosed as being victims of "essential" hypertension, that is, high blood pressure of unknown etiology.[4] On another level, however, reports exist to suggest that, while hypertension cannot be cured, it certainly can be controlled with various therapies.

Epidemiological surveys have established that hypertension is a major risk factor for mortality and morbidity associated with cardiovascular[5] and cerebrovascular[6] diseases. Left untreated, hypertension inflicts damage on the arterial walls, promotes kidney damage, and places a great strain on the heart, which in turn is forced to work harder in order to move the blood against higher-than-optimal pressures. African Americans as a group also tend to experience a disproportionate incidence of these disease-related sequelae (for example, coronary dysfunction and radiographic evidence of left ventricular enlargement) compared to white Americans.[7]

As with many physiological outcomes, BP is very unstable, and it responds to a variety of environmental, cognitive, and physiological variables. Evidence indicates that the impact of these and other factors on BP begin early in a person's life. There is convincing evidence relating BP levels in children to levels in later life.[8] Given this fact, an assessment of factors related to elevated BP levels during childhood may suggest preventive measures that could be introduced at a time when intervention may be most effective.

In order to intervene more effectively, evidence has to exist around two very crucial areas: (1) what salient (antecedent, mediating, etc.) factors are responsible for initiating and/or exacerbating BP levels (especially over time), and (2) given the knowledge of these salient factors, which target group(s) is (are) more vulnerable or at risk for developing hypertension, taking into consideration, for example, age, race, sex, and socioeconomic classifications? Answers to these and other relevant questions can be achieved through the accumulation of epidemiological evidence, particularly using the methodological technique of "tracking." Tracking refers to the phenomenon that a person's relative status on a physiological index is relatively invariant.[9] For example, an individual's elevated BP will tend to remain elevated relative to others in the population. Information from tracking and other sources suggest that BP levels during adolescence and young adulthood have been found to be predictive of later hypertension.[10]

INTERRACIAL DIFFERENCES IN BLOOD PRESSURE AT EARLY AGES

Elevated Blood Pressure and Race

Before puberty, BP levels among whites and African Americans may not differ.[11] After puberty, however, while several reports indicate that there are no interracial differences in BP,[12] several others reported that interracial differences do exist. For example, Voors, Webber, and Berenson, using six BP observations, found that African American children had significantly higher BP than white children.[13] This difference became apparent at around 10 years of age. The distribution of BPs among African Americans is displaced to the upper end of values in comparison to whites; more African Americans than whites may show sustained elevations in BP when rescreened.[14] It has been reported that a significantly greater percentage of African American children than would be expected by chance have BPs above the 95th percentile.[15]

Elevated Blood Pressure, Race, and Socioeconomic Class

The adolescent period, which requires a degree of psychological, physical, and behavioral adjustments, has been the focus of research attempts to identify where interracial differences in BP begin to become more evident. This article will show that stress plays a major role in contributing to interracial differences in BP.

Given the multifaceted nature of the etiology of hypertension, there are several other factors (that is, besides race and stress) that would have to be taken into consideration when addressing the interracial distribution of BP. One such factor is socioeconomic class, where lower socioeconomic class has been reported to be associated with elevated BP.[16]

In a study carried out in Mississippi, it was reported that BP in rural girls was higher than that of city girls.[17] Among African American girls, BP was the highest in the lowest socioeconomic group and lowest in the highest socioeconomic group. BP of African American adolescents was higher than that of whites; however, this racial difference was not evident between African Americans in the upper-socioeconomic class and rural whites. In another study, conducted in Harlem, it was reported that BP levels and the prevalence of hypertension in females did not vary with race, although the highest prevalence of hypertension occurred in African American males.[18]

In still another study, conducted in Washington, D.C., it was reported that African American adolescents had higher BP than whites, and that African Americans attending an inner-city school, which was located in a socioeconomically "deprived" (and, therefore, potentially stressful) area, had higher BP than African Americans attending a middle-class, racially integrated school.[19] Additionally, among African Americans, higher BP was found in children whose parents worked as laborers or were unemployed than in children of parents in professional occupations. Overall, more than 10 percent of African American males, 1 percent of African American females, and no white females or males had systolic BP greater than 140 mmHg (which for this age group is considered relatively high).

Stress, Blood Pressure, and Cardiac Reactivity

African Americans as a group consistently exhibit higher systolic and diastolic BP than whites during adulthood.[20] However, studies assessing BP levels in adolescent populations have yielded conflicting results. Some studies have reported that African

American adolescents have higher BP levels than whites;[21] other studies have reported lower BP levels for African Americans,[22] or similar BP levels in the two groups.[23]Various reasons can be offered for the inconsistency in this body of research. It is argued here however, that a major reason is that most previous reports have not used a conceptual basis to guide their empirical research.

Thus, this article attempts to address this void by suggesting a conceptual framework through which the dynamics of the stress-BP relationship can be explored, especially over time, when the chronicity of BP elevations and resulting organ damage become more evident.

As alluded to earlier, the mechanisms responsible for the development of hypertension and for the racial differences in hypertension have yet to be fully elucidated. Of particular interest in this article are two very important relationships: the impact of African American youths' perception of stress and the impact of such stress on their cardiovascular reactivity and, over time, chronic elevations in arterial BP levels. This emphasis is very appropriate, given the results of previous longitudinal studies that have implicated cardiovascular reactivity in subsequent BP and in the development of hypertension.[24]

It is reasoned that increased cardiovascular and BP reactivity to stress can be a significant risk factor for the development of a disproportionate incidence of hypertension between the races. A brief explanation of the process involved in this relationship is in order. It has been postulated that hypertension develops in susceptible young persons who respond to environmental or emotional stress by having high cardiac output, increased peripheral resistance, or both. When faced with a challenging stimulus, the organism responds with increased output of epinephrine and norepinephrine. The catecholamines cause a rise in peripheral resistance and cardiac output, and acute BP is the outcome. Given the chronic nature of elevated arterial BP, hypertension is likely to occur, over time, since acute increases in BP lead to progressive changes in underlying anatomical structures and changes in BP-regulation mechanisms.[25]

Previous studies have reported racial differences in the hemodynamic responses to stress, when stress was operationalized in terms of maximal voluntary exercise on a cycle ergometer. African American children of both genders demonstrated significantly greater systolic BP (SBP) reactivity (that is, maximal BP level minus resting BP level) than did their white counterparts. These racial differences were manifested even though it was demonstrated that African Americans and whites in the same gender groups showed no differences in either resting SBP or maximal heart rate during exercise.[26]

Racial differences in cardiovascular reactivity and BP still persist even when stress is operationalized from a more psychogenic point of view. For example, when stress was viewed in terms of three conditions of psychological stress using a video game (personal challenge, experimenter's challenge, and experimenter's challenge accompanied by a financial incentive), results indicated that video games provoked significant incremental cardiovascular reactivity across the games. African American children demonstrated significantly greater reactivity than white children. The racial differences, however, were more reliably observed for SBP and diastolic BP (DBP) than for heart rate.[27]

STRESS AND HYPERTENSION

It is argued here and elsewhere by this author that, when viewed from a sociopsychological perspective, stress is perhaps the most salient variable on which to examine interracial differences in elevated arterial BP levels.[28] Realistically, however, it must be said that given the multicausal nature of hypertension, ultimate solutions regarding the etiology of hypertension will, of necessity, have to involve an eclectic approach involving "other" parameters, including stress. Overall, then, it is all these factors working in combination that will act in a synergistic manner, over time, giving rise or contributing to elevated BP. Although these other factors are not of interest to this discussion, they should be acknowledged. Such factors include, for example, genetics,[29] diet (such as excess fat),[30] sodium chloride,[31] age, education, social class, and so forth.[32]

Overview of the Stress Concept

Increased research activity involving the stress concept has brought confusion about the conceptualization and definition of stress. It has been said that

> stress is one of those particular terms which is understood by everyone when used in a very general context but understood by very few when an operational definition is sufficiently specific to enable the precise testing of certain relationships.[33]

A perusal of the literature shows a wide variation in the usage of the stress concept.[34] For example, it has been used as a *stimulus*, that is, an external negative force impinging on an individual; as a *response*, that is, an individual's emotional and/or physiological reactions to internal or external events; and as an *interaction* between an individual and his or her surroundings, that is, as a person-environment problem resulting from perceptions and appraisals of one's internal/external environments.[35]

The dominant view of stress adopted in this article is consistent with the *interactionist* view of stress alluded to in the past by this author[36] and others (for example, Lazarus).[37] Since stress is understood to involve a complex and dynamic process, it is further believed that the onset and perpetuation of stressful experiences are dependent on a host of internal and external predisposing (that is, vulnerability-oriented) and enabling (that is, resource-oriented) factors. With this basic premise in mind, it is reasoned that any attempt to explain the role stress plays in health-related outcomes, for example, cardiac reactivity and elevated BP in young African Americans, should include a treatment of these (and other) parameters in a conceptual framework. This will be addressed within the context of the sociopsychophysiological model of the stress process.

The Relationship between Stress and Hypertension

Although the etiological role of stress in the onset and perpetuation of hypertension is not definitive, the consensus of opinion is that acute stress can elevate BP significantly.[38] However, an issue that is increasingly being addressed, and one most germane to any attempt to understand racial differences in hypertension in the United States, is the contribution of chronic or prolonged stress to permanent elevated arterial BP.

Although the limitations of space preclude a thorough examination of reasons why the stress-hypertension relationship is not more definitive, suffice it to say that a major criticism has to do with the frequent use of structural approaches as a means to test and explain the relationship between stress and hypertension. For example, such approaches have attempted to show that static factors, such as race, gender, education, marital status, etc., are related to stress. Since stress itself involves, not a static, but a dynamic process occurring over time,[39] however, it is reasoned that structural explanations of stress are inherently limiting and reductionistic. This latter point is most germane to this paper, because a purely structural approach fails to explain certain epidemiological intraracial differences. For example, why is it that not all African American adolescents are hypertensive? Theoretically, a pure structural approach would suggest that all African American adolescents should, by virtue of their common race, be hypertensive. This, of course, is not the case! To this end, a process-oriented model is needed, like the one that will be addressed shortly. Such a process-oriented model has the potential to explain interracial as well as intraracial differences in elevated BP.

Sociopsychological Stress and Young African Americans

Given that hypertension is essentially a social disease of modern societies,[40] if stress is viewed as a major contributing factor to its etiology, then it is reasoned that the interpretation of the stress process has to take place within the prevailing social context in which African American youth, especially adolescents, exist. A major argument put forward in this article is that, due to the structural configurations of American society, with its built-in inequities occurring primarily based on race, vast numbers of African American youth are predisposed, individually and collectively, by their life-style experiences (for example, lower educational opportunities, restricted occupational advancement, inadequate medical care, etc.) to realize, over time, chronic levels of stress. Thus, they are also vulnerable to subsequent cardiac and other physiological arousals, which, in time, have the real potential of contributing to sustained elevations in arterial BP.

Any societal system with built-in pervasive inequalities has some very serious implications for the "least" of its citizens. It is argued that the societal system of inequality that currently exists in America routinely and systematically precludes sufficiently large numbers of African American adolescents from learning and developing various requisite skills to promote greater "inoculation." They are thereby rendered prone, in their already age-related vulnerable period, to perceiving many customary day-to-day life experiences as stressful. It is also reasoned that these stressful experiences, with their accompanying cardiac and other physiological reactivity, become chronic, thus subjecting African American adolescents as a specific age-race subgroup to elevated BP and possible irreversible organ damage.

We do not intend to imply that all African American youth will experience a disproportionate incidence of stress and, later, elevated BP. As with hypertension, this is certainly not the case. The mere presence of predisposing sociocultural factors is a necessary but not a sufficient condition to account for permanent elevations in BP. Given that sociopsychological stress involves a subjective process, African American adolescents have to experience discrepancies or stress that derive from the fact that the demands of their life situation outdistance their existing resource capabilities (later to be referred to as the Filter Resource Capability System [FRCS]). Notwithstanding this reasoning, however, the "affective" relative unanimity of African American life-style experiences, especially in the lower-socioeconomic class, must be considered (see earlier discussion of stress, race, and socioeconomic class). It is this unanimity in life-style experiences that seems to contribute substantially to a collective or group manifestation of stress and, subsequently, to elevated arterial BP.

In the wider African American society in general and the more restricted young and impressionable African American population in particular, there is no shortage of evidence, be it real or inferred, that, as a target group, African Americans experience greater degrees of stressful life experiences than do their white counterparts. For example, African Americans face greater demands;[41] are exposed to more insidious status, class, and race-related sources of stress;[42] have earlier experiences of stressful life events; and are more frequently exposed than whites to undesirable and uncontrollable events in their lives.[43] Consistent with the underlying premise of this article, it was reported that racial discrimination has long been postulated to be a stress-creating factor for African Americans in the United States, and it plays a role in the pathogenesis of essential hypertension.[44]

These and other findings have led to the position that, when compared to whites, African Americans (that is, adolescents) have a higher vulnerability to perceived and experienced stress. This higher vulnerability to experienced stress translates, in turn, to a relatively high conditioned physiological (cardiac and BP) reactivity and psychological vigilance, which, in turn, leads to a physiological manifestation as elevated BP. Utilizing a three-stage process of *onset*, *reaction*, and *effect*, the sociopsychophysiological model that follows attempts to show, from a conceptual basis, (1) how it is possible for African American adolescents to perceive events and conditions in their sociocultural environment as stressful (onset), (2) the mechanisms involved in their bodies' physiological responses to such stimulation (reaction), and (3) the possible manifestation of elevated arterial BP or hypertension (effect).

A Conceptual Model of Stress: The Case for Hypertension

It is important to have a conceptual understanding, especially in the case of hypertension, of where all the previously alluded to factors fit in the wider context of the overall stress process. What follows, therefore, is a brief overview of a sociopsycho physiological conceptual model of the stress process. After a brief description of the model, the likely stress-hypertension relationship is discussed as a possible eventuality. (More specific information concerning the stress model can be seen in other publications by Livingston.[45]

Figure 1 illustrates the stress process primarily from an interactionist perspective. That is, African American adolescents' cognitive sense of imbalance or discrepancy occurs when perceived demands placed on them exceed their perceived response capabilities or resources.[46] As can be seen from the model in Figure 1, African American adolescents' cognitive appraisal of their life situation (that is, potential stressors) can be viewed as an important factor in the genesis of subsequent physiological and other reactions.

Other important factors become evident on examining the model.

First, stress is a process that is multilevel, interactive, and dynamic, with input and output variables that may range in organizational hierarchy from the molecular to the behavioral-social. The bidirectional arrows reflect the reciprocal nature of the elements of the model. With respect to its interactive mode — that is, with the possible exclusion of such physiological stressors as internal trauma and environmental stimulants (for example, toxic pollutants) — sociopsychological stress results from the continuous interplay between the adolescent (that is, the individual system) and his or her environmental context (that is, social-environment system).

Second, the model includes the very important variable of time: a short duration of time, such as possibly in the case of acute or episodic stress, or a long duration of time, such as in the case of chronic, unmitigated stress.

Finally, the entire stress process involves three basic sequential and closely interrelated steps: *onset* (or initiation), *reaction* (or bodily response), and *effect* (or behavioral, physiological and psychological outcomes). Because the stress process involves, especially during the onset stage, a good deal of sociopsychological interaction and, during the reaction and effect stages, a great deal of physiological activity, it has been labeled the sociopsychophysiological model of stress.

The Stress Process—Onset. Stress onset refers to the initiation of the complex series of events and processes that must be activated before and during the experience of stress by the individual (for example, the adolescent). Stress is basically a physiological response. In its physiological state, therefore, stress is not synonymous with worry, anxiety, depression, or frustration, all of which are likely precursors or triggers of the stress response. All these and other similar precursors are labeled collectively as *stressors*. A stressor, therefore, is the cause and stress is the physiological response or outcome. Four major factors determine African American adolescents' response to a stressor or the manifestation of the stress state:

1. The nature of the stressor
2. The number of the stressors to be coped with simultaneously

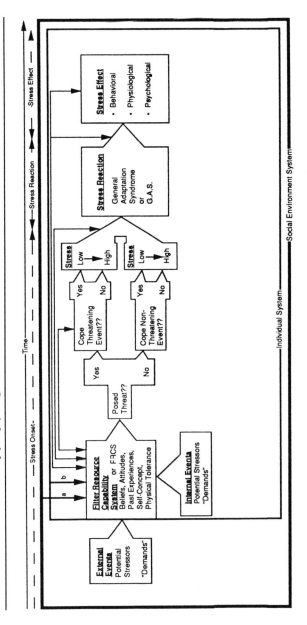

FIGURE 1

A Sociopsychophysiological Model of the Stress Process: Onset Reaction and Effect*

Notes:

a - External environment contributing to the functioning of the FRCS.

b - Internal environment contributing to the functioning of the FRCS.

↔ Bidirectional arrows reflect the reciprocal nature of designated elements in the model.

* Model taken from Livingston, I.L.: Co-Factors, Host Susceptibility and AIDS: An Argument For Stress, Journal of the National Medical Association Vol. 80(1): 49–59, 1988.

4. The duration of the episode
5. Past experiences with comparable stressors

Notwithstanding the various ways in which stressors can be categorized, they can be placed in three broad, but interrelated, categories of endogenous or exogenous events that have the potential to alter organizational structure. These categories include physical factors (for example, internal trauma, external pollutants of urban congestion); rapid-onset, fast-occurring, or sudden factors (for example, witnessing a violent robbery); and sociopsychological factors resulting from the interaction between the individual and his or her sociocultural environment (for example, life change events). Based on the working definition of stress stated previously, this sociopsychological categorization is the one most germane to the model presented in Figure 1. Also, sociopsychological stressors are the most frequent kinds of experiences African American adolescents are likely to have as they act and react to their daily encounters.

As can be seen from Figure 1, adolescents' Filter Resource Capability System (FRCS) (that is, their mind-body enduring capacity) is of particular importance to the interpretation of "threat," successful coping, and further activation of the stress process (that is, reaction and effect stages). In short, the FRCS is the designated *mediator* component of the model and, therefore, it filters and modifies all input and output outcomes.

These factors within the FRCS are known as "enabling" or "mediating" factors and they take on a variety of characteristics. In the case of African American adolescents, for example, these factors may be *physical* (for example, physical tolerance), *psychological* (for example, high self-esteem, ego strength, hardiness, resilience, feelings of being in relative control of life situations), *sociopsychological* (for example, adequate coping skills, having supportive "others" in time of need), and *behavioral* (for example, positive preventive health practices). Given the socialization experiences of low-income, urban African American adolescents, who are more at risk to experience stress in part because they have not learned how to "inoculate" themselves against certain endemic life stressors (for example, unemployment, lack of status advancement, and crime-infested neighborhoods), it is very likely that their FRCSs will be insufficiently reinforced with the above-mentioned positive attributes (See a and b in Figure 1).

Since there is an inverse relationship between socioeconomic class and stress,[47] and between socioeconomic class and hypertension among African American adolescents,[48] it is underscored that African Americans constitute a target group at risk to experience chronic stress. African American adolescents who are relatively poor, unemployed, underemployed, and lacking in certain basic familial, educational, and occupational attainments are the ones who are more at risk to perceive their life circumstances as stressful. These structural as well as learned inhibiting FRCS dispositions are referred to collectively as "dispositional barriers" to change.[49]

As previously mentioned, for stressors to give rise eventually to stress, the perceived demands of the stressors have to exceed the perceived resource capabilities of adolescents (or their FRCSs); the latter have a direct influence on their coping strategies. (See the bidirectional arrows in Figure 1.) The filtering or mediating role of the FRCS is crucial to the subsequent quality and quantity of stress the prehypertensive or posthypertensive African American adolescent experiences.

Given the positive mediating role of selected sociopsychological factors—for example, personal dispositions such as a high locus of control (that is, feelings of being in control of one's life)[50] and having needed social support[51]—any future interventionist efforts should address ways of increasing the presence of these and other mediating factors, especially in the at-risk African American population. The end result of such efforts would be to increase the resiliency of the FRCS for African American adolescents, thereby decreasing their perception of stress and the likelihood of future, related physiological reactions and effects (for example, hypertension).

The Stress Process—Reaction. As is the case with stress onset, stress reaction can occur from the molecular, to the cognitive, to and including the socio-interactive levels. After the onset of stress, a host of bodily reactions or changes are likely to ensue. However, in the case of the stress-hypertension relation, the functioning of the endocrine hormonal system has been found to be a definite part of the body's stress response.[52] Given the vast literature that exists in this area, only a selected overview is presented.

The body's physiological arousal to acute and sustained levels of stress has been relatively well documented, especially through corresponding changes in blood chemistry. Although secretion of corticosteroids by the adrenal cortex and catecholamines by the adrenal medulla have been related to a variety of psychosocial stimuli associated with stress,[53] the involvement of the hypothalamic-pituitary-adrenal cortex axis in the activation and production of corticosteroids is very important. Chronic or repeated hypothalamic stimulation (that is, excitation leading to the elicitation of the "fight-or-flight" response) may lead to (1) a "fixation" of the hemodynamic pattern of selective visceral vasoconstriction and muscle vasodilation, and (2) the possibility of sustained elevations in arterial BP.[54]

A related physiological response associated with corticosteroid hormonal secretion is the presence of a sequential syndrome—the *General Adaptation Syndrome (GAS).*[55] (See Figure 1.) Essentially, the GAS is characterized by three stages or phases.

1. *Alarm reaction*, the first stage, occurs as a result of the African American adolescent's contact with a stressor. It is characterized by rapid physiological and chemical changes, nervous system activation, and hormonal changes.
2. *Resistance*, the second stage, occurs as a consequence of the continued presence of the stressor and attempts by the body to resist the demands of the stressor(s).
3. *Exhaustion*, the final stage, occurs after a relatively prolonged effort by the body to resist the stressor(s). It is the presence of this final stage of the GAS that implies host (that is, the young African American) vulnerability for illness and/or disease.[56]

The Stress Process—Effect. If African American adolescents' FRCSs are not sufficiently strong to reduce or abate the stress that is experienced, the last stage of the stress
process is activated—effect. Hypothalamic mediation of the cardiovascular response to
chronic mentally stressful environmental stimuli (that is, when environmental conditions are conducive to repeated or chronic arousal of the hypothalamic area) is said to
play a significant role in the gradual development of essential hypertension.[57] If this
process is not arrested, for example, through intervention strategies, which should most
definitely include increasing the resiliency of, in this case, African American adolescents' FRCSs, more continuing, chronic levels of stress will be experienced, with
accompanying cardiac reactivity and resulting elevated arterial BP or hypertension.

SUGGESTIONS FOR FUTURE ACTIVITIES

The disproportionately higher incidence of morbidity and mortality associated with
hypertension for African Americans versus white Americans must be addressed more
vigorously than has heretofore been done. As pointed out, the place to start is very early
in the life cycle, where convincing evidence suggests that racial differences begin to
emerge with regard to the direct and indirect experiences of stressful life events,
especially for African American youth.

Policy-Oriented Issues

From a structural point of view, major policy efforts by federal, state and local
governments have to be directed to continue readdressing and finding equitable solutions to the ills of the currently race-class-driven American system. In the current
system, African American youth, as a result of their race and socioeconomic class, are
more frequently exposed to conditions that are potential stressors (for example, poverty
substandard living conditions, inferior education, low and nonexistent occupational
advancement, and the relative absence of quality medical care). The problem begins so
early in the life cycle that it has been reported that various stresses in African Americans begin their insidious influence even in utero, with mothers who are faced with the
vicissitudes of poverty (for example, poor or inadequate nutrition and inadequate
prenatal care).[58]

In terms of more specific policy-oriented directions, the following are suggested:

1. There should be *increased funding* for targeted federal agencies—for example,
   the National Heart, Lung, and Blood Institute (NHLBI)—which are responsible for basic and applied research dealing with cardiovascular and hypertensive disease.
2. With increased funding to federal agencies, such as the NHLBI, *Requests for
   Proposals* (RFPs) should be sent out requesting original research involving the
   etiology of hypertension in the African American population. The research
   agenda should be specific and should include innovative and eclectic empirical

efforts addressing the etiology and distribution of HBP *within* as well as *between* the races. The RFP should emphasize that studies be longitudinal by design, involve tracking, focus on pathogenesis, and, besides stress, other parameters should include, but not be limited to, the following risk factors for hypertension: the role of dietary salt, endocrine factors, renal factors, neural factors, the role of obesity, hemodynamic factors, and epidemiological characteristics.

3. There should be a *renewed emphasis on public education and control of HBP*, starting with the federal government, akin to the National High Blood Pressure Education Program (NHBPEP), which was initiated in 1972. Also, given the duration of time since the NHBPEP was initiated, an evaluation of the program can be made by focusing on a national probability sample, which should most definitely include young African Americans.

4. *National Black Health Providers Task Force* on High Blood Pressure Education Control should be reconstituted to ascertain needed changes that have emerged since the last final report of the Task Force Committee in 1980.

CONCLUDING REMARKS

As we approach the 21st century, the sickness and human devastation associated with cardiovascular disease in general, and hypertension in particular, for African Americans is clearly unacceptable. Given the results of tracking, it behooves all concerned personnel in government, education, and the private sector to play a more concerted role in spearheading preventive efforts against hypertension, particularly during the early periods of the life cycle of African Americans. Given the multidimensional nature of essential hypertension, it is equally appropriate that such preventive efforts be eclectic in nature and culminate in interventionist strategies, such as health education in order to improve control of the disease.

Further, social, behavioral, and medical scientists need to become more aware of the salient contribution *stress* has to the etiology as well as the possible aggravation of elevated arterial BP in the young African American population. Since changes in the structural configurations of an unequal race-class American society may be long in coming, it is more pragmatic to focus a great deal of energy and expertise on increasing the "functional" strength of young African Americans' Filter Resource Capability Systems (FRCSs).

Although the task of increasing the strength of young African Americans' FRCSs is difficult, the demands are by no means insurmountable. By utilizing, for example, high technology audio-video equipment and various media channels popular in the African American community, efforts can be made to literally resocialize or reeducate African American youngsters so that they possess certain selected and desirable psychological qualities (for example, high self-concept, self-worth, feelings of being in control of their lives, and overall resiliency to meet life's challenges and problems). A strenuous effort should also be directed to increasing young African Americans' FRCSs by emphasizing the need to have associations with certain positive sociopsychobehavioral factors. One such factor is the stress-mediating source of "social support," which can be achieved by way of genuine involvement with the family, organizations, and the African American community.

The sociopsychophysiological model of the stress process that has been presented provides a workable framework through which all of the aforementioned (and other) preventive activities can be instituted. The success of these and other efforts should translate, over time, into *lower* degrees of perceived stress, heightened physiological (for example, cardiac) reactivity, and, subsequently, elevated arterial BP for young African Americans.

NOTES

1. I. L. Livingston, "Stress and Essential Hypertension," *Urban Health* 11 (1982): 41–44.
2. D. P. Rice and J. C. Kleinman, "National Health Data for Policy Planning," *Health Education* 1 (1980): 129–41.
3. J. Stamler, R. Stamler, and W. F. Riedlinger, "Hypertension Screening of One Million Americans: Community Evaluation Clinic Program, 1973 through 1975," *Journal of the American Medical Association* 235 (1976): 2,299.
4. H. Weiner, *Essentials of Hypertension: Psychology of Human Disease* (New York: Elsevier, 1979).
5. W. B. Kannel, D. McGee, and T. Gordon, "A General Cardiovascular Risk Profile: The Framingham Study," *American Journal of Epidemiology* 38 (1976): 46–51.
6. A. M. Ostfeld, "A Review of Stroke Epidemiology," *American Journal of Epidemiology* 2 (1980): 136–52.
7. Hypertension Detection and Follow-Up Program Cooperative Group, "Sex and Race Difference in and Organ Damage among 10,940 Hypertensives," *American Journal of Cardiology* 41 (1978): 402.
8. A. W. Voors, L. S. Webber, and G. S. Berenson, "Time Course Studies of Blood Pressure in Children—Bogalusa Heart Study," *American Journal of Epidemiology* 109 (1979): 320.
9. B. Woynarowska, et al., "Blood Changes during Adolescence and Subsequent Adult Blood Pressure Level," *Hypertension* 7 (1985): 695–701.
10. Voors, Webber, and Berenson, "Time Course Studies of Blood Pressure in Children."
11. M. M. Kilcoyne, R. W. Richter and P. A. Alsup, "Adolescent Hypertension: Detection and Prevalence," *Circulation* 50 (1974): 758–64.
12. S. K. Dube, S. Kapoor, and H. Ratner, "Blood Pressure Studies in Black Children," *American Journal of Diseases of Children* 129 (1975): 1,177–80.
13. Voors, Webber, and Berenson, "Time Course Studies of Blood Pressure in Children."
14. Kilcoyne, Richter, and Alsup, "Adolescent Hypertension."
15. Voors, Webber, and Berenson, "Time Course Studies of Blood Pressure in Children."
16. T. J. Coates, "Elevated Blood Pressure and Blood Pressure Reactivity in Children and Adolescents," in *Pediatric and Adolescent Behavioral Medicine: Issues in Treatment*, ed. P. J. McGrath and P. Firestone (New York: Springer, 1983).
17. H. G. Langford, R. L. Watson, and B. H. Douglas, "Factors Affecting Blood Pressure in Population Groups," *Transactions of the Association of American Physicians* 81 (1968): 136–46.
18. Voors, Webber, and Berenson, "Time Course Studies of Blood Pressure in Children."
19. J. M. Kotchen, T. A. Kotchen, and N. C. Schwertman, "Blood Pressure Distributions of Urban Adolescents," *American Journal of Epidemiology* 99 (1974): 315–24.
20. Stamler, Stamler, and Riedlinger, "Hypertension Screening of One Million Americans."
21. A. W. Voors, et al., "Studies of Blood Pressures in Children, Ages 5–14 Years, in a Total Biracial Community: The Bogalusa Heart Study," *Circulation* 54 (1976): 319–27.
22. M. Rowland and J. Roberts, "Blood Pressure Levels and Hypertension in Persons Aged 6–74 Years: United States, 1976–1980," (NCHS) *Advancedata* 84 (1982): 1–12.
23. M. D. Burns et al., "Blood Pressure Studies in Black and White Inner-City and Suburban Adolescents," *Preventive Medicine* 9 (1980): 41–50.
24. B. Falkner et al., "Cardiovascular Characteristics in Adolescents Who Develop Essential Hypertension," *Hypertension* 3 (1981): 521–27.
25. Coates, "Elevated Blood pressure."
26. B. S. Alpert, N. L. Flood, and W. B. Strong, "Responses to Ergometer Exercise in a Healthy Biracial Population of Children," *Journal of Pediatrics* 101 (1982): 538–45.
27. J. K. Murphy et al., "Race and Cardiovascular Reactivity: A Neglected Relationship," *Hypertension* 8 (11) (1986): 1,075–83.

28. Livingston, "Stress and Essential Hypertension"; and I. L. Livingston, "The Importance of Socio-Psychological Stress in the Interpretation of the Race-Hypertension Association," *Humanity and Society* 9 (1985): 168–81.

29. M. R. Vander et al., "A Study of Hypertension in Twins," *American Heart Journal* 79 (1970): 454.

30. M. T. Newman, "Nutritional Adaptation in Man," in *Physiological Anthropology*, ed. A. Damon (London: Oxford University Press, 1975).

31. L. K. Dahl, "Effect of Chronic Salt Ingestion," in *The Epidemiology of Essential Hypertension*, ed. J. Stamler, R. Stamler, and T. Pullman (New York: Stratton, 1967).

32. J. Stamler et al., *The Problem and Challenge: The Hypertension Handbook* (Pennsylvania: Merck, Sharp and Dome, 1974).

33. S. L.Cohen, "Central Nervous System Functioning in Altered Sensory Environments," in *Psychological Stress*, ed. M. H. Appley and R. Trumbull (New York: Appleton, 1967), 27–118, 78.

34. R. L. Kahn and R. P. Quinn, "Role Stress: A Framework for Analysis," in *Mental Health and Work Organizations*, ed. A. McLean (Chicago: Rand McNally, 1970), 50–115.

35. R. J. Burke and T. Weir, "Coping with Stress of Managerial Occupations," in *Current Concerns in Occupational Stress*, ed. C. L. Cooper and R. Payne (New York: Wiley and Sons, 1980), 299–335.

36. Livingston, "Stress and Essential Hypertension"; I. L. Livingston, "Co-Factors, Host Susceptibility, and AIDS: An Argument for Stress," *Journal of the National Medical Association* 80 (1988): 49–59.

37. R. S. Lazarus, "A Strategy for Research on Psychological and Social Factors in Hypertension," *Journal of Human Stress* 4 (1978): 35–40.

38. L. H. Page and W. M. Mawger, "An Overview of Current Concepts Regarding the Pathogenesis and Pathophysiology of Hypertension," in *Arterial Hypertension Pathogenesis Diagnosis and Therapy*, ed. J. Rosenthal (New York: Springer-Verlag, 1982), 2–61.

39. Livingston, "Stress and Essential Hypertension."

40. J. Eyer, "Hypertension as a Disease of Modern Society," *International Journal of Health Services* 5 (1975): 539–58.

41. H. F. Meyers, J. J. Lindenthal, and M. P. Pepper, "Social Class, Life Events, and Psychiatric Symptoms: A Longitudinal Study," in *Stressful Life Events: Their Nature and Effect*, ed. B. P. Dohrenwend and B. S. Dohrenwend (New York: John Wiley and Sons, 1974), 191–206.

42. B. S. Dohrenwend and B. P. Dohrenwend, "Class and Race as Status-Related Sources of Stress," in *Social Stress*, ed. S. Levine and N. A. Scotch (Chicago: Aldine, 1970), 111–40.

43. D. P. Muller, D. W. Edwards and R. M. Yarvis, "Stressful Life Events and Psychiatric Symptomatology: Change Versus Undesirability?" *Journal of Health and Social Behavior* 18 (1977): 307–17.

44. H. A. Tyroler and S. A. James, "Blood Pressure and Skin Color," *American Journal of Public Health* 68 (1978): 1,170

45. I. L. Livingston, "Stress and Health Dysfunctions: The Importance of Health Education," *Stress Medicine* 4 (1988): 155–61; Livingston, "Co-Factors, Host Susceptibility, and AIDS."

46. Livingston, "Stress and Essential Hypertension"; R. S. Lazarus, J. B. Cohen, and S. Folkman, "Psychological Stress and Adaptation: Some Unresolved Issues," in *Selye's Guide to Stress Research*, vol. 1, ed. H. Selye (New York: Van Nostrand Reinhold, 1980), 90–117.

47. Stamler, et al., *The Problem and Challenge*.

48. Kotchen, Kotchen, and Schwertman, "Blood Pressure Distributions of Urban Adolescents."

49. Livingston, "Co-Factors, Host Susceptibility, and AIDS."

50. H. F. Naditch, "Locus of Control, Relative Discontent, and Hypertension," *Social Psychology* 8 (1974): 111–17.

51. S. Cobb, "Social Support as a Moderator of Life Stress," *Psychosomatic Medicine* 38 (1976): 300–14.

52. J. W. Mason, "A Historical View of the Stress Field," *Journal of Human Stress* 1 (1975): 22–36.

53. A. Baum and N. E. Grunberg, "The Use of Psychological and Neuroendocrinological Measurements in the Study of Stress," *Health Psychology* 1 (1982): 217–36.

54. H. Benson, J. B. Kotch and A. B. Crassweller, "Stress and Hypertension," in *Hypertension: Mechanisms, Diagnosis and Treatment*, ed. O. Gaddo and A. N. Best (Philadelphia: F. A. Davis, 1978).

55. H. Selye, "The General Adaptation Syndrome and the Diseases of Adaptation," *Journal of Clinical Endocrinology* 6 (1946): 117–230.

56. M. Shaffer, *Life after Stress* (New York: Plenum Press, 1982).

57. V. C. Abrahams, S. M. Hilton, and A. W. Zbrozna, "The Role of Active Muscle Vasodilatation in the Altering Stage of Defense Reaction," *Journal of Physiology* 171 (1964): 189; J. P. Henry and J. C. Cassel, "Psychosocial Factors in Essential Hypertension: Recent Epidemiologic and Experimental Evidence," *American Journal of Epidemiology* 90 (1979): 171.

58. Livingston, "Co-Factors, Host Susceptibility, and AIDS."

8

Substance Abuse among America's Urban Youth

Omowale Amuleru-Marshall

The substance abuse problem is prevalent among urban youth from ethnic groups that fall outside the ethnocultural mainstream of American society. Urban youth are confronted by life options of idleness, gang membership, crime, violence, pregnancy, drug use, and drug distribution. This is due, in no small part, to the fact that unemployment among them is high, and they constitute a large proportion of America's poor. Current programs for prevention and treatment of substance abuse treat urban youth as a homogeneous group and undermine the complexity of the urban drug abuse problem. To effectively address the substance abuse problem, the integrity of each ethnic group must be respected. There can be no individual self-esteem in the absence of group self-esteem. Personal counseling must, therefore, reinterpret the values, behavior, and experiences of individuals within the context of their groups' collective experiences.

The challenge of discussing substance abuse problems among urban adolescents is complicated by certain societal conditions that make it impossible to view this group as a monolith. The realities of race and class in the United States have configured the contemporary American city in ways that almost force an interchangeability between the terms ''urban adolescents'' and ''national minority youth.'' The majority of the estimated population of 30 million African Americans, 12 percent of the 1988 U.S. population estimate of 246 million, live in urban areas. With ''white flight'' to the suburbs, an increasing number of large cities have gained a majority African American population.[1] When the exploding Hispanic American and Asian American segments are added, the majority of urban youth are found to be increasingly from ethnic groups that fall outside the economic, political, social, and ethnocultural mainstream of this society.[2]

As a consequence, the majority of these young people and the communities in which they live are beset by a variety of socioeconomic deficits.[3] They constitute a disproportionately large number of America's young poor. More than 80 percent of African American youth live in families that exist on the very precipice of desperation, below the federal poverty level.[4] Their educational and employment records are profiles of failure and underdevelopment. The school dropout rate among urban, African American and Hispanic youth is estimated to be 50 percent. Unemployment among African American adolescents hovers around 40 percent. Many of these young people find themselves confronted by life options of idleness, gang membership, crime, violence, pregnancy, drug use, and drug distribution, all of which are, ironically, more feasible in this culture of disempowerment than are the options of education and gainful employment.[5]

These young people live their lives in the midst of a profound psychocultural and spiritual crisis, with features and dimensions that have only recently begun to be discussed. Yet, it is perhaps this phenomenon, more than any other, that predisposes these adolescents to excessive rates of self-destructive behaviors, such as substance abuse.[6] Despite the possibility of a causal relationship between this crisis and substance abuse, there is very little acknowledgment or elaboration of this etiological complex in "establishment" literature and practice. The use of a category such as "urban youth" to label a composite that is actually a heterogeneous mix of political histories, psychocultural dynamics, and socioeconomic realities undermines the complexity of the urban drug abuse problem. Effective interventions with this composite require that the integrity of each group be respected.[7]

The need for culturally specific approaches to effective intervention has been acknowledged for some time, but the issue has not been given the consistent, serious scholarship it deserves. In many cases, little more than lip service has been given to the search for effective models of prevention and treatment of substance abuse disorders among culturally different people. The cyclical process of supporting "innovative" intervention models for high-risk youth only if the models emanate from establishment literature practically ensures that the psychocultural dynamics of the target group will not be addressed in program development, implementation, or evaluation. The Eurocentric monocultural assumption, which still characterizes much of establishment behavioral sciences and human service practice, must give way to new perspectives.[8] While most of the issues presented in this article are probably more aptly suited to urban, African American adolescents, extrapolations to Hispanic American youth are possible, although they should be ventured with the greatest caution and sensitivity.

HIGH-RISK YOUTH AND COMMUNITIES

The recent entry of the term "high-risk youth" in the jargon of substance abuse professionals was spearheaded by the Alcohol, Drug Abuse, and Mental Health Administration's Office for Substance Abuse Prevention. Although this is problematic language for a number of reasons, including those discussed above, the use of this term does represent an endorsement at the federal level that certain segments in this society do experience differential vulnerability to substance abuse problems. Moreover, although it is not explicitly stated, national minority youth are overrepresented in the so-called high-risk category. While there is very little reliable information on the exact extent of drug use among urban youth, anyone who lives or works in these communities can attest to the presence and magnitude of the problem.

In the minds of many, the drug use/distribution problem is the most significant one confronting urban communities.[9] The dramatic escalation of this problem and the proliferation of associated problems have received a great deal of attention recently in the popular press.[10] The value of these articles is found in their effort to grapple with the ecological and phenomenological context in which drug involvement emerges. The following excerpt illustrates this effort.

> Like most young American people, they are material girls and boys. They crave the glamorous clothes, cars and jewelry they see advertised on TV, the beautiful things that only big money can buy. But many have grown up in fatherless homes, watching their mothers labor at low-paying jobs or struggle to stretch a welfare check. With the unemployment rate for black teenagers at 37%, little work is available to unskilled poorly educated youths. The handful of jobs that are open — flipping burgers, packing groceries — pay only minimum wages or "chump change," in the street vernacular. So these youngsters can turn to the most lucrative option they can find. In rapidly growing numbers, they are becoming the new criminal recruits of the inner city, the children who deal crack.[11]

In order to address the urban substance abuse problem among youth, communities must first decide precisely what it is that they wish to prevent. Is it drug use (experimental or recreational)? Is it drug abuse (problematic or addictive)? Is it the negative consequences of drug involvement for individuals, families, and whole communities? The fact is that many urban adolescents, caught up in the drug culture, are enticed by the big money associated with the trade, but not by the drugs. Reportedly, in a hot market like New York City, an aggressive teenage dealer can make as much as $3,000 a day. Even the entry-level 9- and 10-year-old lookouts make $100 a day.[12]

There are major consequences, however. Over the past five years, juvenile drug arrests more than tripled in many of the nation's largest cities. Even more alarming is the escalation of violent and homicidal episodes, which are clearly driven by the proliferation of drug abuse in inner-city neighborhoods. Uzi submachine guns, Magnums, and MAC 10s, easily acquired with the huge profits derived from drug sales, have recently become visibly associated with a frightening increase in juvenile murders. As competing gangs engage in open combat over drug-sales territory, many innocent bystanders swell the homicide statistics.[13]

These patterns of increase in adolescent drug arrests and violence indirectly indicate that the number of urban young people who are being inducted into drug use must also be increasing. Many of the adolescent crack dealers' clients are themselves children. With a vial of crack being available in many places for three to five dollars, there is easy access to an instantaneous high and almost certain addiction.

The patterns of crack distribution and use that characterize the nation's central cities are only the highly reported, dramatic tip of the iceberg. The abuse of other substances, particularly heroin, marijuana, PCP, nicotine, and alcohol, should be equally alarming. The concern about nicotine and alcohol should not be limited to the "gateway hypothesis," which argues that the danger in these drugs lies in the fact that they lead the user to more serious drug use. While there is much support for this hypothesis, nicotine and alcohol are dangerous drugs in their own right.[14]

The addictive potential and health consequences, including high mortality rates, of nicotine and alcohol qualify these substances as two of the most dangerous. Though their effects are often believed to be protracted, alcohol reaps an immediate toll among the nation's youth. In 1983, the age range from 16 to 24, which represented merely 20 percent of the U.S. population, constituted 34 percent of the drivers killed in alcohol-related accidents.[15] Homicide is the number one cause of death among young African American men, ages 15 to 24, and alcohol and other drugs have been demonstrated to be implicated in more than 50 percent of homicide incidents. While the national incidence of cigarette smoking has decreased in recent years, the rate among youth has not declined.[16] In fact, in a recent report on drug use among youth, cigarette smoking is described as the "substance-using behavior" that will take the lives of more of these youth than all the others combined.[17]

ETHNOCULTURAL INTERVENTION STRATEGIES

In practical terms, intervention strategies must be informed by the sociocultural and historical backgrounds of the particular group involved.[18] Addressing such areas as housing, vocational training, remedial education, job development, cultural integrity, peership engineering, and group self-esteem may be more valuable than personal counseling.[19]

This requires a reinterpretation of the values, behavior, and experiences of individuals within the context of their groups' collective experiences. The genius and resilience of the group must be highlighted even as "his-story" is corrected to situate Africa in its true place in history. Africa is the original site of human life and the progenitor of Western civilization. This historical correction is crucial to self-esteem-building among people of African descent. For example, with African American youth, this reinterpretation should be anchored in an intensive analysis of the experience of African people before, during, and after chattel slavery. There can be no individual self-esteem in the absence of group self-esteem. The Africentric view of this matter is: I am because we are and because we are, therefore, I am.[20]

This sense of collective responsibility, or "communitarianism," must be fostered even through those interventions that are specifically targeted to substance abuse themes. For example, presentations of substance abuse epidemiology, highlighting the excessive prevalence of these problems among African Americans, should be subsumed within a discussion of the larger picture of African American avoidable or excessive mortality. The historical emergence of alcohol and other drug abuse among African Americans should also be elucidated, underlining the master-slave relationship that has always characterized supply-demand transactions. More importantly, the complexity of the international narco-industry and the racial identity of its major players must be juxtaposed against the comparatively minor roles of African American petite-dealers.

High-risk considerations affecting the entire racial group must be explained as part of an analysis of macro- and micro-racism (including intrapersonal racism or self-hatred). Finally, a cost-benefit analysis of drug use should not be limited to the individual, his or her family, or even his or her community. It must ultimately be explored at the level of the race.

Clearly, the culturally tailored ingredients that were sketched above would be more effectively implemented in ethnoculturally exclusive groups, with "like-kind" professionals. In situations involving Hispanic American youth, the picture becomes even more complicated since Puerto Ricans are different from Chicanos, who in turn, are different from Cubans, for example. Not only should the content be tailored to reflect the particular historical and collective experiences of the specific group, but also the tasks of preparation and intervention require the participation of "like-kind" professionals.

Prevention and treatment activities that attempt to incorporate the themes and issues presented here will maximize their effectiveness if they are targeted at either youth who are not yet initiated into the use or distribution of drugs (especially crack-cocaine) or whose use has progressed to an advanced stage with major deleterious consequences. Treatment is potentially useful only when the drug-using career is interrupted and a window of opportunity is provided.

CONCLUSION

The harsh realities of life for many adolescents in America's cities unfortunately create conditions that predispose their involvement in many aspects of the lucrative drug trade. The prospect of interrupting, in a helpful way, the drug-distributing or drug-using careers of inner-city youth is remote, indeed. It is particularly unlikely if their involvement is weighted toward drug distribution. Refining our interventions so that they are culturally targeted will enhance their effectiveness with disenfranchised youth who are relegated to high-risk environments. However, in the absence of major social correctives, the special crisis that the escalating drug culture poses for a whole generation of young, national-minority people brings the question of decriminalization within the boundaries of legitimate and timely debate in our communities.

NOTES

1. F. D. Harper, *The Black Family and Substance Abuse* (Detroit: The Detroit Urban League, 1986).

2. Department of Health and Human Services, *Report of the Secretary's Task Force on Black and Minority Health*, vol. 7, *Chemical Dependency and Diabetes* (Washington, DC: Government Printing Office, 1986).

3. R. Dembo et al., "Environmental Setting and Early Drug Involvement among Inner-City Junior High School Youths," *The International Journal of the Addictions* 20 (8) (1985): 1,239–55.

4. Bruce R. Hare, "Black Youth at Risk," in *The State of Black America 1988*, ed. Janet Dewart (New York: National Urban League, Inc. 1988), 81–93.

5. A. Billingsley, "Black Families in a Changing Society," in *The State of Black America 1987*, ed. Janet Dewart (New York: National Urban League, Inc., 1987), 97–111.

6. H. A. Bulhan, *Franz Fanon and the Psychology of Oppression* (New York: Plenum Press, 1985).

7. National Institute on Drug Abuse, *A Guide to Multicultural Drug Abuse Prevention* (Rockville, MD: NIDA, 1981); H. Wash, *Cultural Specific Treatment: A Model for the Treatment of African-American Alcoholics* (Chicago: Jetpro Graphics, 1988).

8. M. A. Orlandi, "Community-Based Substance Abuse Prevention: A Multicultural Perspective," *Journal of School Health* 56 (9) (1986): 394–401.

9. L. P. Brown, "Crime in the Black Community," in *The State of Black America 1988*, ed. J. Dewart, 95–113.

10. "War: The Drug Crisis," *Ebony*, Aug. 1989; "Murder Zones," *U.S. News & World Report*, 10 Apr. 1989; "The Drug Warrior," *Newsweek*, 10 Apr. 1989.

11. J. V. Lamar, "Kids Who Sell Crack," *Time*, 9 May 1988, 20–33.

12. Ibid.

13. G. J. Church, "Thinking the Unthinkable," *Time*, 30 May 1988, 12–19.

14. E. Maddahian, M. D. Newcomb, and P. M. Bentler, "Single and Multiple Patterns of Adolescent Substance Use: Longitudinal Comparisons of Four Ethnic Groups," *Journal of Drug Education* 15 (4) (1985): 311–26.

15. National Institute on Alcohol Abuse and Alcoholism, *Communicating with Youth about Alcohol: Methods, Messages, and Materials* (Rockville, MD: NIAAA, 1986).

16. L. D. Johnston, "Summary of the 1987 Drug Study Results" (Media statement at the national news conference, Office of the Secretary of Health and Human Services, Washington, DC, 13 Jan. 1988.

17. Ibid.

18. D. S. Ford, "Factors Related to the Anticipated Use of Drugs by Urban Junior High School Students," *Journal of Drug Education* 13 (2) (1983): 187–97.

19. Dembo et al., "Environmental Setting and Early Drug Involvement."

20. J. S. Mbiti, *African Religions and Philosophy* (New York: Anchor Books, 1970).

9

The Coloring of IQ Testing: A New Name for an Old Phenomenon

Donna Y. Ford, J. John Harris III, and Duvon G. Winborne

The literature and research swells with evidence attesting to the fact that the dominant European American culture in this nation has a history of judging selected racial-minority groups to be innately or intellectually inferior to European Americans. For more than a century, the dominant culture has tried to prove, using everything from phrenology and craniology to current practices of IQ testing, that its members are intellectually superior to non-European Americans. This article addresses the impact of this ideology on African Americans and Asians. An extensive overview and analysis of scholarly treatises illustrate that IQ testing continues to be one mechanism for maintaining racial prejudice and inequality in the United States. The authors suggest that ''paradigmatic paralysis'' persists among some scholars regarding the intelligence of African American and Asian populations. It is hoped that readers will acquire insight and new paradigms of IQ testing to help eradicate myths about the inferiority of the intelligence of non-European Americans.

The dominant white culture in America has a history of judging readily identifiable minority groups, especially African Americans, to be innately and/or intellectually inferior to whites, and there is an abundance of research and scholarly literature attesting to this prejudice. A particularly blatant example is Terman's 1906 article, ''Genius and Stupidity.''[1] For more than a century, whites have professed and even believed they have ''proved'' by methods ranging from phrenology and craniology to IQ testing, that they are intellectually superior to African Americans.

The literature also reveals a strong prejudice against the Japanese. In California, for instance, there was frequent anti-Japanese legislation. In 1910, the Japanese were forbidden to use or own power engines, or to employ white females, and Japanese inheritance was illegal. The following quotation appeared in the *Sacramento Bee*, an influential central-California newspaper dated 1 May 1910:

> The Jap will always be an undesirable. They are lower in the scale of civilization than the whites and will never become our equal.[2]

In addition, the Japanese were forbidden the right to own land in California under the Alien Land Laws of 1913 and 1920. Similarly, the Immigration Act of 1924 restricted

Japanese immigration and citizenship privileges. According to Kitano, this was a major victory for racists, nativists, and exclusionists.[3] Kitano adds that attacks against the Japanese were not only based on race, but also on nationality, style of life, personal habits, economic competition, and any other grounds that appealed to the emotions as a way to reduce the "yellow peril" rising in the United States. In short, the *New York Times* concluded that the Immigration Act of 1924 was "nativist, racist, and mean."[4]

However, the prejudice toward the Japanese has a different color, a kind of selective racism in which differential explanations are adduced to devalue the persistently demonstrated intelligence of the Japanese. Three arguments have permeated the literature regarding the superior performance of whites over African Americans on intelligence tests: test bias, advantageous environments, and genetics. Many academicians propose that whites perform better than African Americans because the tests are biased in favor of whites, and because whites have more advantageous environments than African Americans, which contribute to higher IQ scores. Still, other academicians continue to propose the nativist (also called geneticist) argument that whites perform better because African Americans are inherently inferior intellectually.

On the other hand, when the Japanese perform better than whites on IQ tests, different explanations are advanced. Hare contends that whites begin to yell "cultural bias," to complain that the IQ tests are biased in favor of the Japanese, and that the Japanese culture produces a more supportive intellectual environment.[5] The genetic argument is not presented. This article will elaborate upon the already-transparent hypocrisy of these arguments.

What accounts for the different and even contradictory explanations advanced by white elites regarding the origin of intelligence of the Japanese, in light of the fact that the genetic theory of intelligence maintains a powerful place in American beliefs, policies, and practices?[6] It is postulated that IQ testing of African Americans in the United States is largely instrumental. The real focus of these tests is to nurture racism, prejudice, and, ultimately, white superiority and African American inferiority. In short, IQ testing represents one way in which white elites suppress African Americans and defend their "dominance" over them.[7] This practice is in accordance with the historical propensity of white elites to support that which affirms their superiority at the same time, negating—despite consistent evidence to the contrary—that which threatens and belies the notion of white superiority.

A HISTORICAL PERSPECTIVE OF THE INTELLIGENCE MOVEMENT

An old adage states: "We do not live in the past, but the past lives in us."[8] The implications of the intelligence movement in the United States extend beyond ethnicity, culture, and economic circumstances. It is a history marred by blatant attempts to stratify society by perpetuating the myth of white supremacy. Lawler states that racism is an institution of U.S. history that has been perpetuated for four centuries, justifying the institution and rendering people blind to its real nature.[9] Such is the case when people, oftentimes whites, argue that racism is nonexistent today. Needless to say, so long as they insist on calling themselves "white," racism will exist.[10]

According to the Harris poll, the data concedes that whites have obviously failed to understand the depth of both the urgency and despair that African Americans feel about their troubles. Thus, the attitude of some whites about the troubles of African Americans is one of vague concern, tempered with a great deal of indifference.[11]

In the 18th and 19th centuries, the subject of race, intelligence, and the superiority of whites occupied the center of much research and debate—not only in the United States, but also in Great Britain, Germany, and other countries. These centuries were characterized by debates between monogenists and polygenists, nativists and nurturists, and craniologists regarding the intelligence of whites versus the intelligence of African Americans and other racial minority people. According to Gossett, many an incipient racist (such as Cyril Burt, who was found to be a fraud) awaited breathlessly some scheme of classification that would withstand the testing of science and, thereby, offer unequivocal "proof" of the superiority of whites to all other races.[12]

In the 20th century, we went from measuring brain sizes to measuring performance on IQ and achievement tests. Gould states that what craniometry was to the 19th century, intelligence testing has been to the 20th.[13] Both craniometry and IQ testing have shared the goal of measuring intelligence and are the basis of legitimizing white superiority. To this end, IQ testing has become a new name for an old phenomenon— racism. To state the obvious, intelligence testing has been a prominent—and effective— means not only of perpetuating bias, as is widely recognized, but also of promoting prejudice. Such prejudice rears its ugly head in myriad ways today, particularly in the form of intelligence and achievement testing, which stratifies or categorizes people as privileged or deprived, as successes or failures, and as bluebirds or blackbirds.[14]

The proposition that IQ tests are biased in favor of whites but racist toward African Americans becomes more evident when one examines the original purpose of the IQ test developed by Binet. In 1905, Binet warned that his IQ test was, for the most part, a measure of school-related abilities and not to be used out of that context.[15] In 1911, Binet argued for a multiplicity of tests when assessing intelligence: "One test has no significance, we repeat with emphasis, but five or six tests do mean something."[16]

According to Berreman, social stratification is based on traditional definitions of innate social equivalence and difference linked to a concept of differential intrinsic worth (for example, racial superiority and inferiority), rationalized by a myth of the origin, effect, and legitimacy of the system.[17] Accordingly, academicians who support the white-superiority myth and who misuse and abuse intelligence and achievement tests—witness Jensen, Jencks, Terman, Shockley, Burt, and Goddard, for example— tend to be nativists or racists or both, who propose that intelligence is primarily or totally biologically determined. Despite popular opinion to the contrary, the belief in the inherent inferiority of African Americans, while archaic in some circles, is firmly held in others.[18] For example, as recently as 1985, Jensen supported the nativist argument—despite evidence to the contrary—that 50 to 70 percent of intelligence is inherited, and that variation in IQ scores is more biological than environmental, psychological, or behavioral.

Not all nativists or racists go as far as Jensen in attributing intelligence primarily to genetics. For example, Jencks states that 45 percent of intelligence is genetically determined.[19] Regardless of the percent cited, many (if not most) nativists (that is, individuals who ascribe intelligence primarily to inheritance) and educators are convinced that IQ testing should continue. Unfortunately, supporters of these perspectives continue to look upon African Americans as intellectually inferior. As recently as 1982, Bernstein argued that

> scientific evidence of racial inferiority simply allows some people to do with better conscience what they would have found a way to do anyway, . . . It would be good to report that all this belongs to some "medieval" past. But as we all know, the spirit of Yerkes and his ilk persists.[20]

Similarly, Howard and Hammond state that African American people continue to suffer racism, discrimination, and oppression, which are the root of many of today's social problems.[21] More specifically, these authors suggest that the high dropout rate and poorer performance of African American students on intelligence measures are two of the most pernicious effects of racism. In short, poor IQ test performances beget more poor performances.

In his Marxist critique of the IQ debate, Levidow argues that the reification or quantification of intelligence is a ploy of racists to scientifically institutionalize capitalist goals.[22] He states that IQ testing is one mechanism for controlling labor. Hence, through the reification of intelligence, capitalists create social classes that are easily channeled into specific jobs. Thereby, African Americans, who capitalists assert are of poor genetic makeup (that is, inferior) and of low socioeconomic status, will remain in servitude and low social standing. Needless to say, IQ testing perpetuates and even glorifies the white superiority myth, and serves as a protective mechanism from the threat of white elites losing their place as "number one." It also serves to confuse poor whites who are conned into identifying with the oppressed.[23]

The irony and hypocrisy of the biological determination theory of intelligence is that whites who support this theory have rarely applied the biological argument to the Japanese, whose performance on intelligence and achievement tests consistently exceeds the performance of whites. Rather, one sees selective racism in which white elites argue that the tests, which are normed on middle-class whites, are biased in favor of the Japanese because the tests measure those abilities valued by the Japanese (that is, analytical thinking, logical reasoning, and mathematics).

But is this not what is valued in most American schools? Hale-Benson,[24] Hilliard,[25] and others indicate that the analytic cognitive style is most valued in American schools. In addition, because the tests are normed on middle-class European Americans, the tests are indeed biased in favor of whites. Yet, advocates of the genetic theory of intelligence selectively apply the genetic theory of those groups whose performance tends to be inferior to white performance, but abandon the argument when a minority group surpasses white performance.

A recent review of the literature revealed that few authors argue that the Japanese are cognitively or intellectually superior to whites.[26] The remaining authors appear to rationalize that environmental factors such as the Japanese schools, the greater amount of homework, the parent-child relationship in Japan, the longer Japanese school year, and the curriculum are the primary factors that influence the superior performance of Japanese students. To quote Hilliard, not only is IQ testing on trial, but so is the very construct of racism and the belief in "race."[27]

THE ROLE OF PREJUDICE TOWARD AFRICAN AMERICANS IN THE UNITED STATES

Jackman defines prejudice as a set of negative generalized beliefs or stereotypes about a group, a feeling of dislike for that group, and a predisposition to behave in a negative way about a group, directly as well as vicariously.[28] IQ testing in the United States has traditionally been a means to justify an end.[29] Lynch also noted that the purpose of prejudice is to achieve status, prestige, and economic rewards and opportunities. Thus, both racial and religious prejudice are used as economic weapons and instruments of social control at the expense of the oppressed group.[30] Burkey concurs, stating that cultural, political, and economic dominance often go hand in hand,[31] and Johnson et al. called standardized tests "self-fulfilling prophecies."[32] Lawler suggested that IQ theory (and by logical extension, IQ testing) attempts to give plausibility to the nativist, *a priori* assumption that intelligence is an essentially biological capacity that is unequally distributed in the population, with the balance beam favorably tilted toward the white population.[33]

Although liberal opinion traditionally rejects the idea that genes determine test scores or that tests measure genetic potential, conservative opinion has frequently embraced the idea, at least when applied to someone else's children. Academicians vacillate from one side to the other, according to the political mood of the times,[34] and, clearly, the failure to create an educational renaissance is hastily explained through resurrected notions of African American inferiority. Hence, even today, if one asks whether African American children score lower on standardized tests because they are genetically inferior, or because their conditions of life have not prepared them for the kinds of knowledge tested by standardized instruments, whites have generally opted for the former explanation. In essence, remnants of the genetic argument continue to prevail.[35]

This hypothesis is also advanced by Lynch, who states that neo-Marxist interpretations of racial prejudice are developed as part of capitalism and nationalism and are associated with the need for a white-supremacist ideology. It may act as a fulcrum for accompanying group solidarity and a legitimator of racist actions.[36] Similarly, the Joint Center for Political Studies (JCPS) argues that student performance on standardized tests measure neither innate aptitudes nor an individual's creative ability, and that to interpret IQ scores and test results in this manner is a dangerous instrument of social oppression.[37]

THE ROLE OF PREJUDICE TOWARD THE JAPANESE

The importance of genetic differences between races is political rather than scientific. As of 1972, white people still ran the world. Those who have power always prefer to believe that they "deserve" it, rather than thinking they have won it by venality, cunning, or historical accidents. Some whites apparently feel that if the average white is slightly more adept at certain kinds of abstract reasoning than the average Black, this legitimizes the whole structure of white supremacy—not just in America but around the world. Conversely, many people seem to feel that if Blacks and whites are born with the same capacity for abstract reasoning, this proves that white supremacy is illegitimate.[38]

Jensen and Inouye published data from their study in which Asian American children (those of Japanese and Chinese ancestry), white children, and African American children were administered a battery of tests to measure IQ, school achievement, and short- and long-term memory.[39] The three groups were compared on factors identified as Level I (memory) and level II (general intelligence). Consistent with findings from many other studies, the results indicated that whites and African Americans differed "significantly" on both Level I and Level II, with whites scoring higher on both levels. Also consistent with literature, whites and Asian Americans differed significantly on Level I with whites scoring higher. However, Jensen and Inouye found that Asian Americans scored as high or higher than whites on Level II (general intelligence).

The researchers attributed the superior performance of whites on Level I (memory) to either the different cognitive abilities in the evolutionary history of the groups, or to cultural origins such as child rearing, values, and motivaton. One might expect a similar explanation for the superior performance of Asian Americans on Level II, but such an explanation was not forthcoming.

> The differential pattern of abilities of Asians and whites, however, might account, at least in part, for the commonly observed differences in the scholastic subject matter preference of Asians as compared to white subjects. . . . a relatively larger portion of Asians who go to college seem to prefer subjects with a high level of reasoning component, such as mathematics, engineering, and the exact sciences.[40]

Clearly, when the scores of whites are inferior, the rationale for the differences changes dramatically. The "logical" conclusion that can be drawn from Jensen and Inouye's explanation is this: if African Americans score lower than whites on IQ tests, then African Americans are innately inferior. If whites score lower than Japanese, then whites are still innately superior.

This tendency of vested-interest groups to defend their dominance over minorities using prejudice and discrimination was studied by Jackman and Muha using national survey data.[41] The results appear to confirm that dominant groups routinely develop new ideologies and practices to legitimize and justify the status quo. In the 18th and 19th centuries, such practices included craniology and biological theories of intelligence. The 20th century witnessed the reification of IQ scores—specifically scores of African Americans—to legitimize white supremacy.

To all objective appearances, nativists and racists distort explanations and invent measures (such as IQ tests) and rationales that produce data predisposed to support the genetic theory of intelligence and, by extension, the myth of white supremacy. Hale-Benson,[42] borrowing from Dr. Anna Grant of Morehouse College, argues that white social scientists engage in a type of chauvinistic ethnocentricism that perpetuates an image of normality in describing whites, but pathology in describing African Americans:

> When Blacks were the principal drug users, they were defined as addicts. Now that drug use is pervasive in the white middle class, we see terms like "drug culture," "chemical dependency," "substance abuse." Out-of-wedlock births were defined as illegitimate when it was thought that they occurred largely among Blacks. As it has been acknowledged that such births are common in the white middle-class community as well, terms such as "single motherhood," "single-parent lifestyles" and even "liberated babies" have replaced the more pejorative ones. Veneral disease (VD) has been renamed STD, sexually transmitted disease. Black children who skip school are truants, but upper middle-class white children might have "school phobia" and require treatment. While poor Black children who do not perform well in school are likely to be moved into classes for the mentally retarded, children from upper-income families who perform poorly are designated as "underachievers," in need of special counseling and educational services. We define and pinpoint their disabilities with diagnosis like dyslexia, and create categories like "learning disability" to differentiate their problems.[43]

Hale-Benson adds that even when African Americans exceed whites in some dimension, African Americans are still regarded by many whites as deficient, deviant, or pathological.

EXPLANATIONS OF JAPANESE "SUPERIORITY"

Rose has observed that "there has been a tendency to gloss over the inglorious history of American anti-Asian attitudes and practices."[44] As such, there is gnawing disquietude about the image of Japan as "number one." As previously stated, the explanations of the superior performance of the Japanese on IQ and achievement tests rarely follow the logic of the explanations regarding the test performance among African Americans. Historically, the poorer performance of African Americans on these measures is oftentimes directly linked to supposedly innate intellectual inferiority.[45]

For the Japanese, however, demographic rather than innate attributes are provided as explanations by whites.[46] A case in point is Weyl, who attributes the superior performance of the Japanese to the "American brain drain" on economically underdeveloped countries;[47] that is, only the most intelligent Japanese immigrate to the United States, which accounts for their high IQ scores. Earlier, Caudill and DeVos surmised that the Japanese are high achievers because they are more endearing to teachers; are punctual, honest, and less troublesome; have higher moral standards, are harder working, and are motivated to get out of poverty.[48] In effect, they appear to be the "teachers' pets." Several researchers also stated that the superior performance of the Japanese may be due to "samples" being primarily from the middle class, or, stated differently, due to sample bias.[49] Other theorists go so far as to advance the proposition that IQ tests are "biased" in favor of the Japanese and against whites.[50]

Still, some academicians propose that environmental factors play a significant role in the development of Japanese intelligence. This explanation is inconsistent with both Jensen[51] and Jencks,[52] who argue that only 20 to 25 percent of intelligence is attributable to the environment. In addition, Jencks states that economic differences explain less than one-third of the variance between the IQ scores of African Americans and whites. The present authors propose that cultural differences, which Jencks and others ignore, may explain far more.

Perhaps a more accurate assessment of the variance in IQ scores (and subsequent explanations for the differences) between African Americans and whites and between Japanese and whites is that some of the variance between IQ scores is due to environmental factors and heredity—the remainder is due to prejudice, racism, and discrimination. In his study, Portenier concluded that racial and religious prejudice and intolerance appear to account for major differences in IQ scores[53]—a hypothesis supported by the persistence of IQ testing despite the staggering amount of data indicating that IQ tests are biased (or even racist) against minorities.

This hypothesis is also supported when one considers the increasing body of data indicating that the Japanese consistently outperform whites on IQ and achievement tests.[54] In general, Japanese students perform better in school (for example, achieve higher test scores and higher grade point averages, particularly in mathematics and the sciences), are more self-motivated to achieve, and are harder working than white students.

According to Divoky, the California Postsecondary Education Commission found that Japanese high school graduates are twice as likely as white students to meet entrance requirements for the state's public universities. Moreover, 33 percent of Asian high school graduates, compared to 16 percent of white high school graduates, qualified for the 1986 freshman class at the University of California.[55] Brunzel and Au found that Asian American applicants actually admitted to Harvard in 1982 had average verbal and mathematics scores on the Scholastic Achievement Test of 742 and 725, respectively, for a combined score of 1,467.[56] That year, white applicants admitted had average verbal and mathematics scores of 666 and 689, respectively, for a total of 1,355 points—112 points lower than the Japanese. Because of the superior performance of Japanese students, admission limitations have been applied and operationalized through administrative fiat.

Other studies report similar results. Lynn reports that 77 percent of Japanese people tested have IQs higher than the average American, defined as middle-class whites.[57] The mean IQ score for the Japanese is 104.9, compared to 100 for white Americans, and the worst-performing Japanese perform better than the average U.S. student.[58] Similarly, it was stated in *A Nation at Risk* that among the top 100 first graders in math, only 15 were American; out of 20 American fifth grade classrooms, not one had a test score equivalent to the worst-performing Japanese classroom, and Americans were overrepresented in the bottom of reading-comprehension classes. Moreover, on 19 academic tests, American students were never first or second, but were last seven times.[59]

For leftover craniologists and phrenologists who continue to attribute brain size to intelligence, perhaps the most disturbing finding is that the Japanese were found to have larger (and by definition, "better") brains than whites.[60]

What explains the variance between the IQ and achievement scores of Japanese and American whites? As previously stated, the majority of the literature reviewed set forth environmental justifications such as the relationship between the Japanese mother and child, the longer school days in Japan, the more-demanding curriculum, and the greater amount of homework. The biological explanation of intelligence is not advanced. The biological theory appears to have died a sudden death when the Japanese began to outperform whites on intelligence and achievement tests. This is not surprising, considering that if whites were to propose this perspective, the myth of white superiority would be forever destroyed. Hence, to view IQ testing in the United States objectively might cast a shadow over the righteous, pretentious, and pious notion of white superiority—the American empire.[61]

Lynn stated that, in general, racial differences in mean IQ have been concerned with the fact that white Americans obtain higher mean IQs than other racial and ethnic groups.[62] Subsequently, three lines of explanations are commonly set forth: test bias, advantageous environments, and genetic factors. However, because the IQ tests that are used to measure Japanese intelligence are normed on middle-class whites, white theorists cannot "objectively" advance the argument that the tests are biased in favor of the Japanese. Moreover, the literature is replete with data indicating that the tests measure the abilities possessed by middle-class whites, and hence guarantee middle-class white children higher IQ scores.[63] The fact that the Japanese consistently outperform whites on tests biased in favor of whites presents a serious embarrassment to whites.

Second, the environmental explanation (such as higher incomes, better nutrition, the parent-child relationship, longer school days, and superior schools) for the performance gap between the Japanese and whites is an equally embarrassing explanation for whites to advance, particularly as the Japanese have had considerably lower per capita income, with less to spend on food, education, and health care. Clearly, then, the advantage should lie with white Americans.[64]

Finally, and perhaps most important, Lynn adduced that test bias and environmental explanations cannot plausibly explain the lower IQ scores of whites in comparison to the Japanese; rather, it is arguable that genetic factors are the most likely source of the performance variance.[65] But it is unlikely that whites will set forth this argument.

Despite evidence to the contrary, elitist white Americans will continue to favor environmental explanations for the superior performance of the Japanese, while at the same time favoring the genetic explanation to account for the superior performance of whites in comparison to African Americans.

CONCLUSION

Paradigmatic paralysis, that is, obsolete and monolithic paradigms, still dominate much of the professional thinking and mask the realities.[66] The IQ testing movement represents the tendency of racists, when a physical parameter (for example, brain size) of measuring race differences eluded them, to assume immense innate physical differences in any way. The literature and other sources of data strongly indicate that whites rarely needed "proof" for what they knew was there.[67] To illustrate, Hilliard stated that it has been well-documented that many leading scientists during the last 100 years have also been heavily nationalistic, or, more specifically, overtly racist, and have been models of self-serving and biased investigations.[68] Carlson and Colburn add that

> No group did more to legitimize race stereotyping than did American scientists. Through their supposedly objective studies of craniology, physiognomy, eugenics, ethnology, intelligence, and social behavior, these scholars . . . attempted to prove that popular images of minorities were scientifically correct. Their work on behalf of Anglo-Saxon superiority, however, only proved that their racial prejudice was stronger than their scientific dedication.[69]

Carlson and Colburn asserted that, unfortunately, Americans have traditionally worshipped at the shrine of scientific objectivity, and few persons questioned the validity of the scientists' conclusions on race. As indicated throughout this article, scientific— and even unscientific—conclusions are seldom questioned. In addition, white Americans traditionally have had a remarkable tendency to "find" data supporting the intellectual superiority of their own race and cultural group.

To illustrate, Terman and Cox went so far as to administer IQ tests to dead people. According to Chase,[70] Terman and Cox solemnly administered IQ tests to Beethoven, Darwin, Goethe, Sir Francis Galton, Washington, Napoleon, Lincoln, and others who had died long before the Revised Stanford-Binet IQ Test had been developed. The results were as follows:

> Sir Francis Galton's IQ was "unquestionably in the neighborhood of 200, Copernicus, Cervantes, and Faraday were awarded between 100–110, Oliver Cromwell and Rembrandt received between 111–120, Charles Darwin received about 135, and George Washington received a score somewhere between 120–130."[71]

As Hilliard aptly concluded, Terman's standardized test was not only able to pierce the boundaries of culture and language, but also the line between the living and the dead.[72]

Our nation's history is marred by a deleterious form of racism and prejudice whose by-product is the stratification of the various races, with African Americans at the bottom of the list, and the Japanese only slightly higher. Perhaps one of the greatest tragedies of this century is that, as our society moves toward increasing racial equality, we have at least a hint that we are maintaining if not increasing racial inequality.[73] This kind of hierarchy persists despite the fact that the Japanese have consistently outperformed the Joneses and the Smiths, as well as the Cohens and Levines, on intelligence and achievement tests.[74] Our society is shaped by actions in consequence of racial differences—actions that usually elevate whites and subordinate African Americans and other minorities.[75]

Rumors of African American inferiority have been around for a long time. It has been based on grounds as diverse as twisted biblical citations, dubious philosophical arguments, and unscientific measures of skull capacity. The latest emergence of this old theme has been in the controversy over race and IQ. The data indicate that genetic explanations have a chilling finality for a nation professing democracy.

Nonetheless, a thread of hope lies in the possibility that people can learn from comparing explanations regarding the academic performance of the Japanese and whites with those regarding the performance of African Americans and whites. Only then can this nation preclude the disaster that has befallen African Americans and other minorities.[76] It is a very thin thread.

NOTES

1. L. M. Terman, "Genius and Stupidity: A Study of Some of the Intellectual Processes of Seven Bright and Seven Stupid Boys," *Pedagogical Seminary* 13 (1906): 307–73.

2. S. D. Gulick, *The American Japanese Problem* (New York: Charles Scribner's Sons, 1914), 188.

3. H. L. Kitano, *Japanese Americans: The Evolution of a Subculture* (Englewood Cliffs, NJ: Prentice-Hall, 1979), 28.

4. *New York Times*, 18 March 1982, A26.

5. B. Hare, "Black Youth at Risk," in *The State of Black America, 1988*, ed. J. Dewart (New York: National Urban League, Inc., 1988), 81–93.

6. Johnson et al., *The Nature of Human Ability: A Historical Perspective on Intelligence* (Eric Document Reproduction no. ED 259 031), 1984, 1–23.

7. J. Lynch, *Prejudice, Reduction, and the Schools* (New York: Nichols Publishing Company, 1987).

8. B. P. Ulrich, *The Slave Economy of the Old South* (Baton Rouge: Louisiana State University Press, 1968), 269; see also T. Sowell, *Ethnic America: A History* (New York: Basic Books, 1981).

9. J. M. Lawler, *IQ, Heritability, and Racism* (New York: International Press, 1978).

10. Hare, "Black Youth at Risk."

11. L. Harris and Associates, *A Study of Attitudes toward Racial and Religious Minorities and toward Women* (New York: Louis Harris and Associates, 1978), 16–19; J. L. Hochschild, *The New American Dilemma: Liberal Democracy and School Desegregation* (New Haven: Yale University Press), 23.

12. T. Gossett, *Race: The History of an Idea in America* (New York: Schocken Books, 1965), 82–83.

13. S. J. Gould, *The Mismeasure of Man* (New York: W. W. Norton and Company, 1981).

14. A. Joseph, *Intelligence Testing, IQ, and Race—When, How, and Why They Became Associated* (San Francisco: R&E Research Associate, Inc., 1977).

15. J. Peterson, *Early Conceptions and Tests of Intelligence* (Westport, CT: Greenwood Press, 1969).

16. Ibid., 229.

17. G. D. Berreman, "Race, Caste, and Other Invidious Distinctions in Social Stratification," *RACE* 13 (4) (1972): 385–414.

18. Johnson et al., *The Nature of Human Ability*, 1; Hochschild, "The New American Dilemma," 18.

19. C. Jencks, *Inequality: A Reassessment of the Effect of Family and Schooling in America* (New York: Basic Books, 1972).

20. J. Bernstein, "Who Was Christy Matherson," *New Yorker*, 12 Apr. 1982, 152–53; M. Snyderman and R. J. Herrnstein, "Intelligence Tests and the Immigration Act of 1924," *American Psychologist* 39 (9) (1983): 986–94.

21. J. Howard and R. Hammond, "Rumors of Inferiority: The Hidden Obstacles to Black Success," *The New Republic*, 3,686 (9 Sept. 1985): 17–21.

22. L. Levidow, "Marxist Critique of IQ Debate," *Radical Science*, 6–7 (1978): 13–72.

23. Hare, "Black Youth at Risk."

24. J. Hale-Benson, *Black Children: Their Roots, Culture, and Learning Styles* (Baltimore: The Johns Hopkins University Press, 1986), chapter 2.

25. A. G. Hilliard, "Standardization and Culture Bias as Impediments to the Scientific Study in Validation of 'Intelligence'," *Journal of Research and Development in Education* 12 (2) (1979): 47–58; A. G. Hilliard, *Alternatives to IQ Testing: An Approach to the Identification of Gifted Minority Children*. (Final report to the California State Department of Education, 1976), 41.

26. R. Lynn "The Intelligence of the Japanese," *Bulletin of the British Psychology Society* 30 (1977): 69–72; R. Lynn and S. Hampson "The Structure of Japanese Abilities: An Analysis in Terms of the Hierarchical Model of Intelligence," *Current Psychological Research and Reviews* (Winter 1985–86): 309–22.

27. Hilliard, "Standardization and Cultural Bias."

28. M. R. Jackman, "Prejudice, Tolerance, and Attitudes toward Ethnic Groups," *Social Science Research* 6 (1977): 145–69.

29. Hale-Benson, *Black Children*; Hilliard, "Standardization and Cultural Bias"; Joint Center for Political Studies (JCPS), *Visions of a Better Way: A Black Appraisal of Public Schooling* (Washington, DC: author, 1989); L. J. Kamin, *The Science and Politics of IQ* (Potomac, MD: Lawrence Erlbaum Associates, 1974).

30. Lynch, *Prejudice, Reduction, and the Schools*.

31. R. M. Burkey, *Ethnic and Racial Groups: The Dynamics of Dominance* (Menlo Park, CA: Cumming Publishing Company, 1978), 58.

32. Johnson et al., *The Nature of Human Ability*, 7.

33. Lawler, *IQ, Heritability, and Racism*.

34. Jencks, *Inequality*.

35. JCPS, *Visions of a Better Way*.

36. Lynch, *Prejudice, Reduction, and the Schools*.

37. JCPS, *Visions of a Better Way*.

38. Jencks, *Inequality*, 84.

39. A. R. Jensen and A. R. Inouye, "Level I and Level II Abilities in Asian, White, and Black Children," *Intelligence* 4 (1979): 1–49.

40. Ibid., 11.

41. M. R. Jackman and M. Muha, "Education and Intergroup Attitudes: Moral Enlightenment, Superficial Democratic Commitment, or Ideological Refinement," *American Sociological Review* 49 (6) (1984): 751–69.

42. Hale-Benson, *Black Children*.

43. Ibid., 179.

44. P. I. Rose, "Asian Americans: From Pariahs to Paragons," in *Clamor at the Gates*, ed. Nathan Glazer (San Francisco: Center for Contemporary Studies Press, 1985), 181–212.

45. C. Darwin, *The Descent of Man and Selection in Relation to Sex* (New York: D. Appleton and Company, 1986); C. Darwin, *The Origin of Species by Means of Natural Selection for the Preservation of Favored Races in the Struggle for Life* (New York: D. Appleton and Company, 1896); H. H. Goodard, *Feeblemindedness: Its Causes and Consequences* (New York: Macmillan Company, 1914); R. M. Yerkes, *Army Mental Test* (New York: H. Holt and Company, 1920).

46. Rose, "Asian Americans," 186.

47. N. Weyl, "Some Comparative Performance Indexes of American Ethnic Minorities," *Mankind Quarterly* 9 (1969): 106–19.

48. W. Caudill and G. Devos, "Achievement, Culture, and Personality: The Case of the Japanese Americans," *American Anthropologist* 58 (1956): 1,102–26.

49. Caudill and Devos, "Achievement, Culture, and Personality," 1,116; H. W. Stevenson and H. Azuma, "IQ in Japan and the United States," *Nature* 306 (17 Nov. 1983): 291–92; P, Sandiford and R. Kerr, "Intelligence of Chinese and Japanese Children," *The Journal of Educational Psychology* 17 (6) (Sept. 1926): 361–67.

50. Jensen and Inouye, "Level I and Level II Abilities."

51. A. Jensen, *Cultural Deficit or Information Processing Deficit?* (ERIC Document Reproduction no. ED 243 918), 1984, 1–15.

52. Jencks, *Inequality*, 14.

53. L. G. Portenier, "Abilities and Interests of Japanese-American High School Seniors," *The Journal of Social Psychology* 25 (1947): 53–61.

54. D. Divoky, "The Model Minority Goes to School," *Phi Delta Kappan* 70 (3) (1988); M. White, *The Japanese Educational Challenge: A Commitment to Children* (New York: The Free Press, 1987); E. L. Yao, "Working Effectively with Asian Immigrant Parents," *Phi Delta Kappan* 70 (3) (1988): 219–22.

55. Divoky , "The Model Minority."

56. J. M. Brunzel and J. K. D. Au, "Diversity, or Discrimination: Asian-Americans in College," *The Public Interest* 87 (Spring 1987): 49–62.

57. Lynn, "The Intelligence of the Japanese."

58. White, *The Japanese Educational Challenge.*

59. National Commission on Excellence in Education, *A Nation at Risk: The Imperative for Educational Reform* (Washington, DC: Department of Education, 1983).

60. A. Montagu. *An Introduction to Physical Anthropology* (Springfield, IL: Thomas, 1966).

61. D. W. Adams, "Fundamental Considerations: The Deep Meaning of Native American Schooling, 1880–1900," *Harvard Educational Review* 58 (1) (1988): 1–28.

62. Lynn, "The Intelligence of the Japanese," 222.

63. J. Kagan, "The Magical Aura of the IQ," *The Saturday Review* 4 Sept. 1971, 92–93.

64. Lynn, "The Intelligence of the Japanese," 72.

65. Ibid.

66. JCPS, *Visions of a Better Way*; J. W. Moore, "Minorities in the American Class System," *Daedalus* 110 (2) (1981): 275–301.

67. Gossett, *Race*, 83.

68. Hilliard, "Standardization and Cultural Bias."

69. I. H. Carlson and G. A. Colburn, *In Their Place: White America Defines Her Minorities, 1850–1950* (New York: John Wiley and Sons, 1972), 32.

70. A. Chase, *The Legacy of Malthus: The Social Costs of the New Scientific Racism* (New York: Alfred A. Knopf, 1980), 236–37.

71. Ibid.

72. Hilliard, "Standardization and Cultural Bias," 49.

73. Hochschild, *The New American Dilemma*, 25.

74. Rose, "Asian Americans," 183.

75. Hochschild, *The New American Dilemma*

76. Berreman, "Race, Caste."

10

Between a Rock and a Hard Place: Drugs and Schools in African American Communities

William B. Harvey, Paul F. Bitting, and Tracy L. Robinson

Traditionally, access to education has been viewed as an escape mechanism from environments of poverty and despair. As a result of the meaninglessness and irrelevance of the American system of education to African American youth, the value and utility of education has decreased while the social acceptability of drugs has increased. Schools, rather than being part of the solution, have become part of the problem. The "cultural mind" or worldview that they propagate is distorted and grounded in false assumptions that do not equip African American youth with the ability to cope with reality. In effect, the consumption of drugs by our young amidst a failure to derive benefit from the nation's classrooms are two critical and intersecting problems. The reconstruction of the American system of education, taking into account the diversity of cultural conditions, is a necessary component of our "war on drugs."

Traditionally, access to education has been viewed as an escape mechanism from environments of poverty and despair. However, the current perception of schooling, especially in the public sector, and particularly in African American communities, is not a favorable one, and, consequently, the belief that education is a way out of limiting circumstances seems to be much less prevalent than it was in times past. The implications of this perception are troubling, because if success in school is not considered to be important as a means of gaining future rewards, then young people will turn their attention away from academic efforts toward other forms of satisfaction and gratification. At that point, the schools, rather than being part of the solution, can become part of the problem. Recent data suggest that this scenario may be more real than hypothetical.

Schools, which have been viewed nostalgically as a place where individuals develop their talents and abilities, are now more likely to be seen as unfriendly, even hostile, institutions. Many African American students seem to feel that there is little genuine concern evidenced for their well-being in school settings, and that there are few, if any, rewards accessible to those who stay to earn a diploma. The National Survey of High School Seniors reported that 40 to 50 percent of African American students in inner-city schools drop out after the ninth grade, and that dropouts tend to have a higher rate of drug use than do young people who stay in school.[1] Thus, an apparent reversal of what would be considered traditional values has occurred, and, as a result, what was bad (drugs) is now good, while what was good (school) is now bad. This pattern is a reflection of the shift taken by the larger culture toward individual satisfaction and personal gain, and away from common concerns or group interests.

The perceived value and utility of education has decreased simultaneously with the increase in the availability and social "acceptability" of drugs. There are important economic factors that have contributed to this turnabout in outlook, such as the increasing poverty and the high unemployment levels that abound in urban depressed areas, which make drug trafficking a viable means of earning money in these locations where few other opportunities are available. Escape and economics, then, emerge as reasons that African Americans are prone to be involved with drugs, and to eschew education. In fact, Helmer and Vietorisz contend that narcotics use has a socioeconomic pattern that has persisted for over a century. The problem of addiction is widespread, recurrent and cyclical.[2]

The educational system itself is not without blame, however. If one were to examine the present educational system with candor, one would conclude not simply that our educational system is imperfect, but that its imperfections are more responsible than we have cared to admit for the grave circumstances in which the culture presently exists. In addition, the system's failure to equally distribute education effectively, which is the unreasonableness of its basic design, bears a great amount of responsibility for social ills in the African American community (drug abuse included). The consumption of drugs by our young amidst a failure to derive benefit from the nation's classrooms are two critical and intersecting problems facing American society as a whole, but particularly African American populations. A plan of reflection and action are definitely needed.

DRUG USE AMONG AFRICAN AMERICANS

Any social problem has to be examined in the larger context in which it is found. From the perspective of a young African American boy or girl, the value orientation that is transmitted by the larger society is significantly different than it was a generation ago. Beginning with a change in cultural values in the 1960s, a general acceptance and even glorification of drugs began that has communicated the message to young people that it is not simply accepted, but even expected, that they will experiment with these substances. The fact that drugs are illegal perhaps adds to their illicit attraction. The recent campaigns that have been mounted against the use of drugs are attempting to reverse a commonly held notion that it is the individual's business, and nobody else's, if a person decides to take drugs. Changing perceptions is usually not an easy task, especially when attitudes have become entrenched over a period of 20 years or more. The situation is not as simple as those who counsel "Just say no" would suggest. According to Kozel and Adams, causes of drug abuse can include peer pressure, curiosity, depression, hedonism, attempts to increase or improve performance, rebellion, and alienation.[3]

TABLE 1
Clients in Treatment
(Persons Aged 15–64)

Race/Ethnicity	Number in Treatment (per 100,000 population)
African Americans	290
American Indians, Eskimos, and Aleuts	170
Others, including whites	90

Source: Beny J. Primm, "Drug Use: Special Implications for Black America," in *The State of Black America 1987*, ed. Janet Dewart (New York: National Urban League, 1987), 148.

The abuse of drugs is not a new phenomenon in African American communities, nor in areas populated by whites, for that matter. Lewis reminds us that "the case of poppy and coca leaf goes back to time immemorial. (So do wine and spirits.)"[4] The most widely abused drug, alcohol, is now overshadowed in terms of its cumulative negative effects on the population by other addictive substances that are illegal to possess and consume. The prevalence of these substances (heroin, cocaine, marijuana, PCP, and sedative hypnotic drugs) has become such that they can be acquired with ease and in the open on many street corners. The consequence of their availability has been what appears to be substantially increased abuse by African Americans, although the data in this realm are far from precise.

Primm cautions that there is little reliable statistical information concerning the number of alcohol and other drug abusers in the United States.[5] Further, he notes that there has never been any reliable epidemiological data supporting the number of African American abusers reported by the media. Official data from the National Household Survey on Drug Abuse identify the overall rate of drug abuse among African Americans to be about the same as it is for whites.[6] Approximately 32 percent of the individuals in each group were reported to have used drugs illicitly at some point in their lives, while 13 percent of African Americans and 12 percent of whites had reported using illicit drugs in the month preceding the survey.

Other figures indicate that African Americans are disproportionately represented among alcohol and drug abusers. Notwithstanding the relative inaccuracy of the numbers of African American drug abusers that are reported, there is widespread agreement concerning the negative impact of drug abuse in African American communities (see Table 1).

Nobles and Goddard assert that drug abuse has reached epidemic proportions in the

African American community.[7] Drug trafficking has been responsible for a significant weakening of the social fabric of African American communities, and in the consequent physical and economic deterioration of these areas. Directly or indirectly, the sale of drugs has led to increased crime rates and the generation of an unsafe and unstable ethos in lower-class neighborhoods, where the problem is at its worst, as addicts engage in various illegal activities in order to accrue the necessary funds to purchase more drugs. Some communities have become virtual battlegrounds, as gangs of teenagers have attempted to establish control over the sale and distribution of drugs through shortcuts and murders.

Nobles and Goddard identify substance abuse as "the single major leading social, economic, and health problem confronting the African American community."[8] The problem has been exacerbated in recent years because of the emergence of a drug known as "crack" that is both potent and inexpensive. Traditionally, marijuana and heroin had been the drugs of choice in African American communities, while cocaine, because of its higher cost, was considered the drug of the wealthy. The introduction of crack, which is a form of cocaine, has made this highly addictive drug available to a larger number of people, and thus increased the incidence and range of drug-related problems, including crime, violence, and prostitution, within African American communities. The data from the Survey conducted by the Department of Health and Human Services on national trends in drug use indicate that 1 of every 25 high school seniors reported having tried crack in the past year.[9] The level of use is considered to be substantially higher among dropouts, thus reaffirming the necessity of providing young people with positive educational experiences so that they stay in school.

While the tragedy of drugs affects both teenagers and adults in a negative way, the situation seems even sadder when one realizes that babies are also the victims when their mothers abuse drugs. The infant mortality rate in Washington, DC, recently increased, so that now 32 babies out of every 1,000 that are born die before their first birthday.[10] The reason for this situation is that there has been a noticeable increase in the use of crack by pregnant women. Further, in New York City, births to mothers who abuse drugs have increased by 3,000 percent in the past 10 years.[11] Figures at the national level reveal that from 9 to 11 percent of babies are born to women who, at some time during their pregnancy, used illegal drugs.[12]

Many addicted mothers simply walk away from their babies, and the children who are fortunate enough to survive frequently have infirmities that can include low birth weights, seizures, respiratory problems, and withdrawal symptoms. Long-range effects might include an abnormally small head size and developmental and learning problems that could cause the child to be a problem to society for as long as he or she lives. Some mothers are so intent on obtaining more drugs that they abandon their children. Beck takes the position that "all women of childbearing age must be persuaded to stay away from addictive drugs, lest their indulgence mean a lifetime of damage to a new generation."[13]

Obviously, the inherent values and operational approaches of the "drug culture" are

TABLE 2
Orientations

African American Family Value Orientation	Drug Culture Value Orientation
I. Cultural Themes	I. Drug Culture Themes
Sense of appropriateness	Anything is permissible
Sense of excellence	Trust no one
II. Cultural Value System	II. Drug Culture Value System
Mutual aid	Selfishness
Adaptability	Materialistic
Natural goodness	Pathological liars
Inclusivity	Extremely violent
Unconditional love	Short-fused
Respect (for elders)	Individualistic
Restraint	Manipulative
Responsibility	Immediate gratification
Reciprocity	Paranoid
Interdependence	Distrustful
Cooperativeness	Nonfamily-oriented
	Not community-oriented
	Self worth = quality

significantly different from what has traditionally been sanctioned and practiced in the African American family and community. It may be that the reemphasis of those traditional values is the only effective way to overcome the scourge of drugs and the associated negative actions. Schools could play a very important role in revitalizing these positive African American values. Table 2 identifies the particular themes and values of the two respective orientations.

It is impossible to overstate the negative impact that drug abuse has on African Americans. The costs, in both social and economic terms, are horrendous. In searching for an answer to this devastating problem, there is a natural inclination to turn to the schools. An analysis of schooling is important in order to determine whether these institutions can or should be used to reduce or curtail drug use in African American communities.

MEANING, REASONABLENESS, AND AMERICAN SCHOOLS

Philosophers, psychologists, politicians, journalists, physicians, social workers, and educators frequently proclaim that the answer to our societal problems is more education. In American society, behind every problem to be solved, so the belief goes, there is a question regarding education that needs to be asked. The questions about education are often philosophical: What is the nature of knowledge, and how is it passed on in ways that will best influence our actions? They are sometimes psychological: How do humans learn? What are the environmental conditions that most enhance learning? They may be expressed in terms of sociology and anthropology: What are the differences in societal structures and cultures that influence ways of learning and knowing?

These questions regarding education, however, cannot be asked or answered simply. They must be pondered and lived with, as a reminder of something essential we seem to have forgotten. The American culture has generally tended to solve its problems without experiencing its questions. That avoidance is its genius as a civilization, but it is also its pathology. Now the pathology is overtaking the genius, resulting in a transformation from social health to social illness. The assumptions of a culture about the principles and powers of the mind may be identified as "a cultural mind."[14] It constitutes the cultural perspective of the world, and both defines the limits and attaches meaning to its operation.

The concept of a cultural mind exists, constituted by a set of philosophical assumptions, whether ever articulated or not, about the principles and powers of the human mind. It shapes the way in which the people of a culture exercise their powers in their efforts to know and cope with reality, and, therefore, it determines the structure of the culture itself. Assumptions can be seen in the way in which a society defines and attempts to solve its problems. Errors in these assumptions can systematically thwart a people in their efforts to know and to cope with reality, and can generate a gap between the culture they develop and the structure of reality. The existence of such a gap leads to what is here referred to as the unreasonable cultural mind.

A culture that has a distorted worldview, one grounded in false assumptions about the principles and powers of a human mind to know and appropriate its world, is unreasonable and possibly deranged. Life lived within such a culture is like the life of a madman. In this setting, one cannot know and cope with reality through the exercise of mental powers because the mental powers are structured by the internalized culture. All efforts to know reality operate from within the culture and thus suffer from the cultural defects. One cannot discover and correct these defects without transcending the distorted worldview and its underlying assumptions about the structure of experience. The educational system plays a vital role in transmitting this worldview.

If we deplore our leaders and electorates as being self-centered and unenlightened; if we decry the moral indiscretions of many of our clergy; if our young concern us in their abuse of alcohol, drugs, and sex, we must remember that all these people are products of our educational system. If we protest, as an extenuating factor, that these individuals are also the products of homes and families, then we must remember that the unreasonable parents and grandparents in such families are likewise products of the self-same process of education. As a culture, we do not require that young people be influenced by reasonable, reflective homes and families. We cannot require that they possess some moral and spiritual center as influenced by religious doctrine. But we can and do require that they all attend some place of formal learning called school. Educators, therefore, bear a heavy responsibility for the unreasonableness of the American cultural mind.

To confront the problems and questions of our culture is never easy because this action relentlessly demands the kind of self-knowledge that educators know to be highly elusive, but that is also indispensable to achieving worthwhile lives and a reasonable civilization. Particularly with regard to education as it is presently understood, any illusions about the benign influence that it may exercise in solving the ills of the culture must be put aside and transcended. Only through critical examination and honest expression can the present role and function of the educational system be clearly understood.

Unreasonableness in the cultural mind, and the problems that follow from it, manifest themselves boldly in the most disadvantaged communities, which are disproportionately populated by African Americans. If such unreasonableness is consonant with the proliferation, for example, of drug abuse in the general culture, such proliferation will show itself twofold in the most disadvantaged communities. Thus, candor forces one to ask: How has the African American child's experience with the American education system induced such unreasonableness? How reasonable and meaningful are their experiences?

MEANING AND EDUCATION

All of us—not just the young—have known what it is for experiences to lack meaning. It is a deeply disturbing situation, much more than simply puzzling. When we are puzzled, we suspect there is an answer somewhere that will yield understanding, but meaninglessness can be terrifying. When African American students sit at their desks and are inundated with factual information that seems jumbled, pointless, and unconnected to their lives, they have a direct sense of meaninglessness. Meaninglessness is a much more fundamental problem than simply not knowing what to believe. African American students who are experiencing meaninglessness desperately search for clues that would give them guidance of some kind.

The mainstream students have mastered the techniques of the "school game" as ways of accommodating meaninglessness. The child's willingness to play the school game is often viewed by educators as "readiness to learn" or as an indication of a "school-oriented child." Smith addresses the absurdity of such concepts through a story.[15] "Dr. Helen Redbird, an Indian faculty member at the Oregon College of Education, visited an elementary school to inquire about the progress of a little American Indian boy, and was told by the boy's teacher that he was doing poorly in class because he appeared disinterested in learning, perhaps unwilling to learn."[16] Dr.

Redbird asked to remove the boy from the classroom for a few days to see if she couldn't get him "ready to learn," and, after a few days of "motivating" the student, Dr. Redbird returned him to class.

About a week later Dr. Redbird inquired about the boy's progress, and "not to her surprise, he was doing excellently and his teacher was amazed with the results. Unknown to the teacher, Dr. Redbird had taught the little boy to do two things; smile and nod his head in response to his teacher."[17] When the boy had mastered these two acts of accommodation, Smith explains, "his teacher was convinced of his willingness to learn! Neither smiling nor nodding was part of the little boy's culture, but until he was taught to behave in ways that signaled his desire to learn, he was abandoned."[18] Smith asks, "how many African American children are lost because they don't know or are unwilling to play the school game?"[19] And, since school is compulsory, many such children, even if they think they fully understand the game, find themselves imprisoned in a nightmare. Smith elaborates:

> When black children do not see themselves in their textbooks, when they are denied the chance to read of their people's accomplishments, when all about them they see only maids and porters, high rises and run-down tenements, when they perceive in the mass media only a replication of the black mentality that is their daily companion, they are trapped by self-doubt and self rejection.[20]

The response to candor is often defensiveness. The defensive educator might retort that the problem lies not in the educational process, but in the fact that so many African American students are apathetic, and that this is a direct result of their home environment. They then appeal to the work of Coleman et al. to support their claim. However, if the home environments were not at least initially stimulating, African American children would come to kindergarten apathetic. They don't. Whatever their home environment, they come to kindergarten bright-eyed, curious, and ready to learn. By about the third grade, however, this inquisitiveness begins to dissipate,[21] and by the middle school years, they are beginning to suspect that they are being compelled to remain in school—not because it does them any good, but simply as a baby-sitting operation and to keep them off the streets and out of the labor market.

The relationship between education and meaning should be considered inviolable. Wherever meaning accrues, there is education. This may happen in school, at home, in church, on the playground, or in any dimension of the child's life. On the other hand, the relationship between schooling and education is a highly contingent one. Schools may or may not educate. But those schools that consider education to be their mission and purpose are schools that dedicate themselves to helping their students find meanings relevant to their lives. Smith elaborates:

> Black children must have proof of their own worth. They must learn about their own worth as a derivative of the worth of their forebears. Black children must be taught to understand and appreciate their cultural heritage by teachers who un-

derstand and appreciate that heritage. Black children must know who they are and they must learn about the racial accomplishments of which they can be very proud.[22]

This sense of meaninglessness is not only expressed through a curriculum from which many disadvantaged children find themselves detached or in the attitude of teachers who do not believe such children can (or have the will to) learn, but it is also expressed through the educational bureaucracy. When one examines the procedures of school systems, one finds that they follow the general pattern that has developed in bureaucratic history. Duties are divided meticulously, and each position in the school is filled by a person who carries out the duties or tasks assigned to that position. Impersonality is the order of the day, and the method of licensure and examination for positions ensures that personality will not enter the picture. Haubrich identified the use of roles and duties in the educational bureaucracy and its effect upon the child:

> A position is set up for a first grade teacher, and one of the duties assigned to that role is to teach the children to read a book that enables them to pass a test which will then admit them to the next level of competition. The child takes the test and does not complete the reader successfully so he is failed and repeats the grade. The sanctions in this entire procedure are impersonal and it always seems that nothing can be done. There is the test (whatever its applicability or validity), there is the rule (whatever its logic or workability), and there is the child who has not passed. There is nothing to be done. While this example may be overstated, . . . the general thrust of bureaucratic organizations is to inculcate in the child and in the functionaries a sense that fairness has prevailed and that no one in the bureaucracy is at fault.[23]

Meanings cannot be dispensed, given, or handed out to children. Meanings must be acquired. It is important to learn how to establish the conditions and opportunities that will enable African American children to use their natural curiosity and appetite for meaning, to seize upon the appropriate clues, and to make sense of things for themselves. Many teachers, while in their defensive mode, will say that they are already doing this, and no doubt they are. But the educational arena, including colleges of education where teachers are trained, generally does not operate in this fashion. African American children must, therefore, be empowered to acquire meaning for themselves. They will not acquire such meaning merely by learning the contents of adult knowledge and of the dominant culture. If they are to be reasonable, they must be taught to reason for themselves because reason is the skill par excellence that enables us to acquire meaning.

REASONABLENESS AND EDUCATION

In what respect has education most greatly disappointed us? Here, the response need not be in the least equivocal. The greatest disappointment of traditional education has been its failure to produce people who approximate the ideal of reasonableness. This is not to say that all who are reasonable must have been educated, but only that whoever is educated ought to be reasonable. It may well be that in centuries past, unreasonableness was a luxury that human beings could afford, even though the costs were high. It should be evident, however, that the costs of a tolerant attitude towards unreasonableness are now far beyond our reach. We now will have to reason together or die together.

Reasonableness should not be expected from people exposed to unreasonableness in their educational institutions. It would be unrealistic to expect a child brought up among unjust institutions to behave justly. Those who have had a history of being abused often turn out to be abusers of the rights of others. Likewise, it is unrealistic to expect a child brought up among unreasonable institutions to behave reasonably. But the unreasonableness of institutions *is* preventable.

The unreasonableness, or "socially patterned defects," which permeate education have to be rooted out, because they do not die out on their own: they have a marvelous capacity for self-perpetuation. This involves bringing a greater degree of reasonable order into the curriculum, into the methodology of teaching, into the process of teacher education, and into the procedures of testing. The adjustments made within each of these areas must be determined by the interrelationships they have among themselves. Alterations in the components of education, as well as the structure of education, depend upon the kind of world we want to live in, since it has much to do with the character of that world. What then, is the ideal that educational practice seeks to approximate? This would seem to be the primary question that the redesign of education must confront.

For the sake of lucidity, one can address the reasonableness of certain classroom practices that appear to affect the reasonableness of African American students, namely, testing and remediation. All too often, the components of education have the kind of bizarre interrelationship for which the best analogy is the tail wagging the dog. Testing, which should have only ancillary status at best, tends to be the driving force of the system. What will be on the tests structures the curriculum, which in turn has a controlling effect upon the nature of teacher education.

As long as the major goal of education is thought to be cognitive learning, as is the case in American society, the model of recall will dominate testing, and teachers will be trained to teach to the tests. It is a sad fact that the information-acquisition model that dominates education, rather than being a model that encourages children to reason for themselves, is a failure even on its own terms. Recent reports raise real concerns about how little our college students seem to *know* about the history of the world, its geography, or its political and economic organization. The effect of this model is to stifle rather than to initiate reasonableness in the student. This does not mean we need to begin by producing better tests. Rather, we need to ask ourselves what kind of world we want to live in, what kind of education is most likely to contribute to the emergence of such a world, and what kind of curriculum is most likely to produce such an education. We must then set about producing the better curriculum.

As far as African American students and remediation are concerned, the disparity in the proportion of disadvantaged students in remediation programs is a byword. Too often, the recourse for inefficiencies in the curriculum continues to be remediation rather than redesign. When the remediation is acknowledged to be inefficient, compensatory approaches proliferate in an effort to remedy the ineffectual remediation. Increasingly, vast sums are poured into efforts to compensate for the inefficiency of the compensatory programs, in an ongoing exercise of futility.

Whatever the deficiencies of an educational system may be, it is apparent that they affect most cruelly and harshly precisely those portions of the population that are disadvantaged. Indeed, the system affects the student populations differently, so that there is significant students vulnerability to systematic unreasonableness. Moreover, it appears that students vary greatly in their susceptibility to the harmfulness of ineffective educational processes. Some cultural groups are not much harmed by inadequate public education, and many of their members may succeed in spite of it, but the system cannot take credit for their success. Other cultural groups may, however, succumb to miseducation very readily, and the system bears some responsibility for their failure. In any event, consideration of the factors to be taken into account in redesigning education must involve the unreasonableness of the educational process that makes compensatory education seem necessary. An analysis of that unreasonableness and its consequences holds more promise than taking as a starting point unsubstantiated allegations of differences in cognitive capacities based upon ethnic or sociocultural differences.

The theory that is implicit in current practice with respect to compensatory education is that the most extreme and obnoxious symptoms of an inadequate educational system may be remedied or redressed by means of a countervailing educational thrust that would make up the ground lost and would bring the lagging population up to par with the remainder of those undergoing educational processing. Unfortunately, the methods employed in compensatory education generally turn out to be much the same as those in the existing system itself. With no clear understanding of the causes of the miseducation now prevalent, compensatory education as currently practiced tends to be preoccupied with little more than the alleviation of symptoms.

The system is not without its critics; but although they are numerous, they are generally unconstructive, perhaps because criticism invokes defensiveness. Defenders of the system point an accusing finger at cultural or at socioeconomic conditions as the true causes of miseducation. And since there are few signs that our society is planning any major improvement in such socioeconomic conditions, the defenders imply that no major amelioration can be expected with respect to the education of those in the society who are disadvantaged.

Reasonableness, however, requires that we begin with a different assumption. This beginning assumes that the only way to make compensatory education work is not to approach it as a merely compensatory device at all, but rather to design it so that it promises educational excellence for all young people. Just as there is no field called "compensatory medicine," there should be no such field as "compensatory education." Just as the intensive care facilities in hospitals are fully equipped for the seriously ill, so, too, the care and attention we give to the educational development of the disadvantaged or highly vulnerable members of our society should be a model of excellence, representing the best in services to all. There is no effective strategy for compensatory education that is not at the same time an effective strategy for all education.

What is clear is that education must be reconstructed so that socioeconomic conditions can never be the excuse for purely educational deficiencies. In turn, educational deficiencies should not be the excuse for the socioeconomic conditions that give rise to problems such as drug abuse. Reconstruction is necessary so that diversity of cultural conditions will be regarded as an opportunity for the system to give proof of its excellence, rather than an excuse for its collapse.

Education, both from the African American child's point of view and from the public's, should be imbued with meaning and reasonableness. The child's claim can be seen as a demand for meaning; the public's as a demand for reasonableness. The existing educational process, however, can only be a disappointment for both, since African American children are neither disciplined to engage in effective reasoning, nor are their school experiences contextually structured so as to make available to them a rich and tempting array of meaning.

An education that has been structured for reasonableness promises to be an academically superior education, in behaviorally measurable terms, and especially more valuable as an instrument for addressing the problems and concerns beyond school, such as drug abuse. There are benefits, in addition to the intrinsic delights, to be found in such processes. It should not be overlooked that the development of children's rational resources can enormously strengthen their self-concept, which in turn intensifies their sense of purpose and direction. It is rather pointless to exhort children to be proud of themselves, to repeat "I am somebody" (that is, to have a "positive" self-image), without helping them to develop those competencies and powers of which they would like to be proud.

It is similarly pointless to assure them that they have the dignity and worth of human beings, when what African American children more immediately and precisely need is to be helped to express the individuality of their experience and the uniqueness of their point of view. This applies with all the more forcefulness to low-income African American children, for they have few other resources to call upon in life than their wits; when these are disparaged, what else are they to fall back upon? Simply identifying problems is never enough, nor is establishing the connection between conditions such as poor schooling and drug abuse. Strategies must be generated to ameliorate these negative conditions.

INTERVENTION STRATEGIES FOR AFRICAN AMERICAN POPULATIONS

African American children must be saved from having to live marginal lives due to inadequate skill attainment; they must be rescued from the toxic waste of drugs that are destroying their minds and bodies. An understanding of human development is an essential and powerful mechanism toward planning effective collaborative interventions within the schools and throughout our communities.

A host of notable public figures, including the current president and the wife of the former president, have informed the nation about the scourge of drugs and their impact on young people, particularly those in our urban areas. Moreover, these same individuals, and others, have been partly responsible for awakening the nation's attention to the educational crisis in this country, which affects the African American population at a disproportionate level. The information about drugs, the reason for their uneven consumption throughout the population, and plans to get rid of them are often based on an incomplete analysis. The information is not even presented with an adequate understanding that has been informed by a relevant context. Most often, the information about the drug problem and what to do about it is representative of a failure to acquire complete information, which often leads to misinformation.

Helmer observed that misinformation is the partial truth that leads to a false conclusion.[24] An excellent example of this is found in the slogan coined by Mrs. Reagan, "Just say no." Clearly, the term *just* is widely used in everyday communication. People probably use the *just* without thinking. Frequently, it precedes a verb, but serves to minimize the difficulty of the action started. For example, Dorothy and her friends (of Wizard-of-Oz fame) were told to "just follow the yellow brick road." As a result, they almost lost their lives. *Just* implies simplicity—failing to adequately take into account the inherent difficulty behind the action required, the motivation needed, the perseverance involved, and the essential support from a caring community.

It is imperative that children say no to drugs. However, it is damaging for children and dangerous for adults to be actively engaged in promoting the pretext of the "Just say no" slogan. The slogan minimizes and reduces the enticing lure of drugs. The truth is that there is significant power in the affirmative—to saying yes to drugs—particularly when there are no reasonable alternatives to take the place of saying no to drugs. As a result of insufficient options and opportunities to which youth can say yes, particularly for disadvantaged children, they are made that much more vulnerable to the lure of the affirmative. What happens, then, when vulnerable, susceptible youth who are constantly exposed to poverty see their peers already using drugs, do not resist the affirmative, and find themselves saying yes? Disinformation results, and falsehood is readily believed. In other words, the victim is blamed for saying yes, when, ostensibly, all he or she had to do was simply say no.

Regardless of a child's gender, socioeconomic status, race, geographic origin, or the type of household in which he or she is reared, there are certain situations that apply to all children and transcend demographic and other differences. That is, children must be loved and they must love. They need meaning, and they need involvement in the lives of others. Essentially, youth must capture the attention of others. Failure to do so will result in their destruction and in society's loss.

Keegan aptly made this point when he said:

> Meaning is, in its origins, a physical activity (grasping, seeing), a social activity

> (it requires another), a survival activity (in doing it we live). Meaning, understood in this way is the primary human motion, irreducible. It cannot be divorced from the body, from social experience or from the very survival of the organism. Meaning depends on someone who recognized you. Not meaning . . . is utterly lonely. Well fed, warm, and free of disease, you may still perish if you cannot mean.[25]

When the essentials for healthy human development are absent, young people are impaired in their ability to make quality choices that will empower their lives. When they are alienated and desperate for something that makes sense, young people in their search for meaning and understanding will try to make sense. When our youth have too little understanding of the relevance of their lives, and the way actions today connect to opportunities in the future, it is hard for them to be motivated, interested, and hopeful about tomorrow. When school, home, and community not only collectively fail to add meaning, but also subtract from life's quality, children are symbolically left with an empty plate, are malnourished, and are utterly lonely.

The process by which meaning is made, and where one is empowered, is born through dialogue and involvement. Children and teenagers are no different from adults in needing and desiring people with whom to talk. The power of dialogue, of reflection upon one's life and one's place in the life cycle, is identity making and self-creating. These acts, in and of themselves, are liberating and represent the beginning ground toward equipping persons with the necessary skills to say no to the things that limit their humanity, such as drugs, and to say yes to the very things that will elevate their humanity, such as getting a quality education.

Schools, as mandated institutions, are an ideal place for this type of dialogue. They are in the communities, and they touch essentially every child between the ages of 5 and 16. An example of a quality program that has community and school links.is in New York. The School Program to Educate and Control Drug Abuse (SPECDA)[26] is based on a social-influence model of prevention where counselors and responsible police officers serve as role models to assist children in acquiring the necessary skills to say no to drugs. The collaborative aspect of the model, with schools, drug counselors, and the community, offers some of the prime ingredients for success. In this program, numerous themes are addressed, but two that are powerful dimensions of the curriculum are self-awareness and positive alternatives to drug abuse.

Throughout the curriculum, which involves 16, 45-minute sessions, students explore who they are. Through self-awareness, they think about their lives, their wants, their fears—their existence. Considering that adolescence is a time of such critical cognitive growth, schools can take advantage of this growth by offering similar programs where questions such as, Who am I in relation to family, friends, and society? are asked. Such questions can strengthen decision-making ability whereby students query themselves and others about the role that education can play, and the role that drug abuse does not play.

Ultimately, students need to feel a sense of respect and worthiness for themselves, which is a tall order during such a turbulent time in the lives of young people. But a sense of admiration for self is essential for youth to be able to take advantage of opportunities that will empower their lives. The schools in the African American community can infuse these values.

At the Chemical Addiction Prevention in Schools (CAPS) program, for instance, students participate in support groups with a counselor. Here, students "learn to explore the reasons behind their own behavior and to understand the effects of their behavior on others."[27] This program does not wait for a crisis to occur as much as it embodies a respect for human development. The foundation of the program is the realization that kids need to talk, that they are pressed by peers, that they need to trust others, and that they need an environment that is supportive and caring.

Another important dimension is the positive alternative to drug abuse. School activities, as well as community leadership opportunities, are presented. Students need to be given a vision of a better way in order to make wise choices. Role models and mentors who will spend time and share their lives with these youth seem to be the only answer, whether or not these persons live in the same communities. More people who will offer some guidance and lend an ear are needed. Such individuals make a significant difference in how children perceive themselves, their schools, and their worlds. When children do not have such a vision, then, at some point, society at large needs to ask itself how it contributed to lack of hope among so many of its young.

A preventative approach entails a knowledge that children will make poor choices if not aided in the process, and if not presented with meaningful and life-sustaining options. In its current form, the American system of education is meaningless and unreasonable for African American students. This meaninglessness is characterized by factual information that seems jumbled, pointless, and unconnected to their lives. The reconstruction of the American system of education is necessary, and its redesign must involve the diversity of cultural conditions. Once this is realized, African American students can say no to drugs and yes to education.

NOTES

1. Beny J. Primm, "Drug Use: Special Implications for Black America," in *The State of Black America 1987*, ed. Janet Dewart (New York: National Urban League, Inc., 1987), 145–58.

2. John Helmer and Thomas Vietorisz, *Drug Use, the Labor Market, and Class Conflict* (New York: The Seabury Press, 1974).

3. Nicholas Kozel and Edgar Adams, "Epidemiology of Drug Abuse: An Overview," *Science* 234 (1986): 970–74.

4. Flora Lewis, "Legalized Drug Advocates Forget the Opium War," *New York Times*, 29 Oct. 1989, sec. E, p. 2–3.

5. Primm, "Drug Use: Special Implications," 145–58.

6. Department of Health and Human Services, National Institute of Drug Abuse, National Household Survey on Drug Abuse, *Population Estimates, 1985* (Washington, DC: Government Printing Office, 1987); Department of Health and Human Services, National Institute of Drug Abuse, National Survey of Drug Abuse, *Main Findings 1982* (Washington, DC: Government Printing Office, 1983).

7. Wade W. Nobles and Lawford L. Goddard, "Drugs in the African-American Community: A Clear and Present Danger," in *The State of Black America 1989*, ed. Janet Dewart (New York: National Urban League, Inc., 1989), 161–81.

8. Ibid., 161.

9. Department of Health and Human Services, National Institute of Drug Abuse, *National Trends in Drug Use and Related Factors among American High School Students and Young Adults, 1975–1986* (Washington, DC: Government Printing Office, 1987).

10. Joan Beck, "Cocaine Babies: A Sad New Problem," *Chicago Tribune*, 26 Oct. 1989, sec. 1, p. 25.

11. Ibid.

12. Ibid.

13. Ibid.

14. Nobles and Goddard, "Drugs in the African-American Community," 171.

15. Donald D. Smith, "The Black Revolution and Education," in *Black Self-Concept*, ed. James A. Banks and Jean D. Grambs (New York: McGraw-Hill, 1972), 47.

16. Ibid.

17. Ibid.

18. Ibid.

19. Ibid.

20. Ibid., 48.

21. D.B. Beane, *Mathematics and Science: Critical Filters for the Future of Minority Students* (Washington, DC: The Mid-Atlantic Center for Race Equity, The American University, 1985).

22. Smith, "The Black Revolution and Education," 48.

23. Vernon F. Haubrich, "Preparing Teachers for Disadvantaged Youth," in *Racial Crisis in American Education*, ed. Robert L. Green (Chicago: Follett Educational Corporation, 1969), 133.

24. John Helmer, *Drugs and Minority Oppression* (New York: The Seabury Press, 1969).

25. Robert Keegan, *The Evolving Self: Problem and Process in Human Development* (Cambridge, MA: Harvard University Press, 1982), 18–19.

26. Robert Blotner and Lilly LeVander, "*Specda*—A Comprehensive Approach to the Delivery of Substance Abuse Prevention Services in New York City School System," *Journal of Drug Education* 16 (1) (1986): 83–89.

27. Ruth Seegrist, "This Program Helps Kids Say No to Alcohol and Drugs," *The American School Board Journal* Sept. 1982: 28–29, 40–41.

11

The College Campus as a Microcosm of U.S. Society: The Issue of Racially Motivated Violence

Dionne J. Jones

The problem of racially motivated violence continues to be of pressing concern for racial minorities, particularly African Americans. Predominantly white college campuses, usually a mirror image of the larger American society, have recently been battlegrounds of racial unrest. The types of racially motivated incidents that occur in educational institutions are similar to those that occur in the larger society. The categories of incidents are broadly described as harassment of minority students, acts of racial or ethnic insensitivity, and physical attack. This article presents an analysis of some of the factors that contribute to racial violence on campus and makes recommendations for programs and training to help alleviate this problem.

Racial violence against African Americans has had a long and ignominious history. It began with slavery. However, multiple lynchings of African Americans have been reported as recently as the 1950s. More recently, several events have captured national attention as headline news, led by the infamous Howard Beach (New York City) incident, the Bensonhurst, Brooklyn, incident, the confrontation in Forsyth County, Georgia, and the problem at Virginia Beach. Similarly, incidents at the University of Massachusetts at Amherst, Duke University, Penn State, and the University of Michigan have been brought to public attention. Thus, racially motivated violence has once again become a public concern.

"Racial violence," "hate violence," or "bias crimes" are terms used to denote words or actions designed to intimidate an individual or a people because of their race, religion, color or national origin. A common definition of racially motivated violence is

> an act or a threatened or attempted act by any person or group of persons against the person or property of another individual or group which may in any way constitute an expression of racial hostility. This includes threatening phone calls, hate mail, physical assaults, vandalism, cross burnings, firebombings and the like.[1]

Because prejudice is at the root of these crimes, they are more serious than comparable crimes. For one thing, racially violent acts are intended to intimidate an entire group of people.[2] And, indeed, the fear generated by these acts can seriously victimize a whole class of people. Even racial slurs and epithets, though in themselves nonphysical acts, cause emotional and sometimes physical harm. Moreover, in addition to their effects on the immediate victims, racially motivated acts can have adverse psychological impact upon succeeding generations of the group as well. As a result of the stigmatization produced by racial slurs and epithets, victims may adopt negative behaviors such as alcohol abuse or even suicide.[3] Since racial slurs inflict pain upon the victim, the motivation and redress for their use should be treated the same way as other forms of racially motivated violence.

In a broader context, racially motivated violence, in any form, against African Americans (and other victimized groups), can be interpreted as an attempt to deny African Americans (and others) their civil rights, liberties, and coexistence in a society that constitutionally affirms equal justice for all. Viewed in this manner, the problem is not only morally reprehensible, but it also jeopardizes the racial progress that has been so vital to the overall society.

Until the very recent Virginia Beach incident, mass media attention to racially motivated violence had subsided, possibly giving the impression that the problem had been resolved and was no longer a cause for serious concern. This is far from the truth. Racially motivated violence against African Americans continues to be of critical concern. However, both for the society at large and the college campus, empirical knowledge about the phenomenon—its incidence, forms, and consequences—is lacking.

This article examines the issue of racially motivated violence on campus, using such data as are available from reliable sources. More specifically, the article has the following objectives:

- To discuss the prevalence of race-based incidents in the nation;
- To illuminate, through case illustrations, the varying forms of race-based incidents on campus;
- To consider some of the factors that contribute to the occurrence of racially motivated acts on campus;
- To recommend measures necessary to improve the current knowledge base and remedial responses to the problem as it occurs.

Although not covered in depth, this brief discussion should, nonetheless, stimulate and further efforts to understand and deal with the contemporary problem of racially motivated violence on campus.

PREVALENCE OF RACE-BASED INCIDENTS

There are no comprehensive national statistics on the incidence of racially motivated violence. Thus, available data originate from state and local sources. However, data collection efforts vary among states and even within governmental bodies at the local level. Further, the processes used provide considerable latitude for subjectivity. Hence, incidents considered trivial by the police may easily remain unreported.

Maryland, the first state to collect statistics on hate crimes, began its efforts as recently as 1981. State police are required to collect the data and provide monthly summaries to the Maryland Human Relations Commission. In 1986, Pennsylvania, too, required its police agencies to file monthly reports on hate crimes with the State Police Bureau of Community Services. Similarly, in 1987, Connecticut, Illinois, and Oklahoma enacted laws that require data collection on hate crimes. Legislation is currently being considered in the states of New York, Virginia, and California. Moreover, New York, New Jersey, and Virginia have established procedures to collect data, although legislation requiring such action has not been enacted.[4] In addition, several private organizations tabulate bias incidents nationally.[5]

While empirical evidence on the nationwide incidence of racially motivated violence is sketchy, existing information on the dimensions of the problem is at least indicative of the trend. In a special report by the Southern Poverty Law Center's Klanwatch Project, it was noted that violence motivated by extreme prejudice worsened in the 1980s, despite a decline in organized hate groups.[6] Relatedly, prosecution of these cases has also increased. For example, in 1987, the U.S. Department of Justice prosecuted 16 cases involving racial violence, with 28 defendants. This was the largest number of cases prosecuted in a single year since 1976.[7] During the period from 1980 to 1986, nearly 3,000 acts of hate motivated violence, harassment, and vandalism were documented by the Center for Democratic Renewal,[8] a multiracial, interfaith organization. This organization counters hate group activities with a program of education, research, victim assistance, community organizing, leadership training, and public policy advocacy.

Similarly, the Department of Justice's Community Relations Service (CRS) was established by the Civil Rights Act of 1964 "to provide assistance to communities and persons therein in resolving disputes, disagreements, or difficulties relating to discriminatory practices based on race, color, or national origin."[9] Thus, this agency has primary responsibility to help communities settle racial and ethnic conflict voluntarily through peaceful means by employing techniques of conciliation and mediation. The CRS documented 2,167 alerts to potentially serious racial and ethnic conflicts in 1986, and 2,046 alerts in 1987.[10] Of the alerts received, 276 resulted in incidents of racial violence and harassment in 1986, and 310 in 1987. Of the total cases from 1987, only 1,265 alerts were accorded conciliation or mediation action by the Community Relations Service.[11]

Between 1985 and 1986, the Community Relations Service responded to a 42 percent increase in the number of racial hate incidents, a near tripling of the cases between 1980 and 1986. Regionally, there was a 32 percent increase in racially motivated crimes in New York between 1983 and 1984, and a 25 percent increase between 1984 and 1985. In California, the Attorney General's Commission on Racial, Ethnic, Religious, and Minority Violence concluded after statewide hearings that hate violence was not only occurring in every part of California, but also was growing.[12] In Maryland, 423 hate acts of all kinds were reported in 1986 by the Maryland Human Relations Commission. In neighboring Pennsylvania, a near-50-percent increase in hate incidents (124) was reported in fiscal year 1986 by the Pennsylvania Human Relations Commission.[13] Finally, in the first eight months of 1987, the New York City Police Department recorded 310 bias crimes, 220 of which involved African Americans and whites.[14]

Considerable disparity characterizes these reports. The disparity among the total incidence of hate activity reported by these jurisdictions is a clear indication of the need for a uniform, nationwide reporting system. Moreover, such legislation would put an end to the ongoing debate between the public and private sectors, particularly between the U.S. Attorney General's Office and civil rights advocates about whether or not racial violence is on the increase.

Since 1986, ethnic, racial, and religious prejudice resulted in publicized incidents of violence on more than 250 campuses across the country. In the 1986–1987 academic year alone, there were approximately 70 incidents on college campuses.[15]

TYPOLOGY OF INCIDENTS

The types of racially motivated incidents that occur in educational institutions are similar to those in the larger society. The categories of incidents are broadly described as (1) harassment of minority students, (2) acts of racial or ethnic insensitivity, and (3) physical attack. These categories overlap, and an incident that begins as one type can easily turn into another. Note the following case examples.[16]

Harassment of Minority Students

Harassment involves intimidation. It may consist of graffiti painting, minor vandalism of property, or threatening phone calls or letters. These cases represent the tip of the iceberg:

- During the 1986–1987 school year, several African American students at the University of Maryland Baltimore County (UMBC) campus were verbally harassed. They were called "nigger" and other derogatory names.
- In March 1988, a white student came into the cafeteria at a high school in Randolph County, North Carolina, wearing a white robe and hood and spoke to an African American student, then left.
- Racial slurs were painted on the walls of two high schools in Charlotte, North Carolina, probably related to the schools' antibusing sentiment.
- Bigoted flyers were heavily distributed at a high school in Catawba County, North Carolina, in October 1988. In addition, a paper depicted an African American student hanging on a burning cross, a grave with a Jewish name on it, and various other Ku Klux Klan and Nazi insignia, as well as slogans calling for the death of African Americans and the rape of Jews.

Acts of Racial or Ethnic Insensitivity

Acts of insensitivity involve the expression of overt racist statements or the display of racist symbols.

- In April 1989, at the University of Michigan, April was declared as "White Pride Time" and featured events such as counseling sessions on how to deal with "uppity niggers."
- At the University of Wisconsin at Madison, the members of the Zeta Beta Tau fraternity held a mock slave auction in which pledges painted their faces black and wore Afro wigs.
- In the fall of 1988 at Stanford University, two freshmen defaced a poster of Beethoven. They gave the image thick lips and hung it on an African American student's door.
- Racist jokes were aired on a University of Michigan radio station.
- In February 1988, a Harvard University history professor read aloud from a white plantation owner's journals, without giving the slaves' point of view. Further, he represented the view that African American men leave their wives because they suffer feelings of inadequacy when African American women leave the labor force.

Physical Attack

This category of incidents involves physical, bodily harm to the victim(s) and can result in death.

- In March 1987, an altercation that began in personal animosity between one white and one African American student ended in a brawl involving several students of both races.
- In July 1988, two teenagers shot an African American high school student in Robeson County, North Carolina.
- In March 1988, a fight over interracial dating led to racial tension at a high school in Alamance County, North Carolina.
- An African American student was stabbed to death with a hunting knife by a white student near a senior high school in Lexington, North Carolina.

AFRICAN AMERICAN STUDENTS' RESPONSE

In response to the racism exhibited on campuses, African American students around the country have rediscovered the militant protest strategies of the 1960s. African American students have sat in, marched, and rallied. However, these actions have gone further than being merely responses to specific racial incidents, and have called for broader action on the part of colleges and universities they were attending.

More specifically, African American students are demanding that universities incorporate intolerance of racial harassment in their disciplinary codes. These students are also calling for mandatory courses on ethnic studies and racial awareness workshops for everyone on campus. In addition, African American and other ethnic minority students are demanding increased recruitment of minority students, faculty, and administrators. Further, they have called for space and funding for cultural centers and programs. Below are some examples of the measures these students have taken to make their demands felt.[17]

- At the University of Massachusetts at Amherst, about a hundred African American students occupied a building after five white students had been accused of beating two African Americans. Among other things, the students demanded a 50 percent increase in minority student enrollment, and the creation of new classes on ethnic studies.
- At Hampshire College, also in Amherst, 40 African American students occupied an office for nine days, winning a 16-point agreement, including the appointment of a "dean of multicultural affairs" and an advisor for the group that occupied the office.
- At Penn State, after 89 students had been arrested for a 15-hour sit-in, the president dropped charges against them. He also agreed to create the position of vice president for cultural affairs for African American students.
- At Duke, when the Faculty Advisory Council rejected a proposal from the Committee on Black Faculty that each of Duke's more than 50 departments be "required" to hire at least one additional African American faculty member by 1993, all eight members of the committee resigned. This evoked a supporting protest by students and faculty, "drawing as many as 500 of Duke's 5,284 students." The result was that the council reversed its decision.
- After a four-day occupation of the president's office at the University of Vermont, that official signed an agreement containing 17 provisions.
- At Williams College, a group of 14 African American students barricaded themselves in a dean's office "to show the intensity of our feelings and the validity of our claims." The result was an agreement by the Williams College administration to review its affirmative action program, to "support a divisional requirement" in minority studies, and to set up a multicultural center with various minority students.

FACTORS CONTRIBUTING TO RACIAL VIOLENCE ON CAMPUS

Racially motivated violence is a complex phenomenon, for which there is no single explanation. Any number of factors, some of them idiosyncratic, may interact to generate a given episode. However, any attempt to understand the larger problem must acknowledge the influence of sociopolitical variables as well as the psychological dynamics associated with group prejudice. Accordingly, the causes are addressed in terms of reactions to cultural differences and the role of the political climate.

Intolerance of Cultural Difference

Prejudice and discriminatory behavior develop in individuals during the socialization process. The prominent sociologist Gordon W. Allport, who pioneered work on racial prejudice, noted that children first learned about racial prejudice from language and words with emotional impact. For example, words such as *wop, nigger, cracker*, or *redneck*, are used to denigrate whole groups of people. Thus, between 7 and 11 years, children learn to reject anyone who is the target of their parents' verbal slurs, and blindly condemn all members of the hated category.[18]

Allport reported that bigoted people go through life feeling threatened and insecure. Thus, they experience fear—of themselves, of their own instincts, of change, and of the social environment. As a result, they are forced to organize their style of life in order to reduce their feelings of discomfort. That is, they must impose structure and order in their lives.[19]

In the American way of life, for some groups, anything that is different from the white Anglo-Saxon Protestant norm is considered to be inferior. Moreover, there is a low tolerance for cultural differences among other groups. It is the lack of awareness of cultural differences, coupled with the lack of *interest in understanding them*, that leads to all types of prejudicial beliefs about other groups and, ultimately, to racial violence.

Trends in race relations in the United States indicate that there has been considerable change over the past 25 years in prejudice against ethnic minorities. However, current research findings are conflicting. On the one hand, some have shown that there is a general rejection of most of the older stereotypes of ethnic minorities. On the other hand, others reveal that intragroup attitudes appear to be stronger than they were a decade ago and that prejudiced attitudes are more emotionally loaded than in the past. That is, it is okay to be prejudiced, and people are feeling more strongly about their prejudiced beliefs.[20] This is in great part due to the sociopolitical climate created over the last 10 years.

POLITICAL CLIMATE

The political climate set by a nation's leaders dictates the social and economic conditions of its citizens and contours the public mood. For example, when the national leadership targets select groups for success, a variety of opportunities and benefits may be made available to them. On the other hand, when there is a negative or, at best, a nonchalant attitude toward some segment of the society, such as African Americans, other minorities, and the poor, programs benefiting these groups are terminated or funds are greatly reduced so that the programs are doomed to failure.

Such was the case demonstrated by the Reagan administration's withdrawal from its federally mandated responsibility to ensure the well-being of African Americans and other historical victims of discrimination. That administration worked aggressively to reverse many of the gains that had been achieved in the civil rights arena. In turn, these actions promoted a broader climate of reaction and retrenchment. Since 1981, the federal government's civil rights enforcement authority has been progressively weakened, its capability to execute enforcement mandates has been reduced, and there has been a broad-scale campaign to undo successful voluntary efforts to eradicate discrimination. These regressive actions were accompanied by the reconstitution, in 1983, of the U.S. Commission on Civil Rights, making it a vehicle through which the administration's reactionary views could be promulgated—a far cry from the original purpose of its establishment in 1957 as the only independent fact-finding and investigatory civil rights agency.[21]

The elimination of, and cuts to, various social programs that were created to assist the impoverished and disadvantaged (who are disproportionately African American) during the 1980s has also sent a message of racial intolerance. "Between 1981 and 1987, the federal government slashed subsidized housing programs by 79 percent, training programs by 70 percent, the Work Incentive Program by 71 percent, and compensatory education programs for poor children by 12 percent."[22]

These are but a few of the actions and practices that occurred during the Reagan administration. These actions expressed that administration's position toward African Americans, minorities, and the poor. The current administration has continued this legacy. In fact, even President Bush's presidential campaign had overtones of racial divisiveness. For example, "the political advertising depicting a black convict, furloughed by Governor Dukakis, who had raped a white woman while temporarily out of jail had all the nuanced messages of crime-race-sex, calculated, some people believed, to appeal to the racist instincts of white Americans."[23]

While many of the incidents of racially motivated violence are not reported, few of those reported are taken seriously enough to be prosecuted. And of those cases prosecuted, even fewer receive convictions.[24] Again, the message at all levels of the legal system is that an African American life is not worth much, and certainly not worth a white youth receiving a criminal record because of a "prank." Thus, it is the belief of many that racial and religious violence persists, in part, because existing state legislation and court systems are failing to adequately deter and punish the perpetrators of these crimes.[25] Indeed, for true racial justice to be achieved in this country, the federal government must act aggressively and consistently to eradicate ongoing discriminatory practices and to overcome the continuing effects of past discrimination.

RACISM AND BIGOTRY

As a result of these political, legislative, and social messages, conflicting findings emerge with regard to discrimination. Some white Americans believe that discrimination is no longer a problem, and that there is equal opportunity for African Americans and members of other minorities. They are, therefore, resentful of social programs designed to increase minority opportunities, since they see such programs as unfair to them. Others who also accept principles of equal treatment reject government policies that help implement these principles.[26] In essence, a clear message has been sent to communities throughout the nation that these subgroups were not and are not of much concern to the previous or current administrations. In addition, and more implicitly, the message was that exclusion of, intimidation of, or even physical abuse of these groups would go unpunished. Hence, there followed a resurgence of violent attacks and acts of intimidation against African Americans during the 1980s.

It seems paradoxical, though, that there would be racial tension on the nation's campuses. In the mid-1960s, colleges were the oases of calm and understanding in a racially tense society. The campus had a tradition of tolerance and fairness and seemed to impose a degree of broad-mindedness on even the most provincial students. Moreover, today's undergraduates were born after the passage of the Civil Rights Act of 1964. They grew up in an era in which racial equality was enforceable by law. There were African Americans on television, as mayors of big cities, as teachers, and even as neighbors. In addition, these students grew up with Sesame Street, and, by virtue of integrated schools, had opportunities to know each other.

Another paradox stems from the notion and practice of affirmative action. Under the Equal Employment Opportunity (EEO) Act of 1972, all state governments and institutions were forced to initiate plans to increase the proportion of minority and women employees (and, for universities, students). However, racial quotas were ruled unconstitutional more than 10 years ago in the *University of California v. Bakke* case.

CONCLUSIONS AND RECOMMENDATIONS

There is consensus among scholars and practitioners in the field that racially motivated violence (both on college campuses and in communities in general) is a dangerously escalating social phenomenon that is national in scope. Further, this phenomenon is not being adequately addressed by the government or by educational institutions. Again, it is difficult to accurately quantify the incidence of racially motivated crimes because such data are not being collected systematically nationwide. Thus, it is imperative to have national legislative policy as well as to initiate educational programs on campuses to help expand students' knowledge about ethnic minorities and, thereby, to improve the way this devastating problem is treated.

Legislation

As mentioned, only a few state governments and community organizations monitor the incidence of hate crimes. Bills to authorize the collection and analysis of data on race and religious violence have been introduced in some state legislatures. There is an urgent need for a national hate crime statistics bill that would mandate a uniform, nationwide system for collecting, analyzing, and reporting these data. The availability of such statistics could provide the basis for more effective law enforcement efforts and for determining law enforcement priorities.

Moreover, these data would also be useful to federal, state, and local legislators in formulating public policy. For example, one benefit of the enactment of legislation would be improved information for developing enforcement strategies. In addition, such data could be helpful in establishing criminal penalties for bias crimes, as well as in providing civil remedies for victims.

Educational institutions need not wait for legal sanctions in order to curtail the proliferation of racially motivated violence on campus. Indeed, many more institutions must follow the lead of those few campuses that have made racial intolerance policy and added it to their disciplinary codes. It is not suggested that legislation will change people's racial attitudes. What is suggested, however, is that when it is known that legislation is enforceable, this serves as a deterrent to many people who might otherwise commit a crime. Racially motivated crime is no exception.

Education

Education is often used as a tool for prevention and remediation of social and other ills. As such, there needs to be ongoing programs at educational institutions to help sensitize students and staff to racial and cultural differences. Such programs are essential both at the junior and senior high school levels as well as on college and university campuses. Token programs, such as a one-day cultural fair with ethnic foods, dress, and music, will not suffice. Major efforts will have to be expended to weave cultural awareness and respect for cultural differences into the infrastructure of eductional institutions. For example, courses on ethnic and cultural diversity in America should be made mandatory for all students. Similarly, there should be ongoing workshops, open to students, faculty, and staff, on the impact of racism in its various forms.

In addition to a programmatic response, university officials can demonstrate their commitment by making intensive efforts to recruit minority students, faculty, and administrators. Another important part of the plan is for school and college administrators to fund and develop multicultural centers and programs, which should be open to the entire student body and faculty. Fraternities and sororities can be most valuable in ensuring student participation.

These are but a few of the ways that educational institutions can take a proactive stance to help eradicate this problem. Although a few institutions have already begun to execute measures such as these, the vast majority of educational institutions have not.

NOTES

1. National Organization of Black Law Enforcement Executives (NOBLE), *Racial and Religious Violence: A Law Enforcement Guidebook* (Washington, DC: NOBLE, Mar. 1986).

2. Peter Finn and Taylor McNeil, *The Response of the Criminal Justice System to Bias Crime: An Exploratory Review* (Cambridge, MA: ABT Associates, Inc., Oct. 1987).

3. R. Delgado, "Words That Wound: A Tort Action for Racial Insults, Epithets, and Name-Calling," *Harvard Civil Rights-Civil Liberties Law Review* 17 (1982): 135–78.

4. National Institute Against Prejudice and Violence, "Legislative Update," *Forum* 3 (1) (January 1988): 2; Finn and McNeil, *The Response of the Criminal Justice System.*

5. For example, the Southern Poverty Law Center Klanwatch Project, North Carolinians against Racist and Religious Violence, the Anti-Defamation League of B'nai B'rith, the Center for Democratic Renewal, and the National Gay and Lesbian Task Force Anti-Violence Project.

6. Southern Poverty Law Center, Klanwatch Project, *The Ku Klux Klan: A History of Racism and Violence* (Montgomery, AL: SPLC, 1988), 57.

7. Ibid.

8. Center for Democratic Renewal, *They Don't All Wear Sheets: A Chronology of Racist and Far Right Violence—1980–1986* (Atlanta: National Council of the Churches of Christ in the U.S.A., 1987).

9. The Community Relations Service, U.S. Department of Justice, *Assistance in the Resolution of Community Conflict* (Washington, DC: Government Printing Office, n.d.) 1.

10. The Community Relations Service, U.S. Department of Justice (Unpublished document, 1988).

11. Ibid.

12. Press Release, Office of Congressman John Conyers, Jr., 27 Mar. 1987.

13. Southern Poverty Law Center, *"Move-In" Violence: White Resistance to Neighborhood Integration in the 1980s. Special Report* (Montgomery, AL: SPLC, 1987).

14. Peter Finn and Taylor McNeil, "Bias Crime: What's Being Done to Fight It" (Unpublished document, ABT Associates, Inc., 1987).

15. National Institute Against Prejudice and Violence, *Ethnoviolence on Campus: The UMBC Study*, Institute Report no. 2 (Baltimore: 1987).

16. Thomas Short, "A 'New Racism' on Campus?" *Commentary* Aug. 1988, 46–50; North Carolinians against Racist and Religious Violence (NCARRV), *1988 Report: Bigoted Violence and Hate Groups in North Carolina*, Annual Report (Durham: NCARRV, 1989); National Institute Against Prejudice and Violence, *Ethnoviolence on Campus*.

17. Short, "A 'New Racism' on Campus?"

18. Cited in Southern Poverty Law Center, Klanwatch Project, *The Ku Klux Klan*, 27.

19. Gordon W. Allport, *The Nature of Prejudice* (Cambridge, MA: Addison-Wesley, 1954).

20. National Institute Against Prejudice and Violence, "Research Notes," *Forum*, 2 (1) (Feb. 1987).

21. Robert McAlpine, Billy J. Tidwell, and Monica L. Jackson, "Civil Rights and Social Justice: From Progress to Regress," *Black Americans and Public Policy: Perspectives of the National Urban League* (New York: National Urban League, Inc., 1988).

22. John E. Jacob, "Black America, 1987: An Overview," in *The State of Black America 1988*, ed. Janet Dewart (New York: National Urban League, Inc., 1989), 2.

23. Charles V. Hamilton, "On Parity and Political Empowerment," in *The State of Black America 1989*, ed. Janet Dewart (New York: National Urban League, Inc., 1989), 111.

24. Finn and McNeil, *The Response of the Criminal Justice System*.

25. Editorial Comments, "Racially-Motivated Violence and Intimidation: Inadequate State Enforcement and Federal Civil Rights Remedies," *The Journal of Criminal Law and Criminology* 75 (1) (1984): 103–37.

26. National Institute Against Prejudice and Violence, "Research Notes."

12

White Racial Nationalism
in the United States

Ronald Walters

Modern American political behavior cannot be understood without taking the resurgence of white racial nationalism into account. This nationalism is a reaction to pressure for social change by African Americans, other disadvantaged groups, and youthful whites since World War II, which caused feelings of disempowerment by a segment of the white population devoted to the preservation of the status quo. This conservative movement has manifested itself on the grass-roots level in the rise of racially motivated violence and on the national level in the rise to power of the conservative wing of the Republican party with the presidency of Ronald Reagan. It will be necessary to reverse the tide of institutionalized racism and white nationalism in order to avoid a fascist future for American society.

An inescapable feature of the past six years of the "Reagan Revolution" has been the extent to which the conservative ideology that fueled it has congealed into a nationalism in the United States, the breathtaking sweep of which has pervaded many aspects of domestic and foreign policy. Ultimately, it has affected the normative character of the American psyche and, thereby, influenced the quality of life and behavior within institutions and neighborhoods. Yet a search reveals few writers who have characterized this phenomenon in its nationalistic dimensions. Perhaps it is easier to see a domestic brand of nationalism when its proponents wield such slogans as "Black Power," causing a flood of articles about "Black nationalism" to pour out into the landscape, as in the 1960s. However, when one is a part of a nationalistic syndrome, it is perhaps more difficult to reveal its manifestations, because people who ostensibly support civil rather than radical processes of social change may be reluctant to admit their support of it. In any case, one cannot understand many aspects of modern American political behavior without taking this resurgent nationalism into serious consideration.

Reprinted with permission from *Without Prejudice* (The EAFORD International Review of Racial Discrimination) 1 (1) (1987): 7–29.

The Reagan Administration has attempted to employ the current strain of U.S. nationalism, for example, to contribute to the viability of U.S. corporations in their struggle with foreign competition, and to destroy the restraints on private capital in an effort to make unbridled capitalism the engine of domestic growth. Moreover, the supporters of this nationalism have sounded a number of moral, social themes such as the preservation of the family, respect for law and order, anti-abortion, prayer in the schools, and others as a basis for restoring a pre-1960s social structure as the substance of "Americanness." They have also attempted to repress public attention to and concern for the disadvantaged class—African Americans, other minorities, women, and others—in order to restore white dominance of the social order through the resurrection of the status of white men.

It is instructive to note that the current wave of American nationalism is chauvinistic not only because it is American, but also because it is white. The domestic indication of this fact is that in attempting to resurrect the primacy of economics and military policy, the Reganites have led the charge for the destruction of the national social agenda aimed at disadvantaged African Americans and others—including African American immigrants, such as the Haitians and Cubans. By posing the domestic dilemma as a problem of government hegemony which required "getting government off your back, to loose you and let you be independent again," Ronald Reagan has shaped a vision of restructuring society, using the framework of a time which not only elevated the interest of the wealthy over the poor, but which also contained white hegemonic dominance. That is to say, whites were not only dominant in an objective sense, there was an explicit ideology and style of such racial dominance.

It has been unnecessary for those supporting the resurrection of white hegemonic dominance to shout "white power"! This crude manifestation of white nationalism has been left to the Ku Klux Klan (KKK), the Aryan Nations, and other such groups. Writers such as Murray Edelman and others have identified a far more sophisticated process which occurs in the transmission of social values through public policy, either as a reflection of a pre-existing movement or as the will of an existing regime in power—or both.[1] Yet, the unmistakable symbolism that the arrival of radical white nationalism has pervaded the culture may be found in such patriotic sounding slogans as "America is back" and "born in America again," slogans which have both foreign and domestic implications.

One of the central social issues which has recently arisen is the increase of incidents of racially motivated violence. Sensational stories, prompted by incidents of racial violence in the Howard Beach section of Queens, New York, and a threatening KKK gathering in Forsyth County, Georgia, have posed the question of why the "resurgence of racism."[2] This means that there has been, in addition to the usual patterns of racism, an apparent increase of incidents of white *physical aggression* against African Americans as a dynamic, highly volatile component of racist conduct.

Why, people have asked, did a mob of whites chase and beat three African American men through Howard Beach until one was killed by an oncoming automobile on the night of 20 December 1986? Why has the Ku Klux Klan been emboldened to the point that it would confront a few hundred and then 20 thousand civil rights marches in Forsyth County, Georgia? The rising tide of these sensational incidents of physical violence against African Americans by whites reminds us of an earlier historical epoch. Yet, a court case brought by the Southern Poverty Law Center settled a Klan lynching in 1987 in Alabama; mobs of whites in southwest Philadelphia harassed a racially mixed couple who moved in in 1985; an elderly African American woman in Harlem, Mrs. Eleanor Bumpers, was shot to death by police in 1986, and several young African Americans have been killed in recent years by the use of police "choke-holds."

The key to the causes of this social behavior lies deep in the post-World War II environment. White nationalism has festered as a reaction to the social movements and changing economic conditions which have provoked a modest amelioration of the social status of some disadvantaged nonwhites and white women, relative to the normative status of white males.

Such conservative and reactionary movements have occurred before and have also carried a strong element of white chauvinism and anti-African American bias in the extreme. White supremacy is an ancient principle whereby those "Americans" who founded this republic—however much they may have differed among themselves on the question of colonialism—agreed as whites when it came to African Americans. One writer has said, "At the heart of Anglo-Saxonism lay the conviction that the Anglo-Saxon (British) race possessed a special capacity for governing itself (and others) through a constitutional system which combined liberty, justice and efficiency. It was a gift that could not be transferred to lesser peoples.[3]

To illustrate this point, at the turn of the century when the Social Darwinists were busily justifying both the manifest destiny of America and the inferiority of other groups, the book *Our Country*, by a minister, Josiah Strong, became very influential. This work, as did many others, championed the idea that the Anglo-Saxon was destined to rule the world.[4] If white supremacy is dead, then shouldn't the idea have seriously eroded that America should be ruled by whites, with nonwhite groups kept in a subordinate position in the social structure? And shouldn't the enlightened view of American pluralism with all groups sharing political, economic, and social power equitably have become the new norm of social practice? The history of current events would appear to speak more loudly in answer to this point, since the practice of racial equality has been dangerously derailed by whites who perceive (I would argue inaccurately) the threatened loss of their social status. This is a powerful motivating factor in generating a conservative ideology and social movement.

Therefore, I want to assert in this article that the current political culture contains a pervasive strain of white nationalism as one of its dynamic features. The origin of this nationalism was the reaction to movements for social change by African Americans, other disadvantaged groups, and youthful whites since World War II, which caused feelings of disempowerment by a segment of the white population devoted to the preservation of the *status quo*. White, conservative populists coalesced with other conservative elements into a nationalist movement dedicated to acquiring social and political power as the instruments of returning the United States to the *status quo ante*.

At the grass-roots level, this conservative movement led to the emergence of an authoritarian populism which facilitated the rise of racially motivated violence. And at the national level, it provided the impetus for a coalition which elected Ronald Reagan to the presidency. One characterizes this movement as "white" in the literal sense that there was a marked absence of substantial African American participation in its activities or support for its values. Moreover, African American progress itself has become one of the primary targets of this movement in the attempt by the Reagan administration to rearticulate the racial problem in society in a way which subordinates African American and minority interests and restores and preserves white supremacy.

THE PERCEIVED LOSS OF WHITE POWER: THE SOURCES OF A CONSERVATIVE POPULIST IDEOLOGY

To suggest that white power was ever surrendered (and therefore needed resurrecting) may appear confusing to many, especially since it is obvious that whites as a group have never lost status in America, a majority white country. However, there is within any society a "balance of attention" to certain issues in a given historical era which defines social power in a public way that both symbolizes and influences the extant distribution of benefit. This determines the relative material condition of groups, and shapes their psyche as well. Whereas sociologist Pitirim Sorokin suggests that the immediate cause of all extreme movements for social change has always been the sense of repression felt by one group, another sociologist, W. I. Thomas, identifies "the wish for public recognition," as one of four specific causes.[5]

Whites, although the dominant sociocultural group, are hardly homogeneous ideologically. In this context, the outcome of struggles for the distribution of benefit among groups of white Americans defines the national power equation existing within society relative to the dominant political formations of whites *and* the status of others–African Americans among them. To the extent that whites differ among themselves over issues, the political system can appear to alter the balance of power by the significance it gives to status and distributive issues. African American demands, on the other hand, have destabilized the system itself, having been portrayed as unsatiable. For example, the Civil Rights Movement appeared to favor African Americans in that the balance of attention focused on what African Americans considered to be the *marginal* alleviation of their grievances due to past oppression. To whites, however, it appeared to be a *substantial* change and, therefore, threatened a serious alteration in the *status quo.*

Of course, there was no better indication of the nature of the public balance of issues which defined the status of any group than those issues with which the national government was seized, since they became the focus of the public dialogue and concern. It was patently clear to any observer that, within the 32 years from 1932 to 1964, African Americans and the white blue-collar working class had begun to benefit from the interventionist policies of Democratic Party presidents, a pattern which could not even be broken by eight consecutive years of Republican administrations.

Isolating the white racial reaction is not difficult, since the 1954 Supreme Court decision in *Brown v. the Board of Education of Topeka, Kansas* touched off a veritable storm which Martin Luther King, Jr., called a return to the "interposition and nullification" postures of the 19th century states' rightists. King's Southern Christian Leadership Conference (SCLC), the Student Nonviolent Coordinating Committee, and the other mainline civil rights organizations went on to campaign throughout the South, bringing the movement into the very heart of the old confederacy, and in the process threatening the *status quo*, both in that area and with the pressures it generated for the promulgation of national legislation.

Danzig notes, however, that the South's "massive resistance" campaign opposing the forward progress of African American civil rights was solidly in defense of the *status quo*, and that

> ideological slogans such as "states rights" . . . permit the segregationist to fight for his privileged position and, at the same time, to regard himself as a latter-day apostle of individual freedom against the tyranny of the state. In this way, he screens his attachment to a caste system by an image carved from the grain of American resistance to tyranny.[6]

Even among the northern Republicans, the writer goes on to suggest that such issues as balancing the budget were not so much championed because they made good economic sense, but because they also were consistent with an ethnic/racial Protestant religious code of personal responsibility, a fact which brought welfare policies under condemnation. Thus, the policy issues were interpreted through the nativist tone of moral values, which established an easy connection with fundamentalist religious sentiments. Nevertheless, a prominent Episcopal minister perceived that the church would become split by those who welcomed change from the basis of a "Christian social conscience" and those seeking to maintain privilege. He asserted that the latter group was attempting "to reassert a past dominance which would deny equal status to others."[7]

Thus, it may be that, for neoconservatists such as writer Clyde Wilson,[8] "well-being" for whites may also have to contain the public assurance that, relative to other groups in society, they are firmly in charge and have not lost—and are not in danger of losing—status due to public policies such as school or neighborhood integration, affirmative action, African American business mobility, or political control.

There is some evidence for this view in the studies of African American and white attitudes in the late 1960s by Cataldo, Johnson, and Kellstedt, who used the "self striving scale" to determine where a group felt it stood on the ladder of life. Strikingly, while whites felt that, in the past, the system met their highest aspirations, more so than African Americans (51% to 4%), African Americans had more confidence than whites that the system was meeting their aspirations in the present (45% to 42%). Future projections for both groups were nearly equally optimistic (59%—whites; 60%—African Americans).[9] Also, data from the University of Michigan's National Election Study confirm this trend as characterized by an increase in political efficacy by con-

TABLE 1
Perception of Internal Political Efficacy by Liberals
and Conservatives 1964-1976
(Percent Different Index)

	1964	1966	1974	1976
Liberals	-10	+15	+30	-15
Conservatives	0	0	0	+ 7

Source: Survey Research Center, *National Election Study Data Source Book, 1952-1978* (Ann Arbor: University of Michigan, 1979), 277.

servatives and a corresponding decrease for liberals precisely at the time when the white populist movement was maturing.[10] (See Table 1.)

When one looks at any graph of average family income in the 1960s, it is remarkable how steadily upward the trend lines appear, leading to the conclusion that as long as the personal fortunes of many middle and upper-class whites were secure, they were willing to tolerate funding the human rights program of the Great Society. However, those fortunes began to fall in the early 1970s, as the rate of growth in American productivity sank and the oil shocks of 1973 and 1975 began to foment economic instability through high rates of unemployment in the critical energy sector and rising prices of many related goods. In addition, as George Dilder has observed: "The American upper classes . . . underwent another 'great depression,'" as wealth was redistributed by an unbeatable rate of inflation.[11]

This "greening" of the white middle and upper classes in the direction of tighter economic, conservative, and individualist notions of opportunity and progress drove them in the direction of the philosophical New Right and the antigovernment populism. At the very least, it made them ripe for reconsidering the entire panoply of government assistance programs to the disadvantaged, especially where they were funded by traditional Democratic-style strategies of taxation. The result was that some were made skeptical and others hostile to affirmative action programs which appeared to provide a federally sponsored mechanism for enhancing the devoluton in the social status in comparison with that of African Americans and others. Senator Paul Laxalt, (R-AZ), a confident of President Reagan who believes affirmative action to be unconstitutional, compounded this extremity with the suggestion that some members of the Supreme Court who affirmed the principle of affirmative action in the *Weber* case (1979)[12] did not expect their own children to work at craft jobs in Louisiana oil refineries. He continued:

But the majority of Americans want and need those jobs, and white collar equivalents. They don't want to see Blacks or anybody else excluded from all the

TABLE 2
Attitudes toward the Power of the
Federal Government, 1964-1978

	1964	1978
Too strong	30%	43%
Not too powerful	36%	14%
Don't know	34%	43%
African Americans	52	-7
Whites	0	-32

Source: Survey Research Center, *National Election Study Data Source Book, 1952-1978* (Ann Arbor; University of Michigan, 1979), 171. African American/white data are calculated using the percent different index (PDI): "too strong" minus "not too powerful."

possibility that America has to offer. At the same time, they don't want or deserve to be confined into an ever-narrowing area of opportunity themselves.[13]

Thus, the competition and resulting social conflict over an ever-tightening job market contributed to heightening tensions over the legacy of the Civil Rights Movement policies such as Title VII of the 1964 Act.[14]

The revolt of southern populist conservatives over civil rights and the economic conservatism of the early 1970s, together with the patriotic counter-reaction to the anti-Vietnam War movement, all made possible what Omi and Winant have called the convergence of the New Right with conservative populism to produce an anti-statist, "authoritarian populism."[15] Since Democrats had been in charge of running the state, the dissatisfaction with the course of the nation came to be lodged at the presidential level of government. Public opinion between 1964 and 1978, for example, exhibited a clear shift in direction toward a negative view of the power of the federal government as Table 2 will show. Table 2 shows historical differences which suggest government has become too strong and that, while African Americans agree with this somewhat, this concept is more strongly held by whites. One source of this alienation is the issue of busing. In fact, one New Right spokesman says: "nothing has contributed more to white populist disillusionment than the breathtaking hypocrisy and condescending arrogance shown by the establishment over the race issue." Citing the activities of some liberal politicians on the issue of busing as a key to this attitude, he continues: "No wonder vast numbers of white working-class Americans have come to believe that the federal government holds them and their children in something approaching contempt."[16] This attitude is supported by the data which show diminishing support for busing in both communities. These data show a significant drop in popular support for busing and a striking decline in support for government efforts to ensure school integration (from 52% in 1962 to 27% in 1978).[17]

Thus, there is some empirical support for the proposition that, in the critical period since the Civil Rights Movement, the white population grew increasingly restive over the various solutions utilized to bring about equality among the races. The goal was to reacquire national political authority in an effort to use government as the instrument for directing basic changes in critical sectors of the society.

THE WHITE CONSERVATIVE POPULIST POLITICAL INSURGENCY

The first substantial white reaction to the attention given by the Democrats to African Americans began in the period 1944–1948, when African Americans became nominal partners in the party coalition. The Supreme Court overturned the white primary in 1944 and the resulting increase in the voting power of African Americans caused the Democrats, in 1948 at their national convention, to adopt platform planks favoring civil rights and fair employment practices. At this signal of the changing balance of attention, Senator Strom Thurmond (D-SC) bolted the Democratic Party and ran for president on the Dixiecrat Party ticket.

This largely symbolic protest marked the important defection of a significant portion of the white South from the party: since then, the white South has given the majority of its vote to only one Democratic presidential candidate, Lyndon Johnson. The Johnson landslide in 1964 buried Senator Barry Goldwater, whose highly ideological campaign, perhaps, signaled the emergence of the radical Right in an attempt to define a conservative reaction to the essential direction of the country. As one writer has noted, however, even polls in 1964 were showing high levels of voter support for such issues as prayer in schools, claims of governmental laxity in national security, trimming the federal government, welfare and relief programs having a demoralizing effect on beneficiaries, and that federal right-to-work laws should be enacted. Also, in the wake of Goldwater's loss, fair housing laws that had recently been passed were repealed in the state of California and in cities such as Akron, Ohio.[18] In part, this was testimony to the growing ideological appeal of Goldwater conservatism, major strains of which were directed against African Americans and other beneficiaries of federal government intervention.

From the description of the Goldwater/Johnson election, it is clear that there was the slow development of a political coalition, both in the North and South, largely among whites with vested interests in at least restoring the *status quo ante* the Civil Rights Movement. Some wanted to eliminate the entire thrust of Democratic Party public policy beginning with the New Deal; however, a much more powerful stimulus would be needed. As is now well known, the first major African American rebellion occurred in Birmingham, Alabama, in 1964 as an outgrowth of the nonviolent civil rights activity of the Southern Christian Leadership Conference. But this movement which had been taken into the depths of the old Confederacy—provoking Governor George Wallace to stand in the schoolhouse door to prevent Autherine Lucy from desegregating the University of Alabama, and to declare "Segregation today, segregation tomorrow and segregation forever"—caused an even greater backlash by whites against the federal government.

The quest for state power by the New Right and conservative populist South was still unable to coalesce by 1968, when George Wallace arrived on the scene to lead the American Independence Party (AIP) in its own strategy of launching a presidential candidacy that would impact upon the Democratic Party and give the election to Richard Nixon. Speaking in the language of southerners and blue-collar northern whites, he propounded the anti-statist and coded-racist doctrine that the source of their problems were northern federal government bureaucrats and "pointy-headed liberals." Although he did surprisingly well in the South, attracting 30 percent of the vote and 13.5 percent in all regions, it was a margin which apparently helped to benefit Richard Nixon. Thus, while Nixon won a narrow victory in 1968 (43.4% to 42.7%), by 1972 his landslide signaled the fusion of the cross-over Wallace white constituency, together with a more conservative group of northern white, middle-class, Republican voters. For, whereas in 1968 the Republicans gained 43.4 percent and the AIP had 13.5 percent, in 1972 the Republican Party landslide vote was 60.7 percent of the electorate, or the combined vote of the two parties.

Between 1968 and 1972, the radical faction made overtures to the Republican Party coalition, but was not strong enough to determine its course. In fact, Nixon attempted to appeal to this constituency without yielding to its political influence. Thus, he began dismantling the funding for Johnson's "War on Poverty" (which had only been instituted three years earlier) and other apsects of the Great Society program. At the same time, he instituted a liberal Republican version of African American economic opportunity in the concept of "set-asides" for minority business.[19] It should be noted that in this period an African American legislator, Edward Brooke, was in the U.S. Senate, and a phalanx of moderate Republicans who shared most of the mainstream African American agenda had been appointed to key posts in the Nixon Administration. This group exercised a slight moderating influence on the racial policies of the Nixon era.

The radical white element joined the conservative Republican coalition in 1972, but it would not gain ascendency within the Republican party until the Reagan election of 1980. It then achieved state power and the ability to go far beyond the Nixon mandate into a serious struggle to eliminate the legislative basis for the status of newly ascendant groups, such as African Americans, and to restore the values of the social structure which made whites able to exercise hegemonic power. Within this coalition, the southern white element has become important as the swing vote, moderating the presidential electoral fortunes of the Republican and Democratic party candidates. As we have seen, it has been largely reponsible for initiating the return to power of the Republican Party, and, provided that African Americans remain in the Democratic column, it could elect a Democrat president as well. This position as a swing vote has set up competition for white southern votes and also influenced public policy in their direction to some extent as well.

THE SURGE OF POPULIST WHITE NATIONALISM

In the studies of revolutionary social processes by Crane Brinton, he refers to a stage in the process as "reign of terror" by the radicals who carry the torch of their particular conception of change, and who light fires to consume the existing icons of social convention maintained by their enemies.[20] There was such a reign of terror which has accompanied the "Reagan Revolution," the initial period of which was the late 1970s and early 1980s, a phenomenon which has extended to the present

Robert Hoy cites a 1975 Gallup Poll showing that, by 1975, the extent of the alienation of the white working class had reached such proportions that "roughly one-third of white Americans feel that violence against the federal government will eventually prove necessary to save 'our true American way of life,' " and that "these people, who love America because they are America" feel "betrayed by a system they see as growing more alien."[21] Then in 1976, Professor Donald Warren identified Middle American Radicals (MARs) as constituting 31 percent of the white American population.[22] In agreement with George Wallace, MARs identified the government, the president, radicals, and big business as enemies of the traditional American values. This group exercised some influence on the racial policies of the Nixon era, though not as much as they would under Reagan.

Intellectual justification proceeded to fuel this movement as several other works of consequence emerged in 1975, such as Robert Whitaker's *A Plague on Both Your Houses*, (Robert B. Luce, 1975) and William Rusher's *The Making of the New Majority Party* (Green Hill, 1975). The concepts these authors espoused helped to legitimize the growth of white populist conservatism. For example, the Populist Forum worked to turn a dispute launched by Concerned Citizens of Kanawha County, West Virginia, over textbooks into a march on Washington which drew five thousand people. This group was later augmented by such anti-busing organizations as Boston's Restore Our Alienated Rights (ROAR) and Union Labor Against Busing (ULAB) in Louisville, Kentucky, which organized 15 thousand people into a similar march.[23] The movement began to build at the grass roots, and the mood of alienation which it embodied often stimulated acts of physical violence against African Americans, minorities, and religious groups.

The Resurgence of the Klan

In addition to these populist stirrings, the orthodox white nationalist came to life in semi-rehabilitated form, as some officials of the Ku Klux Klan began to shed their white robes for three-piece suits to run for election. An example was Tom Metzger, grand dragon of the California Klan, who won the 1980 Democratic Congressional primary, with 13 percent of the vote, however, in a heavily Republican district. Also, a self-described Nazi won 43 percent of the vote in the Republican primary for lieutenant governor of North Carolina, having been defeated by Beverly Lake, who later lost to the popular Jim Hunt in a heavily Democratic state. In addition, "Neo-Nazi" Gerald Carlson actually won the 15th Congressional District primary of Michigan, although voters were not completely aware of his affiliation. When Carlson ran again in the 4th District—which differed from the 15th only in that it contained fewer white-collar and foreign residents—and declared his Nazi affiliation, he only attracted

2 percent of the vote.[24] These voters in themselves, including the Lyndon Larouche associates who won elections for state offices in the 1986 Illinois Democratic Party primary, have exposed the vulnerabilities of the electorate to an increasingly impersonal electoral system. They also may be indicative of the conservative ideological sentiment of many voters.

In any case, outbreaks of violence by the old Klan abated somewhat in the early 1970s, then rose again in the mid-to-late 1970s. Official Justice Department figures show, for example, that cases involving the Klan substantially increased in this period, as we shall see below. As is customary of political movements, this period of the late 1970s was marked by the rapid growth and reorganization of highly ideological, leading-edge, orthodox, white, nationalist groups such as the White Patriot Party of North Carolina, the Posse Comitatus, and the Aryan Nations Church, which was started in the late 1970s to "eliminate the members of the Jewish faith and Black race from society."[25] Linkages were found to exist among the KKK and the various neo-Nazi groups at the World Aryan Congress in July of 1986 involving such groups as The Order, the National States' Rights Party, the White Patriot Party, the Aryan Student Union, etc. This fact suggests their consolidation in an earlier period.[26] This grouping is all the more serious since its tactics apparently involve the use of criminal methods (such as bank robberies, break-ins at U.S. military bases and other weapons storage areas) in order to obtain large amounts of cash and weapons with which to train members for the violent overthrow of the United States and establishment of a white nation.[27]

As one writer said, in 1975 the Klan

> began popping up like crabgrass: throwing its hood into the vice presidential race; infiltrating the Marine Corps; protesting busing in Boston and Louisville; joining textbook fights in Charleston, West Virginia; creating a scandal in New York state prison system; prompting the Illinois legislature to conduct a major investigation; burning crosses from California to Maryland; going to court to sue and be sued; and appearing on national talk shows.[28]

Nevertheless, these orthodox white nationalists have been under attack by the state, and even though they represent a minor threat to it, they constitute a major problem for minority groups. Thus, individuals such as Tom Metzger have been charged with involvement in cross burnings in California, others have been indicted or jailed. And in February 1987, a federal court in Mobile awarded a $7 million judgment against the United Klans of America in a 1981 lynching of Michael Donald, a 19-year-old African American youth.[29]

In addition, just as Klan activity was but the tip of the iceberg which uncovered white nationalist sentiments in Canada, Klan activity in the United States was growing throughout the nation, as witnessed by what was occurring on college campuses. African American students at Harvard in 1980 were subject to the appearance of racist graffiti in a pattern which its Dean of Students, Archie C. Epps III, condemned as

TABLE 3
Racially Motivated Violence in Montgomery County,
Maryland (1981-1983)

Racial Group	1981	1982	1983
Jews	38	95	48
African Americans	34	56	53
Total	72	151	101

Source: Montgomery County Human Relations Commission, "Hate/Violence Incidents," Fact Sheet (Montgomery County, MD: Montgomery County Human Relations Commission, 13 Jan. 1987).

"outrageous" and suggested that it appeared to be part of a national trend. Reports of similar incidents seemed to confirm his view, as cross burnings occurred at Purdue University and Williams College in 1981, and anonymous threats and racial slurs were aimed at African American students at Wesleyan University, Cornell University, and others.[30]

Small wonder that, by 1986, university officials and civil rights leaders would become worried by the widespread pattern of incidents, such as fistfights between African American and white students at the University of Massachusetts after a World Series game; threats against African Americans by a group of Aryan collegiates at the University of Texas; cross burnings in front of an African American sorority house at the University of Alabama (Tuscaloosa); harassment of African American women by white men at Mount Holyoke College and the University of Massachusetts; harassment of an African American student at the Citadel military academy in Charleston, South Carolina; and racial tension over South Africa and other issues at Brown University, Dartmouth, the University of Pennsylvania, and many others.[31]

Diffusion of Racist Violence

In fact, the Ku Klux Klan has been the most visible manifestation of a trend toward racial harassment and violence which has had wide participation by other whites. For example. statistics from the Montgomery County, Maryland, Human Relations Division show that, whereas there were only 13 reported incidents of "Hate/Violence" in the county in 1979 directed against all groups, by 1980 there were 25, a 100 percent increase. Most striking is the fact that incidents against Jews and African Americans continued to increase markedly over the following three years. For Jews, violent incidents increased from 38 in 1981, to 95 the next year. This leveled off to 48 in 1983. Hate/violence directed at African Americans increased from 34 incidents in 1981 to 56 in 1982, and totalled 53 in 1983.[32] (See Table 3.)

The dramatic rise of incidents in Motgomery County from a total of 13 in 1979 to 185 (for all groups) by 1982—stabilizing after 1983—is not an anomalous figure from

TABLE 4
Racial/Ethnic Confrontation Alerts, 1977–1982

	1977	1978	1979	1980	1981	1982
All cases	953	1,353	1,317	1,404	1,548	1,996
% increase	30%	-2%	7%	10%	29%	
Klan cases	NA	NA	44	96	329	(462)
Deadly force	NA	382	108	206	260	289

Source: Community Relations Service. Annual Report (Washington, DC: U.S. Department of Justice, 1979, 1980, 1985, 1986). Table demonstrates the steady increase in racial/ethnic confrontations involving all groups.

a national standpoint, as data in the report referred to above included statistics from the Anti-Defamation League which indicate that anti-Semitic incidents nationwide showed a 200 percent increase between 1979 and 1980 to 377 incidents. Incidents for African Americans and Jews tend to have a similar pattern of increase, although the rate is higher in affluent Montgomery County for the Jewish population, because it is double that of the African American population. Similar increases are also occurring in other cities as recent data from New York City's Human Rights Commission show that, in 1984, there were 245 racial assaults; 298 in 1985; and 253 in 1986, 76 of these occurring after the incident at Howard Beach.[33]

There is a similar pattern discovered in data from the state of California, as the Task Force on Racial, Ethnic and Religious Violence, established by Governor Edmund G. Brown, Jr., issued its report in 1982, shortly before he left office. These data show generally an 80 percent increase in such cases in 1980 over the 1979 level, and a 42 percent increase in 1981 over 1980 cases, with the distribution of such increases generally reflected in the occurrence of a similar pattern in all five cities cited in the California report. Because of the demography of the state of California, these cases reflect incidents affecting groups such as Hispanics, African Americans, and Asians. And while there is some manifestation of intergroup tension among them, the predominant number of incidents occurs between these groups and whites, with the substantial involvement of police and Klan-type groups.

With respect to national trends in racially motivated violence, Justice Department data show a 450 percent increase of incidents of racial violence attributed to the Klan between 1978 and 1979, and a 550 percent increase in the period 1978–1980. Considering the fact that, from all sources, incidents of racially motivated violence increased by 42 percent between 1985 and 1986 with a smaller percent attributed to Klan-type groups, this is an indication that the phenomenon was diffusing into the general population.[34] Table 4 shows racial/ethnic confrontation alerts between 1977 and 1982.

The large increases between 1977 and 1978 conform to the perspective of this article, that a white nationalist, populist attitude within neighborhoods was responsible for the generation of violence. This point is supported by the Justice Department's 1980 Report:

> A factor for much of the racial and ethnic hostility was the perception by many White Americans that minorities, mainly Blacks and Hispanics, were getting a better deal than anyone else, and that *attention and continued effort to bring them into the mainstream threatened their welfare.* Minorities, on the other hand, perceived a creeping indifference and decreasing emphasis on efforts to improve their plight, and cited as justification an increasing number of reverse discrimination suits and charges, and a marked resurgence in the activities of the Ku Klux Klan. [Emphasis added.][35]

There is other empirical evidence which supports this point of view in surveys taken in 1978 and 1981. In 1978, two years after major African American revolts abated that had destroyed parts of northern and midwestern cities, a replication of the 1968 Kerner Commission survey in those areas revealed that 10 percent fewer whites (1968, 39%; 1978, 49%) thought that African Americans were missing out on employment and promotions because of racial discrimination.[36] By 1981, the ABC/ *Washington Post* poll revealed that 65 percent of whites disagreed with the statement that African Americans were discriminated against in securing managerial jobs, and there was strong disagreement (71%) that African Americans should receive assistance from the government "that white people in similar circumstances don't get" because of past discrimination.[37]

Second, the figures for the increases in Klan activity which began to be recorded in 1979 showed increases by 1983 of 95 percent. However, as previously suggested, the phenomenon had begun to generalize and was no longer within the specific purview of the Klan and closely associated groups, as such incidents increased 39 percent over 1982. In any case, the 1983 Report all but suggests that the growth rate was difficult to control when it says: "The second priority, the containment and reduction of racial harassment acknowledges a growing segment of the Community Relations Service (CRS) caseload: the harassment, intimidation, and assault of minorities by the Ku Klux Klan, Nazi Party, and other groups."[38]

Police Use of Deadly Force

Finally, because of the often close relationship between the local police forces and fascist or Klan-type organizations and activities historically, especially in the South, police officers are often suspected to exercise deadly force against African Americans in a manner which highly suggests racial motivation.[39] Whereas, in the early 1980s, the growth of the General Community Service category constituted the majority of CRS cases, in the late 1970s, Adminstration of Justice (police-community relations conflict) cases were the greatest part of its workload. For example, the 1978 CRS Report says that complaints of deadly force against African Americans and Hispanics increased by 50 percent over the 1977 level.[40] The reports are not broken down by race. Nevertheless, figures from the Police Foundation for 1978 indicate that 78 percent of those killed and 80 percent of those nonfatally shot by police were minorities (and most of these were African American).[41] By 1979, the law enforcement caseload was 40 percent of the total, and the growth in the cases of deadly force in particular inspired the statement that policemen had "one trigger finger for minorities and another for whites."[42] Such a sentiment was not without foundation, since the incidents of deadly force grew steadily in the early 1980s with the 1983 figure amounting to 413, or a striking 43 percent increase over the 1982 figure.[43] Such cases of police shootings further inflamed African Americans because prosecutions were rarely brought against the officers involved.

The only factors which appeared to restrain the growth of such *official*, racially motivated violence was not the criminal justice system itself, but the election of sensitive African American mayors who initiated new policies for the use of deadly force. For example, after the election of both Coleman Young of Detroit, in 1973, and Maynard Jackson in Atlanta, in 1975, there were significant reductions in the cases of police use of deadly force there.[44]

So numerous were the killings of African Americans from all sources in the late 1970s, especially in an atmosphere of a resurgence of Klan violence, that African American leaders contacted the Justice Department to complain of a possible national conspiracy.[45] During 1980, 11 African American children in Atlanta, Georgia were murdered, 8 African American men were killed in Buffalo, New York (amid Klan cross burnings), and others were killed by the police, causing African American leaders such as Reverend Herbert Daughtry, head of the Natinal Black United Front, to hold "National Hearings on Racist Violence against Blacks," in February of 1981.[46] In general, it can be concluded that African Americans were suffering harassment, injury, and deaths from a number of sources, both official and nonofficial, in the period of the late 1970s and early 1980s at an increasing rate. The pattern seems to suggest that this fact was related to the increasingly bellicose arrival of the white populist conservative movement which was spearheaded by Klan-Nazi grouping, legitimized to some extent by neoconservative intellectuals and diffused into the general population. The real legitimacy would come when the movement seized state power, as is argued below, through its role in facilitating the election of Ronald Reagan.

LEGITIMIZING WHITE NATIONALISM

Given the strong support for the thesis that the rise of white nationalist populism occurred in the mid-1970s and grew stronger by the end of the five-year period, there is also support for the notion that this was a movement which had two important effects. The first effect is that African Americans began to respond to the growing evidence of racism in their daily lives by increasing the volume of offical complaints. The second was that Ronald Reagan was elected president.

African American Complaints

What may be said to have produced the first effect was the juxtaposition of two movements within the body politic. The militant "Black nationalist" phase of the Black Liberation Movement was just winding down in the mid-1970s, amid the signs that it was to have some salutary effect. For example, a significant African American middle class was being produced through progress in education and employment, and this led in turn to other aspects of social mobility such as suburbanization. At the same time, these gains were under attack by the surging white nationalist movement which had not yet attained state power. The conflict led African Americans to be sensitive to the "stiffening" social environment which began, as we have seen from the polls above, to raise questions about both the sufficiency and method of African American progress.[47]

Within the Title VII category of cases handled by the Equal Employment Opportunity Commission (EEOC), there are such subcategories as race, sex, color, religion, and national origin. Here one observes the categories which heavily involve African Americans charging discrimination based on race and color. The combined data for these two subcategories show that there was a similar increase in such new complaints in the years between 1978 and 1983, with sharp upsurges in the critical 1979–1980 period at the height of the white populist movement and the 1982–1983 period of the Reagan recession. The "Total" figures are essentially evidence of the total number of all Title VII complaints, including the annual backlog, while the "New" figures are annual increases. In general, these complaints of employment discrimination have continued to grow as total Title VII charges to EEOC and the state and localities together were 122 thousand in fiscal year (FY) 1986, a 35 percent increase from the 79,868 the agency received in FY 1980.[48] (See Table 5.)

Added evidence that the neighborhoods in America are becoming a racial battleground is the fact that whites are increasing their resistance to African American movement into certain metropolitan area neighborhoods. It is well known that attendant to nationalist sentiments is a certain feature of "territoriality" wherein the group which believes that it "owns" or desires a piece of land will attempt to defend it from "outsiders," and in some cases attempt to expand their territorial base. Of course, the question of land ownership within a highly urbanized country such as the United States often bears an ambiguous relationship to ethnic or racial residential boundaries, since the economics of urban land distributes ownership to many outside of the neighborhood. Still, neighborhood turf is a "real" nationalist resource to those who live in certain areas, especially where there is an established ethnic or racial residential base involved over a long period of time which may be perceived to be threatened by "outsiders" moving in, and especially if the "outsider" is of a different race.

The 1980 census figures revealed the beginnings of a significant pattern of suburbanization, especially in such major metropolitan areas as Washington, Philadephia,

TABLE 5
Total EEOC State and Local Charges if Race and
Color Discrimination in Employment

	1977	1978	1979	1980	1981	1982	1983
New	47,587	38,236	39,724	45,759	45,367	42,686	50,102
Total	86,029	54,800	55,518	74,141	78,441	72,358	85,384

Source: Compiled from U.S. Equal Employment Opportunity Commission. *Annual Reports* (Washington, DC: Government Printing Office, 1977-1983). "New": new charges by state geographical location; "Total": national total actionable charges.

Boston, Chicago, New York, and Cleveland. Although the African American suburban population only constitutes 6 percent of the entire African American metropolitan residence nationally, this population grew by 43 percent between 1970 and 1980.[49]

Perhaps, then, the small size of this population suggests why it is less well known that African Americans are increasingly facing violence in attempting to move into such neighborhoods. A study by the Southern Poverty Law Center indicates, for example, that between 1985 and 1986, at least 45 such incidents of violence against African Americans were related to "move-in" situations. Some of the more publicized incidents included one in southwest Philadelphia in November of 1985, when a African American couple and an interracial couple simultaneously moved into the Elmwood neighborhood. A hostile mob of 400 whites demonstrated in front of their homes, throwing bricks and bottles and shouting racial slurs in a scene which was repeated in March of 1986, in front of the home of an Asian family.[50] In addition, data from the Civil Rights Division of the U.S. Housing and Urban Affairs Department indicate that general complaints of housing discrimination have continued to rise in the period of the Reagan Administration. Again, this may help to account for the diffusion factor, as the general atmosphere continued to change in a direction which provided greater tendency for such incidents to occur.

Taking Power

The second factor in response to the white nationalist movement was that it provided a solidity to the political coalition inside the Republican Party that made it possible for Ronald Reagan to seize control of its conservative wing and win the party presidential nomination. It should be recalled that, when Reagan first ran for president in 1976, he lost the Republican nomination to Gerald Ford, a sign that the movement had not yet achieved dominance within the party. By 1980, however, Reagan had so successfully played upon the theme of Democratic Party "appeasement" in "losing the Panama Canal" to "a tinhorn dictator," that Jimmy Carter's Iran hostage crisis played right into his hands. This theme, together with the rising crescendo of attacks by the neoconservative side of the coalition on civil rights-coded issues such as affirmative action and busing, and the "vulnerability" of the United States to Soviet military blackmail due to the erosion in defensive capability, all made him electable.[51]

Thus, it is a fact that the white nationalist movement was cresting in the late 1970s and that Reagan was able to find the right symbols to unlock its electoral power which accounted for his election, not—as commonly suggested—that the charisma of Reagan alone was responsible. This powerful white nationalist movement did what other successful movements have done, according to Professors Omi and Winant:

> Racial movements, built on the terrain of civil society, necessarily confront the state as they begin to upset the unstable equilibrium of the racial order. Once an oppositional racial ideology has been articulated, it becomes possible to demand reform of state racial policies and institutions.[52]

They go on to suggest that "the far right attempts to develop a new white identity, to reassert the very meaning of whiteness, challenges of the 1960s."[53] Thus, in posing the question of what the residual rights of white people were in reaction to the demands for African American rights, the ideology of "white rights" developed. The strategy of achieving full fruition of white rights, however, required the advancement of racial politics which would overturn not just the "gains" of the 1960s for African Americans, but the racial frame of reference as well. Hence, it was to rearticulate the very notion of racial inequality in a way which did not continue to threaten white interests.

Inasmuch as the white populist movement did not have the proper voice for this task of rearticulating race, it was left to the conservative and neoconservative intellectuals. And without a full discussion of them here, from Kevin Phillip's *The Emerging Republic Majority* to George Gilder's *Wealth and Poverty*, there emerged an economic policy with a sociopolitical rationale which made possible an attack on "Big Government" as the catch-all synonym for their perceived racial problems, the moral decay of society, and the needs of the defense establishment. In short, a new ideology of "Americanism" developed which made whiteness and its political interests the core definition, such that the patriotic symbols which suggested that "America is back" has a loaded meaning that relates to both foreign and domestic objectives of the new white political culture.

Between 1979 and 1982, a series of works were published proposing "limits" on the ability of government to participate broadly in the development of public goods for the amelioration of social conditions, which anticipated the coming of the Reagan reign. One such work was *Doing Good: The Limits of Benevolence*, by Willard Gaylin, Ira Glasser, Steven Marcus, and David Rothman, wherein the authors leveled a withering attack on the liberal society. They suggest that it had become a *parent* in its paternalistic approach to government's attempt to provide social services for the disadvantaged; and they further argue that such social engineering ignored the often-negative consequences of government intervention.[54] Tellingly, Rothman viewed the service-providing liberals as contributing to government's "power to expand itself and establish *dominion* over people's lives." (Emphasis added.)[55]

The defection of former liberals such as Irving Kristol, Seymour Martin Lipset, Norman Podhoretz, Carl Gershman, Midge Decter, Sidney Hook, and others to the role of neoconservative apologists for the new white political culture lent a certain intellectual respectability to the movement. Indeed, while rejecting the notion that neoconservatism was either a movement or that it was racist in character, Kristol acknowledged that the sources which shaped it were "the campus revolts of the 1960s, the rise of the counterculture, the Great Society programs which many of us felt were misconceived, the reform of the Democratic Party and the takeover by the McGovernite wing, [and] the immense growth of Government regulation."[56] Is it purely accidental that Kristol objects to these enumerated political, economic, and social forces and that they were also instrumental in helping to provide a platform for African American advancement? Such an accident is doubtful, since many of these individuals are also leading Jewish intellectuals and, in 1981, the American Jewish Congress appeared to have joined the conservative movement by calling upon president-elect Ronald Reagan to abolish "'abuses' in 'race-conscious' federal affirmative action programs."[57] In effect, did Kristol, like others perhaps, perceive a "zero-sum" situation to exist with respect to the distribution of attention between Jewish groups and African Americans? In any case, the emerging coherence and impact of this intellectual force in the mid-1970s helps to explain why public policy under Jimmy Carter did not "feel" like the traditional policies of a Democratic president to African Americans.

In fact, African Americans were acutely aware that the first significant cuts in the social side of the national budget were made in the last years of the Carter Administration. Indeed, so many other manifestations confirmed the conservative nature of Carter's administration that one local leader, interviewed in a special feature of the *New York Times* on the African American mood, summed it up by observing what others had been saying.

> Today the coalitions that were so successful in the 1960s are falling apart, partly because civil rights has moved off the national agenda. Vernon Jordan correctly described the new negativism: Because of the illusion of black progress, white people no longer feel that programs should be directly targeted toward black people."[58]

Nevertheless, in the transition from Carter to Reagan social policies would experience an even more abrupt and radical downward slide in profile and substance as the conservative movement assumed power.

The victory of the radical Republicans in 1980 meant that they could implement a broad agenda of concerns in line with their ideology, if one takes seriously the formulation of mandates issued forth from the Heritage Foundation and other far-right think tanks. Among the subjects for urgent attention was a broad-scale attack upon the political and economic foundations of the civil rights revolution of the 1960s. Why? There were many reasons given which ranged from the philosophical concern with the reconstruction of individual rights over corporate—or group—rights, and analyses which purported to show that the social programs which supposedly assisted the disadvantaged in a wide range of areas were dysfunctional. As suggested, none of these rationales were a persuasive pretext for whites to restore what they consider to be the balance of hegemony in the national interests, both domestic and foreign. After the long travail of the white nationalist movement from its populist beginnings to Ronald Reagan's election in 1980, it had arrived at a place where it could utilize the instruments of state power for its interests.

In order to accmplish this, they had to undermine important elements of what they perceived to be the policy foundation of the ascendent minorities and elevate the interests of the conservative movement. This would become the hidden pretext for the influential Heritage Foundation Report, *Agenda for Progress*, issued at the beginning of Reagan's first term, which argued:

> The federal budget, the keystone of national economic policy, is a bastion of immutability in a time of flux and inquiry. No longer a reflection of national goals, the inexorable forces of federal spending have become an obstacle to necessary and desired policy changes. The size and ambition of the federal establishment have become, in many ways, an impediment to the successful fulfillment of the basic obligation of a national government.[59]

The Report went on to recommend in the areas of employment, for example, that temporary public jobs should be eliminated in lieu of a tax cut; comprehensive employment and training programs (CETA) should be "scaled down" and targeted; the minimum wage for youth should be eliminated; that federal provision of training and work experience to the unemployed should be "scaled down"; and the employment and training aspects of the Work Incentive Program should be eliminated.[60]

In general, the philosophy of social service involvement by the federal government which was projected in the report harkened back at least to the early 1960s, when the states and private philanthropy provided as much as 60 percent of the funding for social welfare programs. No credence appeared to be given to the point of view that one reason for the "explosion" in federal funding after the 1967 Aid to Families with Dependent Children (AFDC) amendments was that the states and private philanthropy were not, could not, and would not meet the degree of need for such services, a fact clearly communicated by the exploding cities at the hands of African American protesters.

The Reagan Administration proceeded to follow the advice of the emergent conservative policy establishment in a number of the areas suggested above. Reagan, therefore, rightly felt that he had a mandate from whites to pursue a policy of rearticulating race through the coded strategy of the budget, the Justice Department and other civil rights agencies, and by the attempted isolation of African American leadership. By such actions, Reagan went a long way toward legitimizing what Omi and Winant have considered to be the ultimate objective of authoritarian populism.

Measures under Reagan to roll back legislated checks on white hegemony have prejudiced some of the most fundamental civil rights initiatives. These include the reinstatement of tax exemptions to segregated educational institutions, as in the case of the Bob Jones Academy in 1981–1982. The promotion of a strategy known as "New Federalism" seeks to remove from national responsibility some 45 social programs to the jurisdiction of states. This is in light of the demonstrable fact that, when the balance of power between the states and the federal government has shifted in favor of the former, African Americans have historically suffered.[61] In addition, Reagan's procrastinating on the renewal of the Voting Rights Act also sought to absolve certain southern states of special compliance with the Act, an area of the country noted as a traditional stronghold of conservative, white hegemony. Other noteworthy efforts include the debilitation of the U.S. Civil Rights Commission, contributing to the restoration in the Justice Department of a pro-white, male agenda with attempts, by 1985, to reverse some 50 affirmative action decisions taken by lower courts.[62] Indeed the administration's affirmative action programs were so flawed that Reagan's chief implementor of this strategy, Assistant Secretary for Civil Rights Bradford Reynolds, was rejected for promotion by the Senate in 1985.

The much-discussed question of whether or not, in this modern era and considering the past upheavals attendant to the issue of racism and racial equality, there could arrive in the White House a president who is racist, is historically curious and painful. The question of the president's personal racism is straightforward, if one views the conservative political movement as a manifestation of Reagan's *personal* leadership. However, it is a more difficult question—but I would argue far more important—that the Reagan phenomenon should be more correctly understood as a direct by-product of the conservative movement of white populist nationalism. In this sense, it matters less that the president is personally racist than that he conceives of his political mandate as having racial implications and proceeds to carry them into his policy program through institutions which affect the quality of life for millions of Americans. It may be possible to change the course of policy if the problem is merely personal, but it is extremely difficult to do so where there is a movement which undergirds a political consensus binding individuals of various racial, religious, and political persuasions to a common point of view in a given historical moment.

CONCLUSION

It is, of course, no secret that older nationalist movements have undergone transformations whereby nationalism turns into fascism in the desperate pursuit of rearticulating those aspects of society perceived to stand in the way of the reassumption of power by one disparate group or another. There should be little illusion that, within the current white nationalist movement, there are, indeed, possibilities for the achievement of what Bertram Gross has called "Friendly Fascism"—a nameless, faceless brand of racial (and class) subjugation that would be administered through the major institutions of society.[63] Once the framework has been set, as it appears to be, the 1984 elections having reflected the existence of a racially polarized, political consensus as expressed in one of the largest electoral landslides in history, all that is left is for the natural consequence of institutional racism to work its will in the many fields of society.

This is indeed a formidable problem. Even in the 1960s when there was the greatest admission that America was a racist society, there was an equal optimism that racism could be eliminated through a process that the nation was willing to undergo. This version of institutional racism might be regarded as a benign form, where (it was possible to make the case) racism is insinuated into institutional processes. Then there is the genuine search to root it out which takes into consideration the reprocessing of individual and group behavior and, thus, institutional structures and functions. However, now there is at least the pretense of unconsciousness about racism's presence and effects.

The Kerner Commission Report of 1968, which was written in the throes of an African American violent revolt, set out a vision of American society which could be achieved through the amelioration of the social ills of African Americans. By over-turning this vision—and the possibilities of its achievement—what vision of the social order is being put in its place, and (more important) if it is not viewed by a major segment of the population as just, how will social harmony be maintained? The answers to these questions and others should take us considerably beyond the racial competition of the moment to consider where the current course is heading. This is a task which not only raises the question of responsibility, but calls for leadership of the first order to head off another clear and present danger of social conflict.

The stakes for the elimination of white racism are as urgent as they have ever been, yet society appears to be going in the other direction. When Knowles and Pruitt wrote about "Institutional Racism," they were writing at the time when "there is much less articulation of a diehard defense of racism as a system by business and political leadership."[64] In the late 1960s they were able to observe that

> the mechanisms for subjugating black people have become interlaced with the complex of mechanisms by which power is exercised over both white and black. A root and branch abolition of racism, therefore, threatens the power order as we now know it. This is the fundamental political dynamic behind the institutional maintenance of racism.[65]

However, what is there to be said for an era when institutions are busily implement-ting racist policies knowingly and with rationalizations? What is to be done when students at one of the finest universities throw watermelon at the walls of African American dormitory rooms; when young whites burn pictures of Martin Luther King, Jr., the night before his national holiday celebration, presumably following the exam-ple set by the governor of Arizona who rescinded the holiday altogether; when white teachers from Queens "bristle" at an ameliorative strategy, such as a required course in racism? What is being destroyed now is not only the lives of some African Amer-icans, but the hope that progressive change in the society is possible. It has formerly been this hope which has prevented the descent into an unavoidable spiral of despair which leads in the direction of chaos rather than community.

NOTES

1. Murray Edelmann, *Politics as Symbolic Action* (Chicago: Markham, 1971).
2. "Racism on the Rise," *Time*, 2 Feb. 1982, 18–21. A *Time* poll indicates, in the critical areas of housing, education, and employment, the only area in which whites do not feel overwhelmingly that African Americans have the same opportunity is housing, and here the respondents are about equally divided. These differences may constitute the structural factors in the attitudes which help to maintain white nationalist ideology.
3. Robert Huttenback, *Racism and Empire* (Ithaca, NY: Cornell University Press, 1976): 15.
4. Josiah Strong, *Our Country: Its Possible Future and Its Present Crisis* (New York, 1985); cited in Dorothea R. Muller, "Josiah Strong and American Nationalism: A Re-evaluation," *The Journal of American History* 53 (3) (Dec. 1966), 487.
5. Mark Hagopian, *The Phenomenon of Revolution* (New York: Dodd, Mead and Company, 1974), 169.
6. David Danzig, "Conservatism after Goldwater," *Commentary*, Commentary Report, Mar. 1965: 6.
7. Ibid., 8.
8. Clyde Wilson, "Citizens or Subjects," in *The New Right Papers*, ed. Robert Whitaker (New York: St. Martins, 1982).
9. Everett Cataldo, Richard Johnson, and Lyman Kellstedt, "Political Attitudes of Urban Blacks and Whites: Some Implications for Policy-Makers," in *Black Conflict with White America*, ed. Jack Van Der Silk (Columbus, OH: Charles Merrill and Company, 1970), 49–50.
10. Survey Research Center, Institute for Social Research, *National Election Study Data Source Book, 1952–1978* (hereafter referred to as National Election Study) (Ann Arbor: University of Michgan, 1978).
11. George Gilder, *Wealth and Poverty* (New York: Basic Books, 1981), 19.
12. *Steel Workers v. Weber*, Craft Training Program, 443 U.S. 193 (1981).
13. Paul Laxalt, "Foreign Policy: Facing Reality in the 80s," in *A Changing America: Conservatives View the 80s from the U.S. Senate*, ed. Paul Laxalt and William Richardson (Southbend, IN: Regnery/Gateway, 1980), 63.
14. Until the passage of Title VII of the 1964 Civil Rights Act, African Americans had no effective legal mechanism for confronting discrimination practiced in employment, since most disputes were handled either by labor unions or federal agencies whose only power was to mediate disputes. Article VII established the Equal Employment Opportunity Commission (EEOC), an executive agency with the authority to receive, file, and investigate complaints of employment discrimination. Title VII barred discrimination by private employers or unions with more than 25 workers or members if the employers or unions "fail or refuse to hire or to discharge any individual, or otherwise to discriminate against any individual with respect to his compensation, terms, conditions, or privileges of employment, because of such individual's race, color, religion, sex or national origin." (P.L. 88–352, 88th Congress, H.R. 7152 (2 July 1964); U.S. Senate at Large, 241).
15. Michael Omi and Howard Winant, *Racial Formation in the United States* (New York: Routledge and Kegan Paul, 1986), 120.
16. Robert Hoy, "Lid on a Boiling Pot," in *The New Right Papers*, ed. Whitaker, 99.
17. Survey Research Center, *National Election Study*, 181, 277.
18. Danzig, "Conservatism."
19. Ronald Walters, "Black Survival and Nixon's Second Term," in *The Black Experience in American Politics*, ed. Charles Hamilton (New York: G.P. Putnam/Capricorn Books, 1973), 342–43.
20. Crane Brinton, *Anatomy of Revolution* (Englewood Cliffs, NJ: Prentice Hall, 1952), 135–70.
21. Hoy, "Lid on a Boiling Pot," 91.
22. Donald Warren, *The Radical Center* (Notre Dame, IN: Notre Dame University Press, 1976).
23. Hoy, "Lid on a Boiling Pot," 91.
24. Michael Barone and Grant Ijifusa, *The Almanac of American Politics 1982* (Washington, DC: Barone and Company, 1981).
25. *Washington Post*, 18 Dec. 1984, sec. A, 3.
26. Center for Democratic Renewal, *The Monitor* 5 (Dec. 1986), (Atlanta: Center for Democratic Renewal, 1988).
27. *New York Times*, 9 Jan. 1987, sec. D, 16.
28. Patsy Sims, *Washington Post Magazine*, 22 Jan. 1978, 1. Sims goes on to say that what put the Klan on the front pages of national newspapers and on prime-time television was its sponsorship of a rash of cross burnings in the Maryland suburbs of Washington, D.C. Apparently, some of these incidents were connected to the activities of William Mark Aitcheson, a student at the University of Maryland who preached that the only way the country would revive its laws and the laws of God was through armed violence.
29. *New York Times*, 13 Feb. 1987, sec D, 19.
30. John Ross, "Rise of Racism on College Campuses," *The Challenger*, 4 Feb. 1981, 2.
31. Lena Williams, "Officials Voice Growing Concern over Racial Incidents on U.S. Campuses," *New York Times*, 15 Dec. 1986, sec. A, 18.
32. Montgomery County Human Relations Commission, Fact Sheet, "Hate/Violence Incidents," (Montgomery County, MD: Montgomery County Human Relations Commission, 1987).

33. Raoul Dennis, "Racism on the Rise," *Black Enterprise* 17 (9) (April 1987): 17.

34. Community Relations Service, *Annual Report* (Washington, DC: Department of Justice, 1979, 1980, 1985, 1986). It should be noted that this summary data represents all types of racial conflict involving several different varieties and groups. However within three broad categories into which the data is divided, most of the cases are usually concerned with "General Community Relations" problems, followed by "Administration of Justice" and "Education" (desegregation) cases. The racial distribution is also relatively consistent through these years, which shows that, in all areas, African Americans were involved in 50.6 percent of the cases; Hispanics, 32.5 percent; Native Americans, 7.4 percent; and Asians, 2.7 percent. (*Annual Report, 1980*, 3–4).

35. Community Relations Service, *Annuai Report 1980*, 3.

36. Survey Research Center, *National Election Study*; CBS/New York Times Poll, *New York Times*, 26 Feb. 1978, sec. A2.

37. *Washington Post*, 25 Mar. 1981, sec A2.

38. Community Relations Service, *Annual Report, 1983*, 6.

39. Sociologist Alphonso Pinkney says: "Police are often members of the John Birch Society, the Ku Klux Klan, the Minutemen, and other right-wing groups," (*The American Way of Violence* [New York: Random House, 1972], 152). See also a special issue on "Police Violence," *The Black Scholar* 12 (1) (Jan./Feb. 1981); especially an excellent article by Damu Smith, "The Upsurge of Police Repression: An Analysis," *The Black Scholar* 12 (1) (Jan./Feb. 1981), 35–57.

40. Community Relations Service, *Annual Report, 1978*, 1.

41. Thomas Johnson, "U.S. Agency Moves to Head Off Racial Conflict over Allegations of Police Misuse of Force," *New York Times*, 11 Aug. 1979, 1.

42. Community Relations Service, *Annual Report, 1979*, 4.

43. Community Relations Service, *Annual Report, 1983*, 7.

44. "To Shoot or Not to Shoot," *Time*, 18 Aug. 1980, 44.

45. Nathaniel Sheppard, Jr., "Perception Growing among Blacks That Violent Incidents Are Linked," *New York Times*, 30 Nov. 1980, 1.

46. *The Challenger*, 28 Jan. 1981, 1.

47. Some evidence of this is found in the data of complaints gathered by the EEOC on race and color discrimination in the period from 1976 to 1982. See Table 5.

48. "EEOC Archives Record Enforcement Activity in Fiscal Year 1986," *EEOC News*, 9 Feb. 1987.

49. Bureau of the Census, *We, the Black Americans*, (Washington, DC: Government Printing Office, 1986), 6.

50. Southern Poverty Law Center, "*Move-In*" *Violence: White Resistance to Neighborhood Integration in the 1980s. Special Report* (Montgomery, AL: SPLC,1987), 8.

51. Gary Wills, *Reagan's America: Innocents at Home* (New York: Doubleday, 1987), 334–37.

52. Omi and Winant, "Racial Formation," 86.

53. Ibid., 116–17.

54. Willard Gaylin et al., *Doing Good: The Limits of Benevolence* (New York: Pantheon, 1978), 107.

55. Ibid.

56. Bernard Weinraub, "Neo-Conservatives Today, They Explain All Their Yesterdays," *New York Times*, 28 Dec. 1980, sec. E5.

57. "Affirmative Action 'Abuses' Cited," *Washington Post*, 15 Jan. 1981, sec. A8.

58. "Robert Williams, Executive Director, Fort Wayne Indiana Urban League," *New York Times*, 6 July 1980, sec. E5.

59. The Heritage Foundation, *Agenda for Progress* (Washington: The Heritage Foundation, 1981), *vii*.

60. Ibid.

61. Ronald Walters, "Federalism, 'Civil Rights,' and Black Progress," *Black Law Journal* 8 (2) (Fall 1983), 220–34.

62. Center for Democratic Renewal, *The Monitor*, Dec. 1986.

63. Bertram Gross, *Friendly Fascism: The New Face of Power in America* (Englewood Cliffs, NJ: Prentice-Hall, 1969), 170.

64. Louis Knowles and Kenneth Prewitt, eds., *Institutional Racism in America* (Englewood Cliffs, NJ: Prentice-Hall, 1969), 170.

65. Ibid., 171.

ABOUT THE AUTHORS

OMOWALE AMULERU-MARSHALL, Ph.D., is Director, Cork Institute on Black Alcohol and Other Drug Abuse, and Assistant Professor, Community Health and Preventive Medicine, Morehouse School of Medicine, Atlanta, GA 30310-1495.

PAUL F. BITTING, Ph.D., is Assistant Professor, Department of Educational Leadership and Program Evaluation, College of Education and Psychology, North Carolina State University, Raleigh, NC 27695-7801.

DANIEL BRANTLEY, Ph.D., is Associate Professor, Department of Political Science, Alabama State University, Montgomery, AL 36101.

ROBERT D. BULLARD, Ph.D., is Associate Professor, Department of Sociology, University of California, Riverside, CA 92521-0419.

LYNN C. BURBRIDGE, Ph.D., is Associate Director, Center for Research on Women, Wellesley College, Wellesley, MA 02181.

DONNA Y. FORD, M.A., is Research and Teaching Assistant, Urban Educational Research Center, College of Education, Cleveland State University, Cleveland, OH 44115.

JEAN M. GRANGER, Ph.D., is Professor and Coordinator, Undergraduate Program, Department of Social Work, California State University, Huntington Beach, CA 92646.

J. JOHN HARRIS III, Ph.D., is Professor and Dean, College of Education, Cleveland State University, Cleveland, OH 44115.

WILLIAM B. HARVEY, Ph.D., is Associate Professor, Department of Educational Leadership and Program Evaluation, North Carolina State University, Raleigh, NC 27695-7801.

NORRIS M. HAYNES, Ph.D., is Assistant Professor and Director of Research for the School Development Program, Yale Child Study Center, Yale University, New Haven, CT 06510.

LENNEAL J. HENDERSON, JR., Ph.D., is Professor of Government and Public Administration, William Donald Schaefer Center for Public Policy, Henry C. Welcome Fellow, University of Baltimore, Baltimore, MD 21201.

WILLIE E. JOHNSON, Ph.D., is Associate Professor and Director of the MPA Program, Political Science Department, Savannah State College, Savannah, GA 31404.

DIONNE J. JONES, Ph.D., is Senior Research Associate, National Urban League Research Department, and Editor of *The Urban League Review*, 1111 14th Street, NW, Washington, DC 20005.

IVOR LENSWORTH LIVINGSTON, Ph.D., M.P.H., is Graduate Associate Professor, Department of Sociology/Anthropology, Howard University, Washington, DC 20059.

RONALD J. MARSHALL, M.A., is a doctoral student, Department of Sociology/ Anthropology, Howard University, Washington, DC 20059.

DIANNE M. PINDERHUGHES, Ph.D., is Associate Professor, Department of Political Science and Afro-American Studies and Research Program, and Acting Director, Afro-American Studies and Research Program, University of Illinois, Urbana, IL 61801.

TRACY L. ROBINSON, Ph.D., is Assistant Professor, Department of Counselor Education, College of Education and Psychology, North Carolina State University, Raleigh, NC 27695-7801.

EARL SMITH, Ph.D., is Chair of Comparative American Cultures, and Associate Professor of Sociology, Department of Comparative American Cultures, Washington State University, Pullman, WA 99164-4010.

JACQUELINE MARIE SMITH, Ph.D., is Assistant Professor, School of Social Work, Howard University, Washington, DC 20059.

RONALD WALTERS, Ph.D., is Professor, Political Science Department, Howard University, Washington, DC 20059.

HANES WALTON, JR., Ph.D., is Fuller E. Callaway Professor of Political Science, Department of Political Science, Savannah State College, Savannah, GA 31404.

DUVON G. WINBORNE, Ph.D., is Assistant Professor and Director, Urban Educational Research Center, College of Education, Cleveland State University, Cleveland, OH 44115.

BEVERLY H. WRIGHT, Ph.D., is Associate Professor, Department of Sociology, Wake Forest University, Winston Salem, NC 27109.